Europe through the Prism of Japan

Statue of Erasmus, polychrome wood, 1598.
© *Ryuko-in Temple, Sano*

Europe through the Prism of Japan

Sixteenth to Eighteenth Centuries

JACQUES PROUST

translated by
ELIZABETH BELL

UNIVERSITY OF NOTRE DAME PRESS
Notre Dame, Indiana

Manufactured in the United States of America

The publisher is grateful to
THE FRENCH MINISTRY OF CULTURE — CENTRE NATIONAL DE LIVRE
for support of the costs of translation

© Albin Michel 1997

Library of Congress Cataloging-in-Publication Data
Proust, Jacques.
[Europe au prisme du Japon. English]
Europe through the prism of Japan : sixteenth to eighteenth
centuries / Jacques Proust ; translated by Elizabeth Bell.
p.   cm.
Includes bibliographical references and index.
ISBN 0-268-02761-7 (cloth)
1. Europe—Civilization—Study and teaching—Japan.
2. Japan—Civilization—European influences.   3. East and
West.   I. Title.
CB203.P77   2002
940—dc21

2001004284

∞ *This book is printed on acid-free paper.*

Contents

List of Illustrations

Frontispiece:
Statue of Erasmus, polychrome wood, 1598. © *Ryuko-in Temple, Sano*

Plates beginning after page 72:

1   Johannes Stradanus, Adrianus Collaert, and Philippus Galle, *The Triumph of Caesar.* © *Montpellier Municipal Library*

2   *Twelve European Princes,* early seventeenth century, pair of screens with six panels (132.8 × 308.4 cm). © *Museum of the Prefecture of Nagasaki*

3   *Our Lady of Antigua,* sixteenth-century Japanese engraving, Catholic church of Ohura, Nagasaki.

4   *Saint Peter,* early seventeenth century, oil on canvas (119 × 69 cm). © *Museum of Namban Culture, Osaka*

5   Paul Bril and Raphaël Sadeler, *The Months: May, June.* © *Bibliothéque nationale de France, Paris*

6   *Pastoral Symphony among the Europeans,* early seventeenth century. Pair of screens with six panels (93 × 302.4 cm). © *Eisei Collection, Tokyo*

7   *Battle of Lepanto,* early seventeenth century, six-panel screen (153.5 × 362.5 cm). © *Kosetsu Museum, Kobe*

8   Cornelius Cort, *Battle of Zama.* © *Bibliothéque nationale de France, Paris*

9   *Pastoral Symphony among the Europeans,* early seventeenth century. © *Eisei Collection, Tokyo*

10 Marten de Vos and Raphaël Sadeler, *Paternus.* © *Bibliothéque nationale de France, Paris*

11 Martinus Heemskerck and Philippus Galle, *Pyramus and Thisbe.* © *Bibliothéque nationale de France, Paris*

Plates beginning after page 152:

1   Johann Elias Ridinger and Martin Elias Ridinger, *Falconer with Hooded Hawk Sighting a Heron.* © *Bibliothéque nationale de France, Paris*

Prologue

A vase full of water or a prism, by the interposition of a dense, transparent milieu and the refractive interplay of facets, allows us to see this in action: the free, direct ray is undifferentiated; color appears when there is captive refraction, when matter takes this on as a function of its own. The prism, in the calculated spread of its three angles and the concerted action of its triple dihedral mirror, contains all possible play of reflections and gives back to light its equivalent in color.

Paul Claudel, *Connaissance de l'Est*
(The East I Know), 1900

J like to imagine that "On Light," a chapter in *The East I Know* that seems an incongruous inclusion in the collection, is not entirely unrelated to the chapter in which Claudel compares European artists, who "copy nature according to the feelings they have about it," with Japanese artists, who "imitate it according to the materials with which it furnishes them." The former, he says, "reproduce in detail the sight they behold with a probing and subtle eye; the latter disengage its law with a blink of the eye, and in the freedom of the imagination apply it with scriptural conciseness." Or again: "[Japanese artists] know that the value of a tone results less from its intensity than from its placement; masters of the scale, they transpose as they see fit. And since color is no more than a particular witness that the whole of the visible renders to universal light, it is through color that everything finds its place within the frame, in accordance with the artist's chosen theme."[1]

Despite appearances, in this book I speak not of Japan but of Europe—the Europe of the Classical Era, considered as the "object to paint" but seen for our purposes through the prism of Japan. For the time has come to eject the history of ideas from the age-old national frameworks where it has languished too long, but also, more important, to shatter the perspective handed down from the Renaissance that would have all the lines that lead to an image's vanishing point proceed from the eye of the viewer, the artist, or, in the theater, the king's box.

I will not speak, however, of the way the Japanese in the times of Momoyama and Edo actually saw Europe and the Europeans. Nothing will be said, for example, of the golden skies of the wonderful Kano school screens, which depict with such humor the lives of the Portuguese merchants and missionaries in late-sixteenth-century Kyushu. Nor will I speak of the etchings and ceramics that, in the eighteenth century, accompany with an ironic cast the chronicle of daily life for the Dutch confined to the islet of Deshima, off Nagasaki. The Japanese are the ones who tell this story, and they tell it quite well.

Nor should one expect a history of the intellectual relations between the West and Japan from the middle of the sixteenth to the end of the eighteenth century. Excellent works have been written on this subject, in particular C. R. Boxer's *Jan Compagnie in Japan, 1600–1850* (1936), *The Dutch Seaborne Empire, 1600–1800* (1965), and *The Christian Century in Japan, 1549–1650* (1967), to mention only Western historiography. As a whole, they have only one shortcoming: they focus on the influence the West has had on Japan at various times and the Japanese reception of this influence. The same shortcoming is found in Léon Bourdon's otherwise admirable book on the Society of Jesus in Japan, written in 1949 and published at last in 1993 by the Portuguese Cultural Center in Paris. This shortcoming is called Eurocentrism, and few Western works of cultural anthropology, history, or comparative literature are entirely free of it. An exception is Jacques Gernet's *Chine et christianisme* (1982). Gernet's deep understanding of Chinese culture and language allow him literally to stand on the Chinese side of the immense abyss of noncomprehension that the Jesuits tried to bridge with a few tenuous links in the seventeenth and eighteenth centuries.

I do speak of Europe, as a European, one who loves Japan and the Japanese but does not read or speak their language and under no circumstances would attempt in their regard what Gernet has achieved regarding China. I do not know, even though countless conversations with Japanese friends may afford me some notion of it, how the Japanese *react* in their innermost recesses to the multifaceted influence exerted on them by the West. Still less, for obvious reasons, do I know how their ancestors *reacted* in the past.

There is a large quantity of underexplored documents from which one may try to reconstitute, like a puzzle, the image Europe gave of itself to its Japanese partners, deliberately or otherwise, from the mid-sixteenth century to the end of the eighteenth. The documents, while numerous, are often fragmentary and dispersed throughout publications that may be confidential, written in German, English, Spanish, Portuguese, or Latin. France is not entirely absent from this library, but its place is modest, for the simple reason that it remained almost entirely outside the field of action. Unlike the situation in China in the seventeenth and eighteenth centuries, there were no French missionaries in Japan until the late nineteenth century, and once the Dutch gained a trade monopoly with Nagasaki in 1640, the strategy of the Dutch East India Company left no place for the French in commerce. There were three exceptions, however: Father Guillaume Courtet, François Caron, and Jean de Lacombe.

Father Courtet, born in Sérignan near Béziers in 1589 or 1590, was a Dominican. He served as a negotiator for Richelieu in several delicate diplomatic affairs, notably in the Grisons and the Valteline, then joined the Spanish mission in the Philippines, where he was known by the name Tomaso de Santo Domingo. It was under this name that he arrived in Japan with the Spanish missionaries, and it was in Japan that he was imprisoned and martyred in 1637. A monument to him has been erected in Sérignan; Japanese Christians make pilgrimages to it today.[2]

François Caron was born in Belgium to a Protestant family of French origin. He spent the greater part of his life in the service of the Dutch East India Company and lived for a total of twenty-two years in Japan, until his retirement in 1651. In 1636 he wrote his *Relation de l'empire du Japon*, which was translated from the Dutch and published in French in 1673. Jean-Baptiste Colbert, the French minister at The Hague, who had taken note of Caron, lured him to France; he believed he might use Caron's talents in carrying out his colonial policies. Louis XIV granted Caron French citizenship in 1665 and named him director of the French India Company. Caron established the company in India and Siam and thought to return to Japan in the service of France. He never made it: he went down with his ship off Lisbon in 1673. He had had two sons by a Japanese wife, and both were educated in France. They were Reformed Protestants, like their father, and went into exile in Holland on the revocation of the Edict of Nantes.

Jean de Lacombe, a native of Quercy, was also a Protestant. First a soldier in the Turenne regiment, he entered the service of the French India Company as a captain at arms. He spent some time at Deshima in about 1673 and after returning to France wrote a journal of his travels that remained in manuscript form. It was titled *Le Compendiaire du Levant ou Voyage des Grandes Indes* and was datelined Bordeaux, 1681. The last known trace of it is in a 1937 auction catalog.[3]

For what I will call the "Portuguese period," from the middle of the sixteenth century to the last quarter of the seventeenth, the richest archives are, of course, those of the Society of Jesus. It is chiefly German Jesuits who have availed themselves of this material, because from the political reopening of Japan in 1868 up to the period of World War II, Japan was a mission of the German Province. They published most of their work in the collection *Monumenta nipponica*. It is commendable for its matchless erudition but is narrowly focused on the history of the Society itself, whose honor the Jesuits valiantly defend, at times to the detriment of objectivity and fairness. The Society never forgot, for example, that in the waning days of the sixteenth century they had had competition in Japan from religious orders arriving from the Philippines—Franciscans, Dominicans, and Augustinians—and obviously preferred not to speak about them here overmuch, rather than repeat all the reasons the Jesuits put forth at the time in supplicating the pope not to allow this intrusion.

Jesuit historiography also tends to disregard the fact that the mission in Japan was part of an overall strategy that was both political and ideological. For this reason one must have recourse to other studies, written in Spanish or Portuguese, possibly by Franciscans but also by the laity, to reconstitute such facets as the education of the mission-aries themselves in their countries of origin. This is one of the chapters in which the Japanese "prism" best allows us to discern the true stakes and assumptions behind the missionaries' preaching and catechesis; it was not up to the Jesuit historians to elucidate these completely. I am not accusing them of dissembling: it is impossible to observe the self with enough critical sense to know with certainty whence one speaks, and I consider myself no exception to this rule.

More disturbing is the indifference this historiography has long shown toward sources that are quite accessible, occasionally cited but rarely plumbed to the depths. The best-known example is *História de Japam*, by Father Luís Fróis, who had brought his work up to the year 1593 when he died in 1597. A part of it was published for the first time in 1942, but the first book of the five-volume annotated critical edition did not appear until 1976, in Lisbon; the project was completed in 1984.

Another legacy of the highest importance from the Portuguese period is *De missione legatorum*, published in Macao in 1590 under the guidance of Alessandro Valignano, then the Society of Jesus's Visitor to Japan. These interviews, largely fictitious, with four young Japanese Christians who had returned from a trip to Europe are often referred to in Jesuit sources but rarely quoted exactly, and they have never been translated from their original Latin into a modern Western tongue. We shall see, however, in the discussion in chapter 4 of Counter-Reformation art in Japan, that a knowledge of this text is essential to an understanding of Jesuit policies regarding art. Here again, the prism of Japan allows us to discern, out of the uniform white light of tradi-tional historiography, a singular "note": from Japan, it is easier to see the motives behind a cultural policy with global intents and goals, for Japan resisted and finally rejected it. All at once the intrinsic reasons for an inevitable failure become more perceptible.

An entire chapter of this book is devoted to a third monumental work that has been forgotten: the consultation written by Father Gabriel Vázquez, the famous Spanish casuist of the early seventeenth century, in response to a set of questions sent to him by Valignano from Japan. Vázquez's manuscript slumbered in Spain's archives for more than three and a half centuries before anyone thought to publish or even quote it. Thanks to a Spanish Jesuit in Tokyo, it was published for the first time in 1960–61, in Latin accompanied by a translation and copious annotations in Spanish. The document is as instructive about the mentality of the "doctors" who settled matters of faith *urbi et orbi* from their chambers in Europe as about that of the missionaries confronted in Japan with situations that for them were completely unheard of. Here, too, the irreconcilable contradictions made visible through the Japanese prism reveal the system's limits and digressions better than the most attentive observer could have done in the West, and certainly far in advance of the impassioned denunciation of it by the author of the *Provincial Letters*.

Numerous books, often well-crafted and always magnificently illustrated, were devoted to *japonisme* in Western art beginning in the mid-nineteenth century. Numerous exhibitions were organized in Europe on the topic. Conversely, Japan, Portugal, and the Musée Guimet in Paris presented to the public the masterpieces of *namban* art, the beautiful Kano school screens with gilded backgrounds.

But what is known in France of the Jesuit school of painting and engraving that was opened in Japan in the late sixteenth century and remained active from 1590 to 1614? Japanese art historians and Jesuit historians devoted numerous publications, often illustrated, to the topic, but they are widely dispersed and rarely in French. The picture is much the same for the period from the late seventeenth to the late eighteenth century, dominated by what was long referred to as the "Dutch" influence.

Important works have nonetheless been published, and exhibitions of exceptional interest have treated, variously, religious as well as secular art produced by the Jesuit school in the early seventeenth century, the "Dutch" influence on eighteenth-century Japanese art, or both. A profusion of catalogs resulting from close collaboration between museums and art historians, both Japanese and Western, document these exhibitions. They contain copious illustrations in black-and-white and in color, as well as all the bibliographic information that could be desired to attain a better knowledge and comprehension of the subject. Within this production, a few names stand out: Okamoto Yoshitomo in Japan and Calvin French and Grace A. H. Vlam in the United States. Two international exhibitions were organized around the new material brought to light via this research, one shown in several U.S. cities in 1977–78, the other in Berlin in 1993. The catalogs of these exhibitions were still available recently, the first in English, the second in German. Vlam's 1976 dissertation at the University of Michigan, "Western-Style Secular Painting in Momoyama, Japan," lamentably is available only on microfilm. It is to be hoped that the Musée Guimet, or one of our large national foundations, will one day organize an exhibition on the theme of *européisme* in Japanese art, even if national pride may suffer when confronted with the evidence that France occupies only a very small place in the picture, at least up to the end of the nineteenth century. But things changed substantially by the twentieth century; indeed, the interesting aspect of such an exhibition might be to show, and of course explain, this radical change in perspective.

A revelation supplied by the above-mentioned works is that from the sixteenth to the eighteenth century absolutely nothing of the period's extraordinarily rich and vast European art production reached Japan. The art of the Counter-Reformation introduced by the Jesuits had chiefly catechetical and apologetic aims, and all talent was turned to the service of propaganda, in the secular as well as the religious realm. The Dutch merchants who later served as cross-pollinators for the West and Japan, on the contrary, did not have any concerted policy, but neither did they have artistic taste, and their cultural contribution was always subjected to the vagaries of the market. The situation was also circumscribed by the practical conditions of transportation and exchange. For example, it was easier for them to transport illustrated books and engravings than paintings. Moreover, few Japanese, except for the shogun and a few high lords, had the means to acquire the books offered them at extremely high prices.

For both the Jesuits in the late sixteenth century and the Dutch in the eighteenth, the most easily accessible artistic product, and thus the one privileged in trade, was the engraving. And since the engraving capital of Europe during this period was Anvers, it was almost exclusively Flemish engravings that were brought to be admired, then imitated, by Japanese artists. Here again the prism of Japan casts a revelatory beam. It reveals first the extreme longevity of a means of expression and a style that are also found, in some form, in the plates of encyclopedias published in western Europe in the eighteenth century.

It also reveals the close intertwining of Italian Renaissance taste with that of northern European artists. Most of the Flemish artists and engravers whose works made their way to Japan during this two-and-a-half-century period had lived in Italy for some amount of time, and those who did not go there dreamed of it. The Japanese prism, in exalting this dream, at times took it beyond limits the European artists had not dared to pass, and this is another sort of revelation to us: the genius of classical Europe did not always lead it in the direction of the *rational* and the *mannered;* it also guided it, often unaware, toward the *irrational* and the *fantastic.*[4]

The detour through Japan shows us, finally, that comparative art history cannot ignore the role played by engraving at the time in Europe itself and in the territories it influenced, from the Greater Indies to the two Americas. This opens up a vast chapter that remains to be written in the comparative history of ideas, one addressing the subject of cultural intermediaries in general.[5]

It would be reassuring, or comfortable, in any case, to think that influences pass from master to master, genius to genius, perhaps teacher to disciple, without straying from the sphere of great works and great thought. The fictional dialogues people enjoyed writing in the Renaissance, and those penned in the days when rhetoric was still taught in the colleges, stood in rather well for the ones the pitiless realities of geography or history had rendered impossible. In the domain of exchange between the West and Japan, we might imagine Arai Hakuseki chatting with Rousseau, Miura Baien or Hiraga Gennai arguing with Diderot, Voltaire annotating Ferreira's refutation of Christianity, Dürer opposite one of the Kano school masters, Rembrandt or Rubens versus a Japanese master of "floating world" painting. An art history book titled *Japanese Art in Perspective: A Global View*, by Hirayama Ikuo and Takashina Shuji, was published in Tokyo in 1994. It is profusely illustrated and its focus consciously comparatist. For example, it places side by side a late-fifteenth-century winter landscape and *Hunters in the Snow* by Pieter Brueghel the Elder (1565), *Shrike Calling from a Dead Branch* by Miyamoto Musashi (early seventeenth century) and *Goldfinch* by the Dutch artist Carel Fabritius (1645). This is amusing, at times provocative, but except in cases of direct and clear-cut influence, such as that of da

Vinci's Mona Lisa on Kishida Ryusei's *Reiko's Smile* (1921), most of the similarities are purely formal, leaving the works in their respective exteriority.

Exploring the intersection between the spheres of Western culture and Japanese culture in the Classical Era allows for some surprising comparisons here and there. Thus in chapter 4 I mention Dürer and Jules Romain; in chapter 6, Titian; and in chapters 1 and 2, Æsop and Erasmus, respectively. But one may not conclude, except perhaps in the case of Æsop, that any of them had a long-term *influence* on Japanese thought or art. The cultural ambassadors that Europe sent to Japan in the Classical Era were of considerably lesser scale, and the Japanese who received their credentials were often also minor, obscure, even marginal, figures.

It was not the philosopher from Rotterdam himself who introduced the germs of Erasmianism into Japan in the early seventeenth century but a modest Portuguese Jesuit and an apostate to boot, Cristóvão Ferreira. The first rudiments of Western medicine were introduced in Kyushu in the late sixteenth century by a "new Christian," a Marrano, of the sort who were burned at the stake in autos-da-fé at Lisbon and Coimbra.

I have mentioned the importance of Flemish engraving in the two waves of Western influence that touched Japan during the Classical Era. Through it, and through Dutch engraving, the Japanese discovered, successively or simultaneously, sixteenth-century European cartography; Italian and Flemish Renaissance treatises on perspective and scenography; Italian, French, German, and Dutch treatises on anatomy, botany, and natural history. They did not know Diderot and d'Alembert's *Encyclopédie*, but the Dutch translation of Chomel's modest *Dictionnaire œconomique* served in its stead, and in it a Japanese artist found enough information, we are told, to reinvent the technique of copperplate engraving, which had been forgotten in Japan after the departure of the Jesuits.

Who could have imagined that the *optique*, a French machine that enhanced the effects of perspective in engravings and was very popular in Europe in the late eighteenth and early nineteenth century, would be an instant success when brought to Japan in the mid-eighteenth and would deeply affect the style of fin-de-siècle masters such as Shiba

Kokan and Utagawa Toyoharu, after having amused more modest artist-artisans like Okumura Masanobu?

In the field of medicine, none of the books brought to Japan in the eighteenth century was written by Europe's great figures in medicine or surgery, with the exception of Lorenz Heister. Ambroise Paré was known as early as the seventeenth century, but no one could read him. For a long time, the privilege of meeting with the foreign physicians on Deshima, often humble barber-surgeons, was reserved for the official interpreters of Nagasaki, who were rarely cultivated people and were all entirely lacking in medical training. Nonetheless, it was through these intermediaries that the *spirit* of modern European medicine made its way into Japan, little by little, until from the bosom of traditional Sino-Japanese medicine there sprang a small group of practitioners determined to revise their field from the ground up, on the bases offered by the West. This tells us something about the capacity of the Japanese themselves to create the conditions for what was to them a veritable epistemological revolution but says just as much about that which—beyond schools, beyond barriers of language and national tradition—constituted the very essence of the epistemological revolution that had rocked western Europe, especially northern Europe, from Vesalius and Galileo to Descartes and Newton. It is by the strength and amplitude of the reaction this revolution created in a country like Japan that we may take its full measure, especially—and here is the paradox— in that the participants in its transfer had little stature and little weight, on both the transmitting and the receiving ends.

This round-trip journey between Japan and the West, which in the sixteenth century took about four years and can be done today in twenty-four hours, has the advantage, in the end, of imposing on comparative studies, whatever their object, a geographic framework and a historical framework different from those to which one had been accustomed. For no serious research today can remain within the bounds of a single nation and a single century. As a few young iconoclasts insolently proclaimed in a special issue of the magazine *Dix-Huitième Siècle* (Eighteenth Century) published in 1973, "the eighteenth century doesn't exist." Nor the seventeenth, I would add, nor the sixteenth. The challenge was seen in its time as a provocation. Now the works of Fernand Braudel and the *Annales* school, and those of Michel

Foucault, have been demonstrating for some time the need to open up an extended period and a vast space: Europe, the Mediterranean world, the empire of Charles V. We must go even further, and above all we must learn not to contemplate these expanses from the top of our little tower. The value of comparative studies, ranging the width and breadth of the planet, is to force a confrontation between points of view. Those of the Japanese, the Amerindians, or the Muslim Mughals regarding the West and regarding themselves must be seen as equal in validity to the viewpoint the West once had regarding them, for a long time considered the only one possible.

The prism of Japan also shows us that we cannot safely divide the period from the middle of the sixteenth century to the end of the eighteenth into successive chronological segments. From the point of view of Foucault's archaeology of knowledge, it is a single unit of time. It falls between two epistemological cutoff points: the introduction into Japan of the harquebus and theology in the mid-sixteenth century and Japan's dual discovery of perspective and anatomy in the second half of the eighteenth. In Japan itself, this interval seems to embrace two completely different periods, the Portuguese and the Dutch, separated moreover by a latency period from 1640 to 1720. But from the European end, "Portugal" and "Holland" function rather as two paradigms, two antagonistic entities locked in the merciless combat that pitted the Counter-Reformation against Humanism and the Reformation in the sixteenth century. In the seventeenth century the battle changed shape and place, but not in essence, culminating in the eighteenth century in the struggle between the Enlightenment and Authority, Tradition, Dogmatism, and the spirit of the System, in religion as well as in science and the arts. Its outcome is not certain even today, either in Japan or in Europe.

Chapter One

Æsop's Smile, Aristotle's Substance

They were Japanese but were called Mancius, Michaël, Martinus, Julianus. Not only because they were Christians: it was also the custom for humanists in Europe to adopt Latin or Greek names. They had been chosen by the European missionaries in Japan to represent before Portugal, Spain, and, above all, Rome the young Christendom of Japan. The missionaries expected all manner of benefits to accrue from this visit, and the envoys were to impress their hosts brilliantly with the humanist, Christian culture they had been taught in Japan.

The level of study that had been attained by Mancius, Michaël, Martinus, and Julianus in 1582 is not known. To ensure the greatest advantage, the fathers had not chosen them at random: Mancio Ito was the nephew of Dom Francisco, alias Otomo Yoshishige, "king" of Bungo, baptized in 1578. Miguel Chijiwa was a relative of Dom Bartolomeu, alias Omura Sumitada, lord of Omura, baptized in 1563; he was also the cousin of Dom Protasio, alias Arima Harunobu, "king" of Arima, who was baptized in 1579. Martinho Hara and Juliano Nakaura were lower in rank but of good birth.[1] All were fifteen to twenty years of age. According to a written record of the time, they knew "the Portuguese language quite well, Spanish somewhat, and a good bit of Latin; they [understood] Italian completely, or nearly so."[2]

Passing through Coimbra, the young men were invited to visit the school at which the mission's most prominent teachers had been educated.[3] This visit is described in chapter 31 of the narration in dialogue form of their journey, which was published in 1590 in Macao under the title *De missione legatorum*. This narrative was putatively based on the travel journals kept by the youth themselves, with editing attributed to Father Duarte de Sande. But however brilliant the four envoys may have been, it is highly unlikely that they could have kept their diaries in Latin: the Latin is that of Sande, who had taught it at Braga, then Coimbra. However, the concept, the choice of the dialogue form, and the writing itself are Alessandro Valignano's. He rendered in Spanish a synthesis of the travelers' impressions, recorded on their return to Goa in 1587; Sande translated and structured the work.[4]

The description of the Coimbra College of the Arts contained in *De missione legatorum* is thus a mixture of the impressions received by the travelers and the effect Valignano wished to produce on the minds of those who read it, for *De missione* was to serve as a reader for students at Japanese institutions. Valignano wrote to the superior general of the Society of Jesus in 1589: "The young in our seminaries must assimilate with their milk, so to speak, an awareness of and apprenticeship in the attributes of our home." He added, "The roots of European culture are sunk in Christianity; the better the Japanese come to understand our culture, the more deeply they will know, as well, the values of Christian faith and life."[5] In that light, the "faith" of the travelers, already undoubtedly fortified by the spectacular pomp of Rome and Venice, would reach its zenith at Coimbra.

The Coimbra College of the Arts

The school that the Japanese envoys visited in 1586 had been founded in 1547 by John III of Portugal on the model of the Collège Royal in Paris. The Jesuits, who already operated a school in the city, were invited to take charge of the royal institution in 1555.[6] In 1586, according to *De missione*, all one's studies could be undertaken there, from elementary school to theology. It was frequented by the most intelligent youths from the best families.

The instruction dispensed was both humanist and Christian. Students learned Latin and rhetoric. The best went on to philosophy, Greek, and Hebrew. A small number studied theology; these were for the most part destined to become missionaries to Brazil or the East Indies. The students were instructed by twenty teachers: eleven taught grammar, the humanities, rhetoric, and related disciplines; four taught philosophy; two taught Greek and Hebrew; three taught theology. The school had two thousand day pupils. Nearly two hundred people—teachers, subalterns, and pupils—resided at the school. *De missione* places its annual revenue at fifteen thousand écus, drawn from its own funds and those collected in Portugal and overseas for its operation.[7]

De missione says nothing of the content of the instruction, no doubt because it did not differ from that dispensed at the same time in the overseas institutions, those in India and Japan in particular. According to the Constitutions of the Society of Jesus, the express vocation of its members was to teach letters and languages (beginning with Latin), philosophy (also called "the arts"), and theology. The articles forbade them to practice medicine and law. Law was prohibited so that members would not become involved as judges, attorneys, or lawyers in the countless trials that beset social and ecclesiastical life; medicine, because the profession of doctor or surgeon had been barred to clerics since the Middle Ages. It was not appropriate for a priest to examine the body of a patient, male or female, and in the event that death ensued after an ill-starred intervention or unsuitable treatment, the responsible cleric, guilty or not, became an "irregular," meaning that he was deprived of the right to celebrate the sacraments until the condition of irregularity was lifted. This prohibition had especially heavy consequences in a time when medicine was becoming increasingly an avant-garde discipline, at Padua and elsewhere. The new medicine tended to rely on direct observation of phenomena rather than on the principles of authority and a priori reasoning, and its practice contributed greatly to the gradual erosion of the old scholasticism.

Before coming into Jesuit hands, the Coimbra College of the Arts had been a humanist institution. André de Gouveia, one of the first professors called to teach at Coimbra, had introduced the spirit and methods that had brought renown to the College of Sainte-Barbe in Paris and the College of Guienne in Aquitaine. Things had already reached the point that in 1550 two teachers at the school were accused of "Lutheranism."[8] Under the Jesuits the spirit of obedience replaced a critical spirit, but the course of study inherited from Gouveia was not noticeably altered.

At the time Mancius and his companions were touring the great Christian cities of southern Europe, the Society of Jesus, in keeping with a long-standing tradition (at the College of Goa, founded in 1542; the College of Messina, founded by Ignatius of Loyola himself in 1548; the Collegio Romano, founded in 1551; the College of Saint Anthony in Lisbon, founded in 1553; the College of the Holy Spirit in Évora, founded in 1551; and at Coimbra itself), was studying a general restructuring of its educational system, not so much to change its content or methods as to standardize them and adapt them still more closely to its needs. The commission formed to examine the project was composed of two Portuguese, five Spaniards, three Italians, one German, and one Frenchman. The project was studied further by another commission composed of one Portuguese, one Spaniard, a Frenchman of Scottish origin, an Austrian of Dutch origin, one German, and one Italian. An initial draft was completed in 1591. The proposed text was distributed to the Society's provinces, which had three years to amend it. The final text of what would thenceforth be called *Ratio studiorum* was printed in Naples in 1598 and promulgated in early 1599. It was thus the fruit of a long maturation process; the Society had marshaled all its forces to perfect it. Its authors took into account not only the fund of experience built up by Jesuit teachers but also the experiences of the University of Paris, where Ignatius of Loyola and his early companions had performed their studies, and of the Brothers of Communal Life (Fraterherren in German), whose colleges in Liège, Deventer, Zwolle, and Wesel had also served as a model for Jean Sturm, a Catholic who had converted to Protestantism, when he reformed the University of Strasbourg in 1537.[9]

The Jesuits' goal, as presented by the *Ratio studiorum*, was to teach not so much letters or philosophy as virtue. *De missione legatorum*, in its chapter on the Coimba College of the Arts, uses the term *bonae artes*, which may be translated as "good principles" or "the art of conducting oneself well." In the five classes of letters—three devoted to grammar, one to the humanities, and one to rhetoric—pupils studied

Latin and Greek, poetry and oratory, the national language (taught in Latin), geography, and history. But none of these disciplines was an end in itself; everything was subordinate to the exposition and memorization of good examples worthy of imitation. Students learned Latin (and good examples) via Terence, Cicero, Titus Livius, Virgil, and Horace, purged in advance of anything that might trouble the conscience of a young Christian. Father Cosmo de Magalhães published in 1587 a collection of excerpts selected in this spirit. It included Pliny the Younger, Titus Livius, Cicero, Seneca *(The Trojan Women)*, Plautus *(Aulularia)*, Papinius, Ovid, and Juvenal *(Satire VII)* but also elegies on the death of Christ[10] and an extract of a poem by Jacopo Sannazaro (1455–1530) titled *De partu Virginis* (translated in the seventeenth century as "The Sacred Childbirth of the Virgin"). These selections were intended for the lower grades. In another anthology aimed at the same level, published in 1588, there were extracts from Cicero, Sallust, Pliny, and Ovid and elegies from Tibullus, Propertius, Plautus, and Christian authors. The selections from Greek authors published about the same time contain the discourses of Demosthenes, the idylls of Theocritus, Homer, the dialogues of Lucan, and Æsop's *Fables*. Fables and epigrams were accompanied by their Latin translation, sometimes in prose, sometimes in verse. At times the professors themselves were writers. Thus in 1600 Luís da Cruz, a poet and playwright who taught oratory at Coimbra, translated all the Psalms into Latin and published them. His translation was admired in his time by the literary community but was intended mainly for the pupils of the school and the general public. Rather daringly, the author acknowledged in his preface the translation of one of his predecessors, the Scotsman George Buchanan: he had been an associate of André de Gouveia in the late 1540s and had been arrested and sentenced to death by the Inquisition for "Erasmianism." Thus the tradition of Humanism had not been entirely lost at the College of the Arts, despite the harsh reaction of 1555.[11]

The education provided in letters was primarily a general one and was meant for everyone. Not so the three-and-a-half-year study of philosophy: this was a direct preparation for the study of theology, for which it was to provide a solid rational grounding. It was commonly thought in those times that the Revelation was the endpoint of (and break with) a long process of intellectual development that, starting from the common sense with which the first humans had been endowed, had led to the Greeks, particularly Aristotle. Common sense being by definition shared by all, and Aristotelianism's rigorous formalization of it being near to perfection, this formalization was thus universally valid: it was only necessary for the mind to submit to it and exercise it to be led naturally to admit the supernatural teachings of the Revelation and Tradition as well. That is why the pupils in Jesuit schools, already conditioned by several years of studying an ancient language, were obliged to spend several years in the study of philosophy before taking on theology. The first year of this cycle was devoted to dialectics, the second to logic, physics, and ethics, the third to metaphysics and a few topics in natural hisory. The question of the soul was not broached until the final months.

It is known quite precisely today how philosophy was taught in Coimbra at the end of the sixteenth century. The courses were published in five volumes over the period 1592–1605, under the title *Commentarii Collegii Conimbricencis S.J. in Aristotelem*. This is what is commonly referred to as *O Curso conimbricense*, or sometimes *O Cânone filosófico conimbricense*.[12] The content of these courses was subjected to an analysis by José Sebastião da Silva Dias in volume 4 of *Cultura, História e Filosofia*, published in 1985. The questions addressed are of this sort: "Does God contain all things within His being, or not?" and "Can the void be introduced into nature by means of heavenly intervention?" The question of creation and decomposition is framed on the basis of Aristotelian theories but in reference to the mystery of the Incarnation and the sacrament of the Eucharist. Hence the questions that arise: "Can any accident, by divine intervention, attach to a different subject, or not?" "Can an accident, by divine intervention, exist apart from the subject?" "What must an accident lose, or on the contrary acquire, in order to exist, by divine intervention, apart from the subject?" The question was also posed, regarding the genesis of the first woman, "Is it or is it not possible, by divine intervention, to create something large from something small, without any loss and without the addition of new matter?"[13]

The study of theology at the Coimbra College of the Arts was long dominated by the personality of Father Francisco Soares (or Suárez; he was a Spaniard from Granada). Speculative philosophy, which he taught, predominated over study of the Scriptures, read in the Vulgate version, which moreover were not to be subjected to critical examination, whether philological or historical in nature. On this point the Jesuits were in total opposition to one of the most innovative tendencies of Humanism, which had been banned from the College of the Arts since the early 1550s.[14]

Toward the end of the century, however, there was something of a revival in biblical studies at the University of Coimbra. In 1598 Father Manuel de Sá published *Notationes in totam Scripturam sacram* (Observations on the Entirety of the Holy Scriptures). Four years earlier he had published scholia on the four Gospels. Although it was Jesuit custom to adhere strictly to the allegorical sense of sacred texts, de Sá set out in two parallel columns the literal meaning and the mystical meaning. A year later, in 1599, Father Sebastião Barradas (1542–1615) published in four large folio volumes his commentaries on the concordance of the evangelical narratives.[15] The same year, Father António Fernandes published his commentaries on narratives of visions in the Old Testament, and in 1601 Father Brás Viegas came out with an exegesis of the Apocalypse: this was a course he had taught successively at the University of Coimbra, the College of Goa, and Saint Anthony's in Lisbon. In it he brought into play literal or mystical meanings as the case required.

The choice of a teaching method is no less important than the material being taught. At all levels and in all things, the Jesuit instructors privileged memorization over personal reflection[16] and abhorred new opinions. In philosophy, they privileged logic and metaphysics over the life sciences or natural history. They spoke at times of "experiment" but always to support an argument, never in the spirit of experimental science that was beginning to arise here and there in Europe. For them, "physics" itself was nothing more than fuel for their ontological speculations. Even when they spoke of "natural philosophy," their arguments were based on the sacred texts or Tradition. Meanwhile, at Padua philosophical discourse was making progressively louder demands for autonomy from the realm of theological discourse, and the natural sciences found it increasingly difficult to submit to the authority of the Bible, the Church, and the Ancients in general.[17]

When Nicolaus Copernicus published his treatise *De revolutionibus orbium celestium* in 1542, the Church of Rome condemned it for the supposition that the earth revolved around the sun, rather than the other way around, as had always been believed. Copernicus did not go unnoticed at Coimbra; in fact, he was known there quite early, as of 1546. But the practice was to remain silent about him, or to cite him in order to refute him, as was done for example by Father Cristávão Clavio, a Jesuit of German origin, in his treatise *In sphaeram Joannis de Sacro Bosco commentarius* (On the Sphere), published in Rome in 1570.[18] John Holywood, known as Joannes de Sacrobosco, was a thirteenth-century mathematician and astronomer whose treatise was a classic of pre-Copernican astronomy. Yet in the treatise *De sphaera*, the first item in an anthology produced in Japan in 1584 for scholastics in training there, Clavio uses Holywood's argument to counter the newly emerging Copernican concept of the world.[19] It preceded in the collection an abridged version of Aristotle's theory of the soul, which itself served as an introduction to a summary of "Catholic truth" intended for the Japanese brothers of the Society of Jesus. The anthologist was Father Pedro Gómez, a Spaniard who had studied at Coimbra after 1555, and again, he used the work to teach Latin to Japanese pupils in 1594. In reality, the goal of *De sphaera* was not to dispense to students the scientific knowledge of astronomy; it was meant to conduct them from things visible to things invisible, in the spirit of the Nineteenth Psalm: "The heavens are telling the glory of God, and the firmament proclaims his handiwork."[20]

The syllogism was generally considered the form best suited to transliterate the natural functioning of human understanding. Along with elocution and composition, debate was an important component of the students' exercises, but the best debaters were those who could construct a line of argument citing authorities considered indisputable and present their positions most convincingly. The elite students were admitted to "academies" where they could deploy their talents among their peers. The sessions were sometimes public. There was one for "grammarians," one for "humanists" (those studying the humanities) and "rhetoricians," and one for "philosophers" and "theologians."[21] All these exercises were performed, of course, in Latin.

Although hostile to the critical current of Humanism, the Jesuits were humanists. They came to Japan with books and were constantly bringing more from Europe, Goa, and Macao. As soon as they received permission to remain in Japan, the Dominicans did the same, through Manila. When Valignano's envoys returned from their European journey in 1590, they brought back from Macao a press with movable metal type, and beginning in 1591 the Jesuits were able to print locally the works they needed. The press operated successively in Kazusa, Amakusa (1592), and Nagasaki (1597). It ceased operation in 1614 when the anti-Christian persecution became widespread and was most likely shipped back to Macao.

As their educational mission was not solely religious, the books the missionaries imported and printed were not restricted to devotional works. From the 1500s on, Plato and Aristotle shared shelf space in their library with Saint Augustine and Saint Thomas, as naturally as they had in Goa or Coimbra. Particularly popular among Aristotle's works were the *Ethics* (which they considered to be "natural ethics" par excellence) and works of "physics." The Jesuits also encountered Aristotle's thought in the *Compendium naturalis philosophiae*, by the philosopher Titelmans (ca. 1502–37) of Louvain. He was as passionately fond of Aristotle as he was inimical to Erasmus. His book, published in 1530, was reprinted countless times. Since Aristotle could not serve as a foundation for belief in a single, personified God, the missionaries turned to Plato. It is not known which of his works were found in the catalog of the Jesuit library in Japan, but his authority was invoked in various polemics to prove the existence of God and to explain Creation.[22]

In keeping with their own humanities studies at Coimbra, Goa, or Macao, the Jesuits used in their teachings the Latin primer written by Antonio of Lebrija or Nebrixa (1444–1532). Antonio was a good humanist who had worked in Alcalá on the translation of the polyglot Bible *(Poliglota complutense)* and had published in Salamanca in 1481 a didactic work titled *Institutiones latinae*. This was a grammar offering examples drawn from Cicero and Virgil. For several centuries it served as the textbook for nearly all the schools and seminaries in Portugal, Spain, and the Asian missions. Since, in Europe, the national tongue was taught via classes conducted in Latin, the first Japanese grammar books were also based on "as reglas de António (the rules of Antonio)."[23] Antonio's book was reprinted in France as late as 1859.

The number of works printed in Japan on the Jesuits' press between 1591 and 1614 is estimated at about sixty,[24] of which fewer than half still exist. Of the twenty-nine titles identified by Matsuda in 1965, three are very good illustrations of the policies of cultural penetration then in practice by the Society of Jesus. The first, *Fides no dôxi*, is a Japanese adaptation of a book published in Salamanca in 1582 under the title *Introducción al sámbolo de la fé* (Introduction to the Symbol of Faith). Its author was a Dominican, Friar Luis de Granada, and it had been translated into Japanese by Father Pedro Ramón. The latter was a Spaniard from Saragossa, educated in Alcalá, Salamanca, and Rome, who arrived in Japan in 1575 to serve as master of novices. The work, written in Japanese but printed in Latin characters, was published in Amakusa in 1592. It was, of course, like all "good" theology books of its time, founded on Aristotle.[25]

The second work, *Heike no monogatari* (Tales of Heike), was also written in Japanese, set in Latin characters, and printed at Amakusa in 1592 or 1593. It is an adaptation, in the dialogue form commonly used by European scholastics, of a thirteenth-century Japanese saga, written in popular language and intended for those who needed to gain familiarity with the language and history of Japan. The author of the adaptation was a Japanese Jesuit brother named Fabian. Appended to the main text of *Heike* were maxims drawn from the great Chinese classics of Confucianism, especially *The Great Learning* and *The Doctrine of the Mean*, suitable for adding color to a homily. The third part of the collection consisted of seventy fables from Æsop, translated from Latin and altered here and there to adapt them to a Japanese context: thus "The Olive Tree and the Reed," which inspired La Fontaine's "The Oak and the Reed," becomes "The Palm and the Bamboo." And the moral of "The Cicada and the Ants" is reversed, so as not to offend Confucian sensibilities. Certain fables attributed to Æsop are, moreover, actually excerpts from *Le roman de Renart*, also adapted: because water does not often freeze at the latitude of Kyushu, when Renart is fishing for eel with Ysengrin, he surreptitiously loads with stones the bucket he has tied to his partner's tail.

It was of little concern to the Jesuits that Christian tradition was entirely foreign to the Chinese philosopher and the Greek fabulist; all that mattered was to inculcate in the lay reader as well as Japanese and European theology students the principles of what they understood as "natural morality." For such purposes Æsop was inseparable from Aristotle, and both resonated with Confucius across space and time: the very diversity of the sources "demonstrated" the universality of the message.

The missionaries' desires were fulfilled: Æsop was the sole Western author who was not swept away in the turmoil of 1614–39. His *Fables* quickly became classics and were published in Japanese no fewer than eleven times during the Tokugawa period. They were reissued in 1929, 1939, 1959, and 1960.[26]

PREACHING AND CATECHISM

Not a single copy of the first catechism put together by Francis Xavier during his stay in Japan has survived. One can only imagine what it might have contained, based on the one he had used previously in the Moluccas. This was a chronological exposition of the facts revealed in the story of Christianity and the New Testament, from the Creation to the Last Judgment, introducing according to Tradition the great truths of the Credo, the institution of the sacraments, the Decalogue, and the commandments of the Church. The apostle stressed the logical nature of this Revelation and this Tradition, for he wished his teachings to be accessible to anyone able to reason correctly. For example, after having "demonstrated" the necessary existence of a creator, he justifies the prohibition against the adoration of idols by saying, "Sound reason teaches us clearly and distinctly that we must, in life, allow ourselves to be led only by the one who has given us life."[27]

The Japanese version of Francis Xavier's catechism had been simplified. It laid even more stress on those elements of preaching and catechism that, he believed, could be understood by any reasonable individual: the idea of God as creator, the notion of the immortality of the soul, the declaration of eternal punishments and rewards.[28]

Somewhat later, Matteo Ricci, as apostle to China, did much the same thing in what came to be called in 1604, after several reworkings, *The True Meaning of the Lord of Heaven.* He wrote: "This work does not [treat] all the mysteries of the Holy Faith, which should only be explicated to catechumens and Christians, but only a few of its principles, particularly those which can be proven in some way by natural reasons and apprehended by natural insight itself . . . , such as the presence in the universe of a Lord and Creator of all things, which he constantly maintains in existence; the immortality of the human soul; God's recompense of good and evil acts in the next life; the falsity of the transmigration of souls into the bodies of other humans or of animals, a belief to which many here subscribe; and other things of this nature."[29]

Francis Xavier's successors perceived early on that he had been imprudent in seeking in the vocabulary of Japanese religions notions equivalent to the Aristotelian or Christian ideas on which his teaching was founded. In so doing, he had consciously or unconsciously multiplied the points of comparison and parallels between Christianity and Buddhism, and many of his listeners might have wondered in good faith whether this religion which claimed to be new was not simply a variant of the old one. Thus one of his successors, Baltasar Gago, undertook to reform the vocabulary. To translate these specific concepts, he returned to the Latin or Portuguese words in usage in the Society and transliterated them into one of the Japanese syllabic alphabets (*hiragana*), so that the faithful would have no difficulty pronouncing or writing them, or, above all, memorizing them. In this way he "naturalized" *anima, sustancia, persona:* they were read *anima, susutanshiya, perusona.* He transliterated a total of about fifty words and expressions.[30] Father Fróis, in his *History of Japan,* reports that in about 1560 a Japanese Jesuit named Lourenço preached on *quintessence:* that of the Orientals, which was pure nothingness, and that of the Occidentals, which was, he said, "the principal cause and most efficacious motive that could bring to our climes the Fathers, whose homeland is so far away." He went on to expound on *quintessence,* which is but an "element" added to the four known ones, the Supreme Essence, infinitely distant from them and also called Deos, with neither beginning nor end, all-powerful and all-good. Then he addressed the "rational soul, an invisible and immortal substance," and the invisible "spiritual substances" that are the angels and demons.[31]

Apart from the vocabulary, Friar Lourenço did not deviate from the path forged by Francis Xavier; it still came down to a demonstration "by natural reasons understood and apprehended by natural insight itself." Neither Lourenço nor Fróis thought to wonder whether it sufficed to argue according to scholastic rules to be truly understood. For even if the words used in the reasoning have been "naturalized" in pronunciation and writing, they do not necessarily have meaning outside the cultural context from which they have been drawn.

Despite his laudable attempt at linguistic *aggiornamento*, Gago did not stray from the established path either. Around 1556, he collaborated with Father Belchior Nunes Barreto in the creation of the *Treatise of Twenty-Five Instructions*, of which only the Japanese title has survived. The treatise remained in use until about 1570. It appears to have been in two parts, the first a refutation of Japanese religions and the second an account of the philosophical and theological aspects of "Christian" doctrine. It began by positing an "infinite principle, the primary cause of all good, creator of all things visible and invisible," then showed that "human beings were constituted of two substances, one corporal and perishable, the other spiritual and immortal, and that they received in the latter, called *anima*, reward or punishment according to their works." Only then came an account of the facts of the Revelation and Tradition. The demonstration of the immortality of the soul was made by structured reasoning rather than by relying on authority, either of the Scriptures or of the Ancients. The soul is immortal (1) because it is a simple substance without intermixture (the "mixed" substances, composed of several elements, break up and die); (2) because all people desire to be saved (all hold funerals for their dead); (3) because all people aspire to prolong their lives indefinitely; (4) because each person desires to perpetuate his name; (5) because all would like to accede to perfection; and (6) because good and evil do not necessarily find their just recompense on earth.[32] As time went on, Barreto's twenty-five instructions were reduced to seven, for practical reasons. But nothing was altered in the progression: reasoning led to Revelation. And the theory of the sphere still came before the Scriptures.[33]

The Council of Trent, which finished its work in 1563, was obliged to set down the doctrinal bases of the Catholic Reformation in the form of a catechism. The task of writing it was conferred on Cardinal Carlo Borromeo (1538–84), who had taken an active part in the Council. His work was completed in 1566. Under the title *Catechismus romanus*, it was introduced into Japan in 1568, which is to say, very rapidly: in those times, it took about two years to send a communication from western Europe to Japan. *Catechismus romanus* was an abridged version of the Italian original, translated into Japanese, and its use was initially restricted to preachers and coadjutors.[34] The complete Latin text was reprinted later, in 1596, at Amakusa.[35]

But the Visitor to Japan, Alessandro Valignano, did not think the *Catechismus romanus* could be used in its original form in the Far East. He had taken office in 1572 and had visited Malacca, Macao, and several Indian territories from 1574 to 1578, had stayed in Japan from 1579 to 1582, and was acquainted with Fathers Ruggeri and Ricci, who were working in China.[36] He ordered Ricci to prepare a catechism especially for China (Ricci finished the first version of it in 1581) and himself undertook to write one for Japan. This appeared in Lisbon in 1586 under the title *Catechismus christianae fidei, in quo veritas nostrae religionis ostenditur, et sectas japonenses confutantur* (Catechism of the Christian Faith, in which the verity of our Christian religion is demonstrated and the Japanese sects refuted).

This catechism was in two parts, divided into eight and four discourses, respectively. Of the eight discourses in the first part, only the last three deal directly with divine law, the Credo, the Trinity, the Fall, and the Revelation through the intermediation of patriarchs, prophets, saints, Jesus, and the apostles. Of the first five sections, the fourth and fifth are devoted to a critique of Japanese religions, a refutation of the belief in metempsychosis, and the denunciation of customary crimes in Japan such as sodomy, suicide, infanticide, and abortion. The philosophical base of the whole is set forth in the first three discourses. In them are enunciated the rational premises from which all the rest will flow.

Valignano, born in the foothills of the Abruzzis in what was then called the kingdom of the Two Sicilies, had studied at the University of Padua but in law: the new spirit was not so strongly felt in that discipline as it was in medicine. He entered the novitiate of the Jesuits in Rome in 1566 and performed his philosophical studies, beginning in 1567, at the Collegio Romano in the company of Claudio Aquaviva, the future superior general of the order. His professors there included, in physics, Father Klau, or Clavus in Latin (mentioned earlier under the Portuguese name Clavio in connection with the Coimbra College of the Arts). Klau published his treatise *De sphaera* in Rome in 1570, while Valignano was studying theology. When he was named Visitor to the East Indies, Valignano had five years of philosophy and theology behind him. He had also been for a brief time master of novices, then rector, at the College of Macerata.[37] In other words, he was as deeply imbued with the dominant culture in philosophy as were his colleagues at Coimbra.

The first discourse in the *Catechismus christianae fidei* begins by refusing to grant the slightest intellectual plausibility to the "first principle" of the Japanese. This, by its claims, is perfect in all ways and endowed with wisdom but has no intelligence, remains in total stasis, and is wholly unconcerned with occurrences in the material world. It is said that this principle is present in each human being but on the death of the individual does no more than return to its source, and there is no punishment or reward waiting in the beyond. It is absurd, and contrary to reason, to speak of wisdom in an entity lacking intelligence. And, Valignano reasons, first, if this "first principle" is present in all human beings, then its capabilities—its intelligence, for example—are not superior to those of humans; indeed, "nothing can confer or give what it does not possess in itself, in actuality or in potential" *(quod ipse re, aut potestate non habet);* second, if it is perfect, the "first principle" is necessarily intelligent; third, if it is entirely passive, it is no better than a stone; and fourth, if it is not intelligent, then truth, insight, reason, and thought are foreign to it, "for truth, clarity, reason, and thought have their home and their seat in the mind and in intelligence, but whatever is lacking in mind and intelligence cannot have any of this" *(qui vero mente, et intelligentia vacat, nihil horum prorsus habere potest).*

The existence of the universe necessarily presupposes the existence of a creator, and the latter must possess perfect intelligence. Every object made by human hands presupposes the existence of a worker, and every being engendered necessarily has a progenitor. This world is so great, so beauteous, so vast, that the one who created it can only be endowed with superior intelligence. Nothing moves by itself; everything requires a prime mover. Last, each being has its own finality: the arrow would not find its mark were it not aimed by the archer. The first discourse of the *Catechismus christianae fidei* ends, without a single word having been said about Christianity per se, in a hymn to the glory of a wholly constructed concept. And Valignano concludes, "From all these reasonings and arguments it emerges clearly that Japanese religions make a declaration that is false and completely absurd when they teach, in regard to the supreme principle, that the entity from which the whole makeup of the world ensues has no intelligence."

The second discourse begins by explaining that if the Japanese, who are no more foolish than other people, have fallen into such grave error, it is the fault of the Buddhist priests, who are ignorant and stupid. Returning to the perfection of God, Valignano goes on to insist that God is One. Aristotle, he recalls, did not think that there was one single substance: "It is contrary to reason *[nulla ratione fieri potest]* that the first principle be identified with the very nature of all things and with their substance." Aristotle and other philosophers have shown that a first principle that is a sort of soul of the world would be absurd. Its substance cannot be identified either as that of the totality of all created things or as an isolated part of them, and the principle does not act in them and through them as though they were instruments. Here he presents the classic Aristotelian distinction between *matter* and *form*. Form, says Valignano, is "that which gives to things either their meaning, their life, or their movement: it is that by which things accede to the state of being." All things found in nature, he continues, "are constituted of two principles, matter, certainly, but also form." A third principle, the *principium efficiens* (the efficient cause or driving force) makes matter, the material cause, take one form or another. All observable movement is a combination of matter and form and proceeds in the final analysis from the impulsion of a single prime mover, which has neither beginning nor end and is beyond space, movement, and time. For Valignano (but not for Aristotle, as we shall see later), this prime mover must be called God: "We say that God is the author of this world, the worker par excellence, the prime manufacturer of all things in existence. It is God who, through an act of will and through his power, creates and gives form to everything that exists. He assembles, he constructs, either out of his own core or through the intermediary of efficient causes." Clearly, the Japanese did not understand how these efficient causes act; they were unable to grasp the principles correctly. That is why they thought the "first principle" could indeed exist in each being, either as matter or as form.

Valignano's properly philosophical demonstration closes in the third discourse with a traditional exposition on the immortality of the soul, the necessity of which must seem obvious to anyone concerned about the postmortem recompense of good and evil actions. From the Aristotelian conception of the soul—the first degree of achieved life, the union par excellence of matter and form—and from the (non-Aristotelian) identification of the "prime mover" with the Creator, Valignano, like all his colleagues, draws his definition of the spirit, or soul, as "spiritual form and substance" *(substantia quaedam et forma spiritualis)*. This spiritual substance must be immortal, like the "first principle" from which it emanates, and because it is immortal, the good and evil acts it has committed in the course of its earthly sojourn can be sanctioned after its separation from the body.[38]

One may apply to this entirely typical "demonstration" the critical remarks made by Gernet in *Chine et christianisme* regarding Father Ricci's catechism for the Chinese. For Valignano as for Ricci, to imagine that matter in itself can be endowed with movement, and even with intelligence, is scandalous. Neither of them seems to conceive that the Chinese or Japanese might think in different mental categories than do Europeans. They really believe, because humans are actually or potentially rational under all skies, that notions such as *form, principle, matter, substance*, and *soul* are truly universal. They do not admit that the Chinese and Japanese may not only be saying things with different words, but rather, and more important, may actually think about them differently, with different concepts, articulated with different modes of reasoning, in a different logic. On this level, the question is not Aristotle, or scholasticism's greater or lesser fidelity to the Peripatetic tradition; it is the inability of the missionaries, despite their attentiveness to the particularities of cultural context, to call into question the presuppositions of their own intellectual processes.

In Japan, however, when Valignano wrote his catechism, the missionaries took a step in the right direction in deciding, along with Gago and thereafter, that the content of thought proper to the Christian West could only be expressed in a European language, ancient or modern. But although the best among them made an effort to study and master the Japanese language, they did not understand that Latin or Portuguese words transliterated into that tongue, but excised from their original semantic domain and poured into an altogether different syntactic mold, suffered a tremendous loss of meaning at best and a total denaturing at worst. Valignano, who never learned Japanese, excluded any consideration of having his catechism translated into Japanese; its use was reserved for those of the Japanese who understood Latin. This fact notwithstanding, when the Visitor wrote the first three chapters of his book, he set out to furnish its users with arguments useful against *Japanese* adversaries. He imagined, then, that the mental categories in which they thought would be the same as his own.

Likewise, in making scholastic philosophy the indispensable base of their evangelical work, Valignano, Ricci, and their companions did not seem to doubt the concordance of what they considered Revealed Truth with the teachings of ancient philosophy. This could be justified perhaps for that portion of the Scriptures written in Greek: it is certain that Luke and Paul were culturally Greek, even if one of them was a Syrian who spoke Aramaic and the other was a Jew and a citizen of Rome. But if it is true that some books of the Old Testament, like the books of Wisdom, were influenced by Hellenism, it also seems that between the ancient Hebrews and even the Jews of Palestine in Jesus' time, on the one hand, and the great Greek philosophers of antiquity such as Aristotle, on the other, there was a considerable distance, both linguistically and even in modes of conceptualization. It would be quite difficult to find in the Old Testament, or even the New, any equivalent to what Aristotle understood as substance, form, matter, first principle, or efficient cause. The sixteenth-century missionaries were less apt to suspect this pitfall in that, even if they had a vague knowledge of Hebrew or Greek, they ordinarily read the Bible in Vulgate Latin.[39]

Valignano's catechism was published during the time that Mancius, Michaël, Martinus, and Julianus happened to be in Portugal.

They asked to enter the Society after their return, and in July 1591 all four donned the novice's habit at Amakusa. Thus it is not impossible that they read Valignano in the course of their training. Unfortunately, no evidence of this reading exists. It is known, however, that Mancius, at least, read in Latin the *Compendium catholicae veritatis* by Father Gómez. This *Compendium*, now found in the Vatican Library,[40] is the sole surviving example of an unprinted "literature" that was, it appears, very rich. It consisted of versions freely and diversely adapted for use by Japanese students from the philosophy and theology courses taught at Coimbra, and it may be supposed that each instructor had his own. The manuscript that remains is in three parts, which are, in order, *De sphaera* (fols. 1–38), the *Breve compendium eorum quae ab Aristotele in tribus libris de anima, et in parvis rebus dicta sunt* (fols. 42–108), and the *Compendium catholicae veritatis* itself (fols. 122–432).

Gómez entered the Society of Jesus in 1553 at Alcalá. By 1555 he had left Spain for Portugal and had spent fifteen years there. He benefited from the instruction in philosophy and theology dispensed by the Coimbra College of the Arts and became an instructor there. Ordained a priest in 1559, he went to preach in the Azores for a time. He departed for the Far East in 1579 and beginning in 1582 was the superior of the Bungo district on Kyushu, under the direct authority of the vice provincial. As such, he was charged with designing instruction in philosophy and theology aimed at European theology students of the Bungo school. In 1590, the same year the "ambassadors" returned, he himself became vice provincial. He died in 1600.

A letter from Mancius, written in Rome in March 1594, proves that by that date the course written by Gómez ten years earlier had been passed on from the hands of the European scholastics to those of the Japanese. Within days of Mancius's writing, however, Gómez wrote to one of his own correspondents that Japanese brothers could not be trained the way others were, because they were older and, more than anything, because they had to learn Latin. The *Compendium*, therefore, served primarily as a study text for learning the language. Gómez was fully convinced of the need for them to learn the distinctions between the rational soul, the vegetative soul, and the sensitive soul and to be able to contrast the potentiality for becoming or doing with its actualization. A letter written later in the same year shows that, at Bungo as at Coimbra, the verities of the faith were introduced only after philosophical training, and always in Latin.

Here is a brief résumé of the progression of the course, after the treatise *De sphaera*, which served as its introduction. The second part of the collection dealt chiefly with the soul, defined in Aristotelian terms as "the realization or first entelechy of a natural organic body, which has life in potentiality" *(actus primus corporis physici organici, potentia vitam habentis)*. The soul is a function having three classes ordered hierarchically. In its lowest degree, it is vegetative. Its existence is expressed by the natural warmth of the body; this level exists in all living beings. In its second degree, it is sensitive, allowing all animals to perceive and to acquire a representation of the external appearance of things. It also endows them with the power to move *(potentia locomotiva)*. The highest function of the soul is reserved for human beings, the function of reasoning.

The mental act by which one rises from the sensitive and vegetative functions to the reasoning, intellectual function is judgment. This act of the intellect consists of discerning intelligible forms among the perceptible ones. But human intellect is limited to receptivity, passivity, and potential *(intellectus possibilis)*; another intellect *(intellectus agens)* must illuminate and actualize intelligible forms for it. This is not of humans; it resides elsewhere than in matter. It is immortal; it is divine intellect. For the Jesuits and for Gómez in particular, the *intellectus agens* alone can procure for humanity a knowledge of God. To lead the young Japanese to the threshold of this "enlightenment," and to a precise comprehension of the conditions of its possibility, rigorous philosophical training had to be dispensed before unveiling the revealed truths.

The second part of the collection ends with the expected exposition on the emotions, free will, and the immortality of the soul. Its properly theological part *(Compendium catholicae veritatis)* conforms to the directives of the Council of Trent. Its teaching addresses five points: the God of the Credo, the commandments of God and of the Church, the sacraments, Christian life, and the virtues and vices.

Gómez's *Compendium*, probably much the same as those that have been lost, was principally a guide to preaching. It was addressed, through the preacher, to people to whom the Christian religion was unknown. Its aim was a practical one. For this reason questions of dogma were not treated separately and as such. Once the Dominicans and Franciscans were authorized to settle on the archipelago, they, too, composed "manuals," also inspired by the *Catechismus romanus*. These manuals were intended to train young people in the spirit of the Coimbra College of the Arts or the Collegio Romano and to lead them eventually to the priesthood. It is not surprising that one wished to give them instruction as similar as possible to that given in the best European institutions. More surprising is that the arguments and reasoning in currency within these institutions were also used in the missionaries' debates against the philosophers and non-Christian clergy who consented to confront them.

The first debate whose content is known with any precision took place in 1551, with Father Cosmo de Torres (1510–70) opposite the Buddhist monks of Yamaguchi. Torres was a priest of Spanish origin, born in Valencia. Ordained into the priesthood in 1535, he had initially become a teacher, then embarked for New Spain. He went from there to Asia and met Francis Xavier in the Moluccas in 1546. He entered the Society of Jesus in 1548 in Goa, where he was assigned to teach grammar. He was among those Francis Xavier took with him to Japan in 1549.[41] The content of the argument has survived, thanks to Brother João Fernandes (or Juan Fernández), who knew a little Japanese, in three letters written by Torres in late September and early October 1551. Two of them were published in Portugal before the end of the century. There is also a letter from Fernández to Francis Xavier, dated October 20, 1551, excerpts of which had reached Europe.

At the outset Torres situates the argument on the terrain of reason alone. The Japanese, he says, "may be led by reason just as well as and even more willingly than may Spaniards." Then he intrepidly broaches the subject of *principle*, understood as both foundation and origin, and registers his surprise that the principle admitted by the Buddhists is pure nonbeing, foreign to distinctions of good and evil, life and death. Humans, the monks reply, have in themselves the capacity to distinguish good from evil; reason teaches them this. If they can reason, they need not be concerned with the beyond. Those concerned about their salvation are simple people. The sages know that the passions are extinguished along with life, and at death the body returns to the elements of which it was composed. But, Torres retorts, only animals are satisfied when their appetites are sated; humans aspire to eternal joy. Their passions turn them away from it, and they fear punishment. After the question of *principle* comes that of the *soul*. What is that? ask the monks. What is it made of? Torres replies: The one who made the sun, the moon, and all that exists, solely by his word and his will, has also made the soul. It is created out of nothing. It is not seen or felt, it has neither shape nor color, yet it exists, like the wind, like air, which likewise cannot be seen. And this God of whom you preach, who is he? The principle of all things. He had no beginning and will have no end but is at the origin of all things; it is in him that they have their beginning. Does he have a body? Can he be seen? He has created the elements, but he himself is not composed of elements. Will the souls of the just, separated from the body after death, be visible? If so, why can the just not see them while alive? Because a gem, however brilliant, does not shine when buried in mire, and so on.

This was the style and the tone: these were academic debates. And they go on in this vein for pages. In one of the rare moments when the polemic rises above such quibbling, the Buddhists introduce into the discussion notions specific to their own philosophy. But when Torres writes the word *Qu*, it is impossible to know what he really understood by it and still less the actual meaning of the word. He translated it far from rigorously as *form*, which made sense to him in the context of Aristotelian philosophy. But to the Buddhist monks?

The best polemicist of the period is Fabian Fukan, author of the adaptation of *Heike monogatari* printed at Amakusa in 1592 or 1593. He was Japanese, born in the Kyoto region in 1564 or 1565. The numerous quotations he uses from the classics of Buddhist and Confucian literature indicate that he had received a good education in this domain, perhaps in a Buddhist temple. He converted to Christianity quite young, perhaps in 1582, and in 1584 joined the ranks of the Society of Jesus. He became a coadjutor in the Society in 1586. In 1592 he was still coadjutor, teaching the Japanese language at the College of Amakusa.[42]

Fabian was about forty years old when he wrote the dialogue *Myôtei Mondô*, named after his two characters, ladies named *Myôshu* and *Yûtei*. Fabian defined the aim of his work, in a sort of postface to the dialogue, in these words:

> The *Myôtei Mondô* was written because noble wives and widows may not easily receive visits from a man, even an ecclesiastic; they have therefore no means of obtaining instruction in religious matters; were they to wish it, their desire would be in vain. Thus I have composed the present volume so that such people may read and understand these truths, and may know, in consequence, how desirable Christianity is. It is divided into three volumes: the first assails and refutes Buddhism as a perverse law, since it rests on the void; the second argues against the doctrines of Confucianism and Shintoism and establishes that there is a great difference between them and Christianity, the true religion; the third reveals and exalts the truth of Christianity, our religion.[43]

Naturally, the dialogue was written in Japanese: it had to be understood even by the ladies of the court. Indeed, by all indications in the text, Myôshu belongs to the aristocracy and has enjoyed an enviable lot in the past, but no longer. Yûtei, who is Christian, is apparently of somewhat lower rank.

The first and second volumes, devoted to the Japanese religions, are rather technical, but there were at the time in good society women cultivated enough to follow all the subtleties of Confucian philosophy and the teachings of the Buddhist sects. Much more surprising are the first three parts of the third book, which could be mistaken for a rendering into dialogue form of a philosophy course from Goa or Coimbra. The first Aristotelian concept introduced in the propositions of Yûtei is that of *materia prima* (in Latin in the Japanese text). This is, she says, a "being created by the Lord of my religion . . . of which he has made the substance of all things." And to make it quite clear to Myôshu, she explains that it is the equivalent for Christians of the *in-yo* of Shintoism (or the Yin and the Yang, the two opposing and complementary forces whose perpetual interplay engenders the elements). The traditional demonstration follows: no created thing can exist without a creator, and so on. The Creator and Lord of the Universe is necessarily unique. This is demonstrated (1) by his perfection, (2) by his omnipotence, and (3) by the orderliness that reigns in his creation. And he has no beginning since he himself is at the origin of everything.

A second Aristotelian concept is then introduced by Yûtei, that of the *spiritual sustancia* (this time in Portuguese in the text). "Which means," she explains, "substance without color or form. [But the fact] that the eye cannot see it nor the hands feel it does not necessarily mean that it does not exist. In fact the general law is that one finds through its properties the essence of things, which may not be seen with the eyes or touched with the hands." *Property* and *essence* are two more classical Aristotelian concepts that are not explained and whose use in the definition of "spiritual substance" renders it incomprehensible. As was probably the practice in teaching Japanese theology students at the time, Fabian gets around the problem by illustrating Yûtei's proposals with examples: the boat that seems to glide across the waters, although we know it requires a captain and rowers; the stone that flies through the air, which someone necessarily has hurled. Thus it is with the heavens and the earth, which an invisible being one day hurled into space.

From the philosophical "demonstration" the text proceeds to theology, as does the *Curso conimbricense*. The invisible hurler, God, *spiritual sustancia*, is traditionally *sapientissimo*, *misericordissimo*, *justissimo*, and *omnipotente*, all qualities that are deduced from his essence. None of them is to be found in the *materia prima*.

The third part of the book deals with the *anima racional* (in Portuguese in the original). For Aristotle, this is the third term of a series that includes the *anima vegetativa* and the *anima sensitiva*. Yûtei, alias Fabian, adds a fourth, which serves as the foundation for the whole: this is *being*, the simple fact of being (in Portuguese or Spanish, *ser*), a small addition with far-reaching consequences, when one knows, as Fabian obviously did, the importance of the notion of *being* in Western thought. Here I must quote Gernet, who himself is commenting on Benveniste:[44]

Benveniste demonstrates that Aristotle's ten categories (all that can be enunciated about a subject, or in a more restricted sense all possible primary and irreducible types of being) are a set of noun and verb categories that are particular to the Greek language. . . . And he adds this, which is capital to the explanation of the general differences between the conception of the world in China and in the West: "Beyond Aristotelian terms, above this categorization [Fabian would think it more accurately below, rather than above] lies the notion of 'being,' which encompasses everything. Not only did Greek have a verb 'to be,' which is in no way requisite to all languages, but [Aristotle] used the verb in entirely singular ways. . . . The language allowed 'being' to become an objectivizable notion, which philosophical reflection could manipulate, analyze, and situate as it could any other concept."

Benveniste's analysis, Gernet goes on to say, "points up two characteristics of Greek thought—and Western thought in general—that bear a close relationship to the structure of the Greek and Latin languages: first, the existence of categories whose characteristics of being evident and necessary rely unconsciously on the usage of language, and second, the fundamental importance to Western philosophical and religious thought of the notion of being. Throughout its history, the West has been seeking being beyond appearances."[45] Symptomatic of this is the fact that Fabian, writing in Japanese for a relatively broad public, was unable to express it other than in Portuguese, *without explanation*. The illustration he offers for it ("the category of beings") does not do justice to *ser:* the totality of beings (sky, earth, sun, moon, stars, metals, stones) is not a notion identical to *being*.

Appearance, form, essence, all the Aristotelian notions brought into play in the text to render Chinese and Japanese philosophical notions as nearly as possible, suffer from a fundamental weakness: they are analytic; they separate; they distinguish between categories. The Japanese, like the Chinese, "reject any radical distinction between nature and its power to order and to generate, [they do not admit] the existence of a world of eternal truths separate from the world of appearances and transient realities." For the Christians, on the contrary, "heirs to Greek thought and medieval theology, these distinctions were . . . so basic, so obvious and natural, that their historical character and their links to certain categories of language could not be perceived."[46]

As a good pupil to the Jesuits, Fabian obviously cannot conceive— or if he can conceive, cannot admit it, although he will do so years later—that the "differentiation of beings" might be a phenomenon that is its own explanation. He needs a primary cause, external and in no way immanent in the perceptible world, that imposes forms and diversifies objects. He needs above all to "demonstrate" that the *anima racional* "does not come from the body," that its *essence* comes from elsewhere, that its *substance* will survive its mortal remains. When, at this point in the debate, Myôshu at last admits that all that has been shown to her is grounded in reason, her Christian education may commence: this is the object of the fourth, fifth, and sixth parts of the dialogue, which concern heaven and hell, the instruments of salvation and damnation, and so on. But the essential has been played out in the philosophical part of the debate: reason and reason alone can, at the endpoint of a rigorous dialectic, lead the ignorant person acting in good faith to the threshold of revelation. The fourth part of the dialogue begins, indeed, with these words, placed in Yûtei's mouth: "Generally speaking, the teachings of this religion hold points that are decided by reason and others that have no recourse to arguments but resolve a question by invoking tradition. The truths set forth here, the existence of a lord of heaven and earth, the presence in human beings of a life principle that is called the *anima racional* and may continue in another life, are those proven by reason. The same is true for this: that the Lord, as the source of justice, must reward the good and punish the wicked." And Myôshu concludes the dialogue by saying, "Among all the reasons you have put forth in reply to my questions, I see none that is not right and convincing; now, then, lead me to the temple."

Shortly after having written this edifying dialogue and having defended it in debate against a celebrated neo-Confucianist philosopher, Hayashi Razan (1583–1659),[47] Brother Fabian renounced his faith. Several years later, in 1620, he wrote a refutation of Christianity titled *Ha daiusu* (The God of the Christians Confuted), which was a complete reversal of the theses upheld in *Myôtei Mondô*.[48]

Of the four Japanese who traveled as ambassadors to Europe in 1582–90 and were initiated into the Society of Jesus on their return, only one became a martyr for professing his faith. This was Julianus, who died on October 18, 1633. Nothing is known of Mancius and Martinus except that they died in 1612 and 1623, respectively. Michaël, like Fabian, became an apostate.

After the eradication of Christianity, there was no more Aristotle in Japan until the Meiji Restoration. But Æsop, a naturalized Japanese, continued to enchant the literate and small children. The story of Christianity, revisited and revised by oral tradition and cut off from the philosophical and theological bases the missionaries had given it, continued to nourish the piety of older Japanese Catholics, who held out until the middle of the nineteenth century against the persecution and pressures of a cultural milieu fundamentally hostile to the path they had chosen.[49]

Chapter Two

The Worm in the Fruit
Marranism and Erasmianism

Father Valignano's four envoys had been well prepared before their departure and were closely escorted during the course of their journey; they did not suspect for an instant what the facade of the grandiose monument they were admiring might conceal. The seventh of the dialogues recounting their trip is titled "Dialogue concerning the things of Europe in general and in particular the sacred or ecclesiastical monarchy, and other lesser offices." It lauds the glory of the successor to Peter, of the Curia and the Roman hierarchy, of the religious orders, and of those who make the greatest sacrifices to carry the Gospel to the ends of the earth. One searches the document in vain for any trace of the great upheavals then wracking the continent. This was an idealized Europe, gathered in its entirety under the wing of the Catholic church, with no Protestants, no Jews, no religious wars, no Inquisition. At most, the distant threat of Islam could be perceived.

However, the imperium the Church of Rome claimed to impose on Europe and the world was threatened in Portugal itself by two much more immediate dangers, ones that even "Christian" Japan would not entirely escape. The first came from what were known in Portugal as the "new Christians," who were numerous and active in mission lands overseas; the second consisted of the remnants of the intellectual movement labeled "Erasmianism," which had supposedly been eradicated on the Iberian Peninsula since the middle of the sixteenth century.

THE "NEW CHRISTIANS"

Portugal came to anti-Semitism later than other European countries, but once it took hold, the country threw itself into it with a passion. At first Portugal welcomed the Jews expelled from Spain in 1492. They joined communities already established in Lisbon, Coimbra, Porto, and elsewhere, places where they traditionally enjoyed relative protection. Portuguese Jews were often rich and occupied enviable positions in society. Among them were mathematicians, cartographers, astronomers, and seafarers, as well as doctors, who were highly esteemed as a class.[1]

But the hospitality John II showed the Spanish Jews was not disinterested. He extracted from them as much money as possible in exchange for temporary authorization to remain in the country and assistance in departing to settle elsewhere. After which he brutally turned against them. In 1493 he had Jewish children between the ages of two and ten kidnapped and deported to Africa. Nearly all of them died in transit or on arrival. His successor, Emmanuel I, needed Spain's support to pursue his dynastic interests. He ruled in 1496 that Muslims and Jews must leave within a ten-month period, on pain of death and confiscation of property. Then, seeing that many were indeed preparing to depart, he took extreme measures: he first ordered that all Jewish children under the age of fourteen be rounded up and raised in Christian families, then had all the adult Jews in the country forcibly baptized. This was in 1497. Many attempted to escape the terror by fleeing to Italy, Anvers, Africa, and the eastern Mediterranean. Others committed suicide or killed their children. Those who remained and survived the forced baptism were known thereafter as "Christians." But for the native Portuguese—the "old Christians," whose resentment was constantly rekindled by the sermons of priests and monks—they were still Jews. The authorities also suspected them of continuing to practice Judaism in secret and hounded them relentlessly. Thus the "new

Christians" often fell victim to the excesses of a popular hatred stoked by religious and civil authorities. In 1506 four thousand of them were massacred by the inhabitants of Lisbon, who divided among themselves their gold, their jewels, everything they possessed. Adults were burned alive, children hacked to death. The king himself was moved by this. He authorized those Jews who so desired to leave the country. But for those who could not leave, things were much the same.

After the death of Emmanuel II, John III adopted a different tactic with regard to the "new Christians." In 1536 he obtained from Pope Paul III a bull establishing the court of the Inquisition in Portugal. The chief function of this new institution was to monitor closely the acts and movements of the community and prevent the bourgeoisie of Jewish origin from regaining their former power.

For its part, Spain set in place "blood purity" statutes ratified by the pope (1555). These obliged any person who wished to enroll in a university, exercise a public office, or enter a religious order to present a genealogy free of all traces of "impure blood." When Portugal was united with the Spanish crown in 1580 on the accession of Philip II, the "blood purity" law applied forthwith in Portugal as well.

There remained to Jews only two possible sources of livelihood: banking and trade. They set about these activities all the more ardently since after the Great Discoveries Portugal had been opened up to significant trade with the Americas and Asia. The dispersal of Jewish exiles throughout the world favored the creation of financial and commercial networks that were both far-flung and reliable. They made use of this resource with intelligence. But their new prosperity redoubled the hatred of their enemies: the more successful they were, the more the Inquisition harassed them, in Europe and overseas.[2]

Spiritually, these "new Christians" were no longer entirely Jews, but they were not really Christians either. They practiced the externals of Catholicism but most often remained attached to customs and rites handed down within the family through the women. This was their downfall: to take Saturday as one's customary day of rest, keep a lamp burning on Friday evening, or openly refuse to eat pork was sufficient grounds for accusations of "Judaizing." Denunciation was vigorously encouraged and false testimony favorably received; the trials were countless. They most often concluded with vigorous autos-da-fé:

Lisbon, 1540, 1541; Goa, 1543; Évora, 1557; Coimbra, 1567. The "new Christians" who had amassed fortunes tried to buy their lives at a high price, either from the Inquisitors, not all of whom were deaf to their arguments, or from the pope. At one point the king proposed on his own initiative to ease conditions for the "new Christians" in exchange for an extremely elevated lump-sum payment. They paid it; their lot was unchanged.[3]

The ever-present issue of these "new Christians" was a blight on university life as well. The Jesuits and judges of the Holy Office, the Visitors of the Society, the rectors of the university, and the various religious orders were always quick to accuse each other of being irresolute in the face of their common enemy. At first, the Jesuits were not in favor of discriminating between "old" and "new" Christians. Ignatius of Loyola, the first superior general of the order, soon came into conflict on this point with the archbishop of Toledo and the provincial superior of Portugal. He wrote to the latter in 1554: "Being from a family of new Christians is no impediment to taking part in the Society." This pronouncement was renewed a year later. Loyola merely advised that discretion be used and that the parties in question be sent *outside Portugal*. In a country in which popular prejudice had been inflamed and the authorities were unbending, one had to avoid any discredit to the faith, but no fundamental objection was invoked.[4]

Loyola had studied at the Sorbonne with one of these "new Christians," Diego Laínez. He had made him his vicar general, and it was Laínez who succeeded Loyola as superior general of the order. Laínez was from a family that had converted three generations earlier, and there is no cause to doubt the sincerity of his faith. He quickly drew notice, however, by his strong emphasis on absolute obedience within the Society. His insistence reached the point of intransigence, a frequent attitude among converts, who took pains to avoid the slightest suspicion of heterodoxy. This very stance, evil minds insinuated, was the one best suited to concealing a lack of personal faith. Many "new Christians," their faith fresh or long-standing, were thus torn between the tendency toward blind reliance on faith and Machiavellian temptations.

The Church and its religious orders had quite a few "new Christian" members at the end of the sixteenth century, both in Portugal and in Spain. Despite the intransigence of Simão Rodrigues, the first provincial superior of Portugal, a "new Christian" by the name of Manuel Lopes, who was born in Porto in 1525 and had studied at the Coimbra College of the Arts, was allowed to enter the Society of Jesus. He was one of the first members of the College of Alcalá in Spain, rector of Alcalá in 1556, provincial superior of Toledo from 1565 to 1568, then superior of the Professed House in Toledo. He then went to the province of Castilla, was teacher and rector of novices at Villagarcia, and finally superior of the Professed House at Burgos. He died peacefully at Alcalá in 1603. He had spent his entire career in Spain, and thus caused no stir in his native land. His brother, Henrique Henriques, was also a Jesuit. He entered the Society in 1552 and became a theologian of some repute, but again in Spain; he taught at Córdoba and Salamanca, among other colleges. Unlike his brother, he was known for his heterodox opinions. The general survey of moral theology he published in Salamanca in 1588, which had several reprintings, was criticized for containing theses opposed to those of the famous casuist Molina. His theses on ecclesiastical immunity, which defended the rights of the king against those of the Church, were condemned in Rome, and the work that contained them was seized and burned in 1603. He also caused friction within the Society when the *Ratio studiorum* was still under scrutiny: he objected to it for departing from the strictest Thomist tradition, of which he was a confirmed partisan. He even left the Jesuits for a time to become a Dominican.

Manuel Lopes and Henrique Henriques had two other brothers, who also became Jesuits. Their father, Master Simão, was a physician from a large neo-Christian family in Porto, the Bemtalhados. The family also included two Franciscans, one Dominican, and one Benedictine. But an uncle of the four Jesuits, Manuel Bemtalhado, was burned by the Holy Office in 1602 at Coimbra, and several other members of the family who were rounded up and sentenced at the same time confessed, willingly or by force, to having "Judaized" in secret. For the Portuguese "new Christians," the broad avenue to honors and riches was never far from the narrow path to jail and the stake.[5]

As Loyola had suggested to Rodrigues, expatriation could be a convenient resort for the "new Christians." There were illustrious examples in Asia, such as Father Pedro Gómez. Valignano often had dealings with Gómez during his second stay in Japan, after the return of the young Japanese "ambassadors" from Europe. And it seems that not the slightest fault was ever found with Gómez's duty to his order or to Catholic orthodoxy.

There were also numerous physicians among these expatriates. The practice of medicine was an ancient tradition in the Jewish communities of Spain and Portugal. It continued unbroken with the converts. Toward the end of the sixteenth century, it was estimated that a third of the doctors practicing in the East Indies were of Jewish origin. In 1581, at Goa, the Jesuit headquarters in the area, there were one physician and two surgeons, all three of them "new Christians." This situation did not please the authorities. Valignano was perturbed by it as early as 1575. He wrote to the superior general to request that he stem this possibly perilous tide.[6]

The situation was detrimental to Portugal itself, and in quite a different way than the authorities thought. Thanks to the long tradition maintained by Jewish doctors, Portuguese medicine and surgery had been brought to a high level by the early sixteenth century. Books were written and published in Portuguese on the treatment of wounds.[7] The works of Guy de Chauliac, from Montpellier, were well known in Lisbon and Coimbra. The same was true of the works of Ambroise Paré, although they did not have wide circulation.[8] The chair in anatomy at the University of Coimbra was held by a professor of no small merit. His name was Alfonso Rodrigues de Guevara, and he was familiar with the research of Vesalius in anatomy. Later, in 1596, the Castilian Rodrigo Reinoso introduced the practice of dissection to the university and hospital at Coimbra.

Nonetheless, because the incessant persecution of the "new Christians" drove off its best practitioners, medical studies continued to decline in Portugal. They went to study in Salamanca, Valladolid, Bologna, Paris, and elsewhere. Thus we find the names Francisco Sanches and André Lourenço Ferreira on the roll books at the University of Montpellier and that of Estevão Rodrigues at Pisa.[9]

The "new Christians" were not attracted to medicine solely because of the tradition of their "nation." Another draw was the pragmatic character of the discipline, increasingly oriented toward direct observation and concomitantly less subject to the yoke of authority.

From the Middle Ages on, there had been a tendency in Spanish Jewry toward skepticism and rationalism, particularly pronounced in the financial aristocracy and among physicians and philosophers. Later, in the "convert" community, it was doctors, again, who went furthest in their critique of Christian dogma and in questioning traditional Jewish beliefs.[10] If one may speak of a "Marrano religion," as does Israël Salvador Révah, the eminent historian of Portuguese Jews, the term must not be used to mean only the external observation of Catholic practices and the attachment in private to a few customs peculiar to Judaism. Marranism is characterized first and foremost by the negation of all orthodoxy, Jewish or Christian.[11] It is understandable that the civil and religious authorities who had trusteeship of the East Indies were disquieted to see so many Marrano physicians exercising their considerable talents there.

The Jesuits were confronted with a real problem. Their status as priests and the Constitutions of the order forbade them, in principle, to study, teach, or practice medicine. But they were not forbidden to come to the aid of the sick, the poor, and the infirm. On the contrary, the order recommended the practice of charitable works. Faithful to this vocation, the missionaries created charitable establishments at Yamaguchi and Funai in 1555, at Hirado in 1557, at Nagasaki in 1583, at Sakai and Osaka in 1591–92. But where were they to find a doctor, and how were they to encourage the exercise and instruction of medicine within the Society, without contravening the will of the Church and the founders of the order?

Luís de Almeida

The relative tolerance shown by Ignatius of Loyola in regard to the Portuguese "new Christians" found recompense—an almost miraculously fortuitous one for the Jesuits in Japan—when in 1555 Luís de Almeida arrived in Hirado from Malacca. Who was he? Not much is known, and the mystery seems to have contributed in no small measure to his legendary status. He was born, it is believed, to a rich family of "new Christians" in Lisbon in 1523 or 1525. Thus he would have been of Jewish origin, some say Moorish. He is thought to have studied to become a surgeon at the Todos-os-Santos hospital in Lisbon. The establishment had been founded in 1498 by John II. Apprenticeship there lasted for two years and was followed by a practical course, on completion of which the candidates were tested by a head surgeon appointed by the king. It is recorded that Almeida received his diploma at Lisbon in 1546. Nothing is known of the level of instruction he was given, but it was probably more practical than theoretical and the short duration indicates it had to be rather superficial. In those days, in any case, in Portugal as elsewhere, *a surgeon was not a physician.*

It is not known what Almeida did between 1546 and 1555, or why fate drew him to the Far East. But whatever his personal motives, he was following a path trodden by many of his peers before him. Did he engage in trade during his stay there? Did he amass a fortune from it? Some have believed, and have written, that he did, but there appears to be a mix-up between two different Almeidas, an adventurer with extensive business enterprises in Asia and the surgeon who graduated from Todos-os-Santos. Given that the adventurer also frequented the Japanese coast, the confusion is understandable.

Whatever the facts of Almeida's past, Gago took a liking to him, and shortly after his arrival in Kyushu Almeida asked to enter the Society of Jesus. He became thenceforth Brother Luís de Almeida. He had been a trained surgeon well before becoming a Jesuit, and because he was not a priest as yet, none could reproach him with violating the regulations. Those who had recourse to his services had no sense that they were violating them either. Must not every good Christian perform works of mercy? Feed the hungry, give drink to the thirsty, shelter the wayfarer, clothe the naked, care for the sick, visit the imprisoned—all acts that, to go by chapter 25 of the Gospel according to Saint Matthew, serve the Lord when performed for one's neighbor. The Jesuits' cloth did not exempt them from obeying this law. Indeed, this was why they founded Confraternities of Mercy everywhere they were able as soon as they arrived in Japan.

In 1555 Gago opened a sort of dispensary in Funai that he called Our Lady of Mercy of Bungo, after a chapel in the cloister of the Lisbon cathedral, which had been the seat of a charitable brotherhood since the thirteenth century. Only the most basic care was administered there. The following year the superior of the mission tried to have it replaced with a real hospital. The "king" of Bungo, Otomo Yoshishige, approved the project, and a part of the Jesuits' residence was divided into two facilities, one for the sick who were able to be treated, the other for the incurably ill, mostly lepers. In 1559 it was necessary to open a third facility, a true clinic, with rooms for the sick having two beds each, a wing for the convalescing, and lodgings for nursing and service staff. Whom better to entrust with the directorship of the overall operation than Brother Luís de Almeida, an accredited surgeon? He accepted the post with alacrity and set to practicing the art he had learned in Portugal. Better yet, he taught it to Japanese pupils, thus becoming the founder of the first school of Western medicine in Japan. The Japanese called it *namban-ryu*, School of the Southern Barbarians.

Almeida himself performed operations on chancres, ulcers, abscesses, and gunshot wounds and trained several Japanese students who in a few years became prized practitioners themselves. He was extremely cautious when it came to internal medicine, however, and for this he had recourse to Chinese traditional medicine and its pharmacopoeia. One of his first concerns was to establish a pharmacy. He sent for traditional products from China, Malacca, and Goa and conferred the task of preparing remedies and unguents on Brother Paulo, a Japanese Jesuit and former Buddhist monk who owned some Chinese manuals. On Paulo's death, the pharmacy passed into the hands of Brother Miguel, also Japanese. As Almeida would not dare to practice Chinese medicine himself, he had the sick examined by a practitioner from Funai.

From the little we know of Almeida's activities as head of the hospital at Funai, we recognize the pragmatic intelligence then customarily associated with doctors of Jewish origin. It is observable particularly in his separation of the practices of internal medicine and surgery, in his absence of any prejudice toward traditional Chinese medicine, and in his care to educate Japanese students identified early on as capable of reaching the same level as their European teacher. One more detail is worthy of note: the sick who hoped to be cured at Funai often came from far away, and most were not Christians. But Almeida made it a rule that a patient could not be baptized until he or she had been cured. This may be seen as an example of the pastoral caution the Jesuits generally exhibited in their evangelical work. One may also speculate that a "new Christian" would have been averse to the idea of more or less blackmailing people into baptism.

Unfortunately for Almeida, and for the Jesuits' mission in Japan, Rome at last took umbrage at the liberties taken by the missionaries there with the decisions of the ecumenical councils. They were sternly called to order. Almeida left the directorship of his hospital in 1561, and from 1562 on there was no mention of any *medical* activity in Jesuits' letters from Japan. They spoke readily of Confraternities of Mercy, which continued to grow, but their purpose was assistance rather than healing. The hospital at Funai remained in operation until 1586 but under the direction of a Japanese brother, and if Almeida exercised his talents there, as is likely, he did so with the utmost discretion. Moreover, he was not ordained a priest until the 1570s, in Macao, well after the period when he had been most active.[12]

When Valignano released his report *Sumario de las cosas de Japón*, on "things concerning the province of Japan and its government," in 1583, the same year Almeida died, it contained not a single word about his work of a few years earlier. He said nothing about the charitable brotherhoods then active in several cities. He wrote as if everything had yet to be begun: in each region a house of charity would have to be opened, as well as a "hospital to take in poor and sick Christians, and also children whom the mothers customarily kill." One would entrust the management of said hospital to "outsiders" under the supervision of a brother, exclude the incurable, such as lepers, whom the Japanese found repugnant, and admit only "educated Christians from honorable and noble families."[13] With the last two recommendations, Valignano was issuing a stinging rebuke to Almeida, without naming him, and to those who, like Gago and Torres, had encouraged and abetted him. All the evidence concurs on these points: the incurable patients admitted at Funai were not all lepers; syphilitics were also taken in; and the majority of the sick were poor people, not all of them Christians.

No one thought to reproach Almeida for his origins at the time. But the hour of suspicion toward the "new Christians" and their subsequent ejection from the Society were not long in coming. The Society had been resigned to the fact that Loyola rejected discrimination against clergy of Jewish origin. That Laínez, his successor, was in fact one of them was accepted (not without difficulty in Spain). But when in

1572 Juan de Polanco, also a "new Christian," was in line to become the third superior general of the order, all of European Catholicism raised an outcry as one. Polanco had been secretary to Loyola and Laínez successively; he was known, identified, stigmatized. One faction of Portuguese Jesuits, the king of Portugal, the cardinal infante Dom Enrique (Inquisitor and brother of the king), all the Spanish Jesuits, and the pope himself expressed their reprobation. The Society, ever protective of its autonomy, disregarded them all. At last it chose for its fourth superior general a Belgian of presumably "pure" ethnic origin.

But it would be twenty more years before the order renounced its founder's wishes. In 1592 Superior General Aquaviva, who was Italian, established an ordinance forbidding provincials superior from receiving "new Christians" into the Society. Finally, in 1593, the fifth General Congregation established a "blood purity" statute *(estatuto de limpieza de sangre)* that brought the Jesuits firmly in line with Portuguese and Spanish common law. This statute allowed for no exemptions, even at the behest of the superior general himself. It remained in force among the Jesuits until 1948.[14]

PORTUGUESE ERASMIANISM

Erasmianism never reached as broad an audience in Portugal as it did in Spain between 1520 and 1530. Marcel Bataillon states confidently that in Europe in that era, "all the local forces for intellectual and religious renewal" had rallied around the name of Erasmus.[15] There were no fewer than fifteen works by Erasmus published in Spain as of 1531, in Latin or Spanish, some of them reprinted several times.[16] There were two categories of people among the readers of Erasmus, although any given individual may have fit both: the "Illuminists," or spiritual readers, who privileged the believer's personal relationship to God over any form of external piety (and swore by Erasmus's *Handbook of the Militant Christian* and the Bible), and the *conversos,* or Christians of Jewish origin, torn between two dogmas and two traditions, Jewish and Christian.

The tide began to ebb during the 1530s in all the countries of western Europe. The abdication of Charles V in 1566 and the discontinuance of the Council of Trent in 1563 marked the end of the Erasmian movement in Spain. And the Society of Jesus had played no small part in bringing it about.

Portugal had at its disposal, earlier than Spain, powerful means to exorcise the Erasmian devil, considered merely an avatar of the great Lutheran devil. As early as 1527, at the theological assembly held at Valladolid, the representatives of Portugal, Dom Estevam de Almeida and Diogo de Gouveia, drew notice for their anti-Erasmian attitudes. Their animosity was all the greater in that they suspected, not without reason, that the "new Christians" were attracted to Illuminism and Erasmianism. The ambassador from Portugal, who attended the assembly, declared that nearly all the theologians present at Valladolid were "of Jewish blood."

For Almeida and Gouveia, at least, things were clear: Erasmus was a negator of the dogma of the Trinity, a drum beater for Arius, who twisted the meaning of the Scriptures in order to support heretical propositions.[17] The establishment of the tribunal of the Holy Office in 1536 and the placing of the Coimbra College of the Arts under Jesuit control in 1555 were the principal steps leading to the enactment of a system of constraints intended to contain both the crypto-Judaic tendencies of certain "new Christians" and the Erasmian or Illuminist inclinations of certain recalcitrant intellectuals, university professors, men of letters, or simple members of an order. Portugal was also notable for its zeal in creating or ratifying Indexes to aid censors and Inquisitors. The state ceded all responsibility in this domain to the Church.

The first Portuguese Index Librorum Prohibitorum was published in 1547, and, as Révah has noted, from 1547 to 1597 Portugal was "the Catholic country most strictly protected, by far, against heresy and literary 'immorality.'" The Pontifical Index of Paul IV (1558–59) was so harsh that even Spain would not ratify it, nor would the majority of Catholic countries. It was accepted in Portugal and reprinted at once at Coimbra. On March 24, 1564, a papal bull from Pius IV approved the new Index established by the Council of Trent. It was accepted in only three countries: the Netherlands, Bavaria, and Portugal. It limited the use of translations of the Bible into popular idiom, requiring the laity to gain written authorization to read them from a bishop or Inquisitor on the recommendation of a priest or confessor. Another Pontifical

Index was published by Clement VIII in 1596. It was reprinted in Lisbon the following year, accompanied by an order from the Inquisitor General granting it the force of law throughout the kingdom.[18] The sheer number of precautions, plus the need to constantly renew the prohibitions, is of course suspicious: why would the censors and Inquisitors have had to go to so much trouble unless the hydra they were pursuing kept growing new heads?

What is conventionally termed Erasmianism actually had several facets. There was Erasmianism in the narrowest sense, which embraced those few people who had had personal contact with Erasmus outside the country and had studied his works. Then there was Erasmianism in the broad sense, more diffuse and elusive. It was, one might say, in the air of the times. The need for deep reform within the Church and society was so apparent that certain ideas cropped up among thinking people everywhere, even when they had no contact with each other. A quotation one happened on in a work of refutation sufficed, or a phrase snatched up in passing, a remark repeated, a summation of a book or debate in a university course. And books circulated, despite censorship and the Inquisition's petty officers. When one of Erasmus's works was burned at the Jesuit school in Naples (which was a dependency of the Spanish crown), officials immediately took steps "to obtain authorization to redeem this book, so valuable to men of study."[19] Moreover, if certain books were not published in Portugal, it was easy for a Portuguese who had studied humanities to read them in Spanish. For Portuguese intellectuals in those days traveled a great deal and often remained in other countries for years; the mobility of individuals often compensated, fortunately, for the stagnation and brittleness that characterized institutions.

The three Portuguese figures who best represent the Erasmian current in the strict sense, André de Gouveia (1497–1548), André de Resende (1500–73), and Damião de Góis (1502–74), belong to this family of voyagers. Góis had traveled to Anvers; northern Europe; Wittenburg, where he met Luther; Louvain; Freiburg, where he was the guest of Erasmus; and Padua, spending a total of twenty-two years outside Portugal's borders. Resende had been to Alcalá de Henares, Salamanca, Paris, and Louvain. Gouveia was living in France when he was called to the Coimbra College of the Arts in 1547.[20]

If Diogo de Gouveia, André's uncle, was a fierce adversary of Erasmus, his nephew had an open mind. He was the principal of the College of Guienne, where Montaigne met and admired him, then in 1537 a lecturer on the Holy Scriptures at the University of Coimbra. He favored a sound theology grounded in the Scriptures and the church fathers, as opposed to the scholastic, formalist, abstract theology of which his uncle was a perfect product.[21]

Resende published in 1531 at Basel his *Eulogy to Erasmus (Erasmi Encomium,* just as Erasmus had written the *Encomium matrimonii),* whose title is a manifesto in itself. The theology of Erasmus was in perfect accord with Resende's sentiments: he appreciated its attachment to the Bible, its philological groundwork, its Christ-centered approach, its ever-watchful critical spirit. He, like Erasmus, had no temptation to follow Luther, whom he reproached for having ruptured the unity of the Church and for interpreting the Scriptures too subjectively.[22]

Góis was in Holland when he was recalled to Portugal by John III in 1545. He had already met and befriended Luther, Melancthon, and Erasmus. He was also acquainted with the provincial superior of the Society of Jesus, Simão Rodrigues, who had been his classmate at Padua and would become his sworn enemy. It seems that in 1533 Góis had mentioned to the king the idea of bringing Erasmus, whom he had just met, to Coimbra.[23] When Góis returned to Lisbon in 1545, he quickly fell under suspicion of "Lutheranism." He was finally arrested and condemned to life imprisonment in 1572. He died suddenly the following year. The chief transgression imputed to Góis was having shown a suspicious interest in the religion of the Ethiopians. At the time, Ethiopia had diplomatic relations with Portugal. A bishop from Ethiopia had been sent as an envoy to John III, and Góis was keen to meet him. Two books resulted from their discussions, one on the mission of the great "Emperor of the Indies," the other on the religion and customs of the Ethiopians. They caused a scandal in Lisbon and Rome. For Góis, not content simply to express a typically "Erasmian" sympathetic curiosity for a Christian faith that fell outside the sway of Rome, went on to deplore the rupture of Church unity, admiring Ethiopian Christianity for surviving for so many centuries beyond the civilized world and suggesting that the Christians of Ethiopia had found the means to reconcile the irreconcilable: they were Catholic in the main body of dogma, Protestant because they took communion in both species and their priests could marry, Jewish and Muslim in several of their ceremonies.[24]

Among the Erasmians in the strict sense was another notable, Juan Fernández. He was not Portuguese but Spanish, perhaps from a family of *conversos*. He had arrived at Coimbra in 1536 after spending time in Alcalá and Salamanca. He taught at the monastery of Santa Cruz, then at the College of the Arts. He was named to the college's chair of rhetoric in 1542. But most important, he produced an edition of Erasmus's *Colloquies*, published at Coimbra in 1545 or 1546. The work was in Latin, and Fernández had adapted certain parts of it for Portuguese readers. He had softened the attacks against monks, ceremonies, and the worship of saints, and the authorities of the Faculty of Theology had seen nothing amiss in that. But the Inquisition was ever watchful. *Colloquies* appeared in the Index Librorum Prohibitorum of 1547, and the book was forbidden thenceforth. It had already been condemned once by the Sorbonne in 1526 and twice by the Spanish Inquisition, the Spanish version in 1536 and the Latin one in 1537. However, Fernández's edition continued to circulate in Portugal after 1547.[25]

It would be extremely difficult to flush out Erasmianism anywhere the Inquisition did not succeed in finding it, and it is highly improbable that everything imputed to crypto-Judaism and Lutheranism had some connection to Erasmus. Transcripts of the trial of Brother Valentim da Luz, which took place from 1560 to 1562 and ended with a sentence of death (he was burned in Lisbon in an auto-da-fé), offer a clear look at the way Erasmianism was understood at the time in its larger sense.

Valentim da Luz, born in 1524, belonged to the order of the Eremitas de Santo Agostinho at the Convento da Graça in Lisbon. He completed his philosophy courses at Coimbra but, probably out of distaste for scholasticism, did not finish his studies in theology. He became a preacher, but his preaching was not well received. He was nonetheless named master of novices for his order in Lisbon in 1553 or 1554, then became prior of the Convento da Graça of Tavira, in the southeast corner of the country. If this was not exile, it was the closest thing to it.

Brother Valentim had traveled to Italy in 1551 to attend the General Chapter of his order in Bologna. He also passed through Rome, remaining absent from his country for a total of eight months. The first phase of the Council of Trent had come to a close four years earlier, and Italy was all abuzz. New ideas—Erasmianism, Christian Humanism—were debated everywhere, there was sympathy with Protestantism here and there, and it is more than likely that the monk made crucial contacts there. Other members of his order were also inclined toward reform: not that of Luther or Calvin (they had no thought of abandoning the cloth, or of departing from the Church of Rome) but a true Catholic reform that would bring the Church back to the blessed days of early Christianity. There were two tendencies within the order. The first and more moderate called for greater asceticism. The other, bolder and "penetrable by the polemical language of Calvinists and Lutherans," was quite close to Erasmian Humanism. Brother Valentim was of the latter tendency.

Had he read Erasmus? The Inquisitors did all they could to find out, but they failed. However, many of his opinions resembled those expressed in Erasmus's writings: the critique of false devotions, of saint worship, of images, of relics: the marked preference for a spiritual worship as opposed to useless ceremonies and rituals. Like Erasmus, he preferred to speak of God's mercy rather than his justice and detested the formalism and abstractness of scholastic philosophy. He favored a theology rooted in the Bible and the church fathers. In his eyes, faith was a matter not of belief but of trust; it was a practice, a lifestyle, a way of being.

However, Brother Valentim was a Catholic and a monk and intended to remain so. He wished not to eliminate the religious orders but to reform them from within. He wanted the ecclesiastical hierarchy to cease to mimic the hierarchy of civil authorities. He railed against the taste for pomp and adornment whose excesses he had no doubt witnessed in Rome. He asked that the money spent on sumptuous ceremonies be used instead to ease the lot of the poor. And he was opposed to the Inquisition: *Heretici non sunt comburendi* (Heretics should not be burned at the stake). He was made to understand the scope of his error by being sent there himself.

Valentim da Luz was convicted of the charge of "Lutheranism" and sentenced to die for it, although nothing in the records showed evidence of the slightest concession on his part to the Lutheran theses concerning justification by faith alone, which was usually the litmus test for this line of inquisition. So that there would be no doubt about the accuracy of the charges, he was forced to sign a last confession before his torture and death: *Confesso que fui muito affeiçoado a Lutero e a suas cousas* (I confess that I was very devoted to the cause of Luther). He further confessed having believed that "Erasmus was a good teacher, and holy, and [that] those who condemned him were in error."[26]

CRISTÓVÃO FERREIRA

Cristóvão Ferreira was born in 1580 in Zivreira, near Torres Vedras in the archbishopric of Lisbon, to Domingo Ferreira and Maria Lourenço. He entered the Society of Jesus on Christmas Day in 1596. On that date the "blood purity" statute had been in force for three years for all members of the order, and there is no reason to doubt that Ferreira came from a family of "old Christians." The name Ferreira is not uncommon, however, among the descendants of converted Jewish families. Ferreiras are found in "Portuguese" communities in Bordeaux, the Antilles, and South America, but this proves nothing: many "new Christian" families were obliged to exchange their last names for more "Catholic" ones chosen at random.

In 1597 Ferreria entered the newly created novitiate in Lisbon, opened on December 18. The class consisted of fifteen novices who had come from Coimbra and Évora. The master of novices was Father António Mascarenhas. It is not known what Ferreira did there. We know only that he stayed for two years and that his fellow students included João Baptista Machado, later martyred in Japan, António de Andrade, the future explorer of Tibet, and Pedro da Rocha and Paulo Rodrigues, who went on to become university professors.[27]

On completion of his novitiate, Ferreira made his first vows and requested to be sent to the Indies. He embarked from Lisbon on April 4, 1600, for Goa and Macao in the company of Brother Pedro de Almeida. He was barely twenty years old. What had he read? What had he been taught? If, as is likely, he had studied humanities and rhetoric first at Coimbra and later at Lisbon, he would have been shaped in the mold of the *Ratio studiorum*. But he had not begun his philosophy studies. What did he know of the deep disturbances that had shaken Portugal, the Society of Jesus, and the College of the Arts and the university at Coimbra throughout the century? Had he heard about the autos-da-fé in which books and sometimes men and women were burned in the squares of large cities? Did he know that when he was a child four Japanese youths had traveled twice across his country, with extended stays in Lisbon and Coimbra? Had he been shown the tomb of Bernardo, the Japanese man who had come to Coimbra for his novitiate in 1553, had gone to Rome, been received by Ignatius of Loyola, and then returned to Portugal, where he had died in 1557 at the Coimbra College of the Arts?[28] Nothing is known of all this. It is quite likely, however, that before his departure Ferreira was shown etchings depicting the torture of twenty-six adherents martyred in Japan in 1597, the year he had entered the novitiate. All of Christian Europe had seen them. But even this spectacle could not divert an ardent, pious Portuguese youth from his vocation.

The registries of the Society of Jesus show Ferreira's name again in 1603 and 1604 at Macao. He completed his philosophy studies then. In 1606 he was a second-year theology student. In 1609 he was ordained a priest and prepared to leave Macao for Japan. He arrived in Nagasaki on June 19, 1609, and was assigned to the seminary of Arima to begin studying the Japanese language. The instruction in philosophy and theology that he received at Macao was not significantly different from what he would have been taught at Coimbra at that time.

For twenty-three years, Ferreira's conduct in Japan was completely honorable and even, after 1614, heroic. When the great persecution began he was thirty-four years old, had been in the Society for eighteen of them, and knew Japanese well. His preaching in that language, how-ever, was only "passable."[29] In 1617 he took his final vows. In 1620 he was professed of the four vows and was friend, adviser, and admonitor to the provincial superior in Japan. But most of the time he had to carry out his activities clandestinely and in constant danger. From time to time he was called to testify in beatification procedures for martyred co-religionists and colleagues: in 1623, for the fifty Christians burned at the stake by the third shogun, Tokugawa Iemitsu; in 1627, for the Chris-tians executed that year at Shimabara; in 1632, after the exemplary death of a Jesuit of Japanese origin who was first tortured in the sulfur pits of Unzen, then burned alive in Nagasaki with five other priests.

Ferreira was captured on September 24, 1633, and on October 18 was subjected to the pit torture. The victim was suspended, head downward, over a pit filled with excrement. The body was very tightly bound to prevent blood from flowing to the brain. The temples were slit to provide a certain amount of drainage and prevent cerebral hemorrhage. The toxic gases emanating from the pit had a slightly anesthetic effect, allowing the victim's sufferings to be prolonged. The Japanese Inquisitors would have the victim decide between unending, inhuman pain and apostasy. The only escape was to signal with a gesture that one wished to end the torture; one hand remained unbound to allow for this. Ferreira held out for five hours. At the end of the fifth hour, he moved his hand.

The apostasy of Father Cristóvão Ferreira sent a shock wave throughout the Society of Jesus in Asia and in several European countries. The Jesuits made every conceivable effort to contact him again and lead him back to the right path. They failed. In late 1655 they spread the word, based on vague information from Tonkin, that he had renounced his errors in the end and had died a martyr in Nagasaki. This one could read as late as 1964 in a book by Father Josef Franz Schütte.[30]

After his apostasy, Ferreira went into the service of the Japanese Inquisition. He took the name Sawano Chuan, enrolled in a Buddhist temple, and began a new existence. He left no personal writings, and no testimony has come down to us that could explain his behavior. One may only ponder the fact that his path resembles in many ways the one taken before him, under constraint, by so many of his compatriots of Jewish origin.[31]

Three years later he wrote, under the title *Kengiroku* (Deception Unmasked), a brief refutation of Christianity whose content allows us to lift a corner of the veil. It is a sort of guide for Japanese Inquisitors, designed to help them trip up suspected Christians during interrogation, demonstrate to them the pointlessness of their faith, and conduct them to an awareness of the mortal danger they represented to the harmony of Japanese society and the security of the state.

The outline of *Deception Unmasked* is simple.[32] It follows the order of the catechisms used in Japan and China at that time. Ferreira first addresses one by one all the major dogmatic affirmations of the Catholic church. Next he enumerates the Ten Commandments in the form handed down by the Tradition: the Second Commandment, "Thou shalt not make idols," vanishes, but the last is divided in two in order to redouble the sixth: "Thou shalt not be lustful / Thou shalt not covet thy neighbor's wife." Then the author narrates the life of Jesus with his own commentary but retains only the beginning and end of the story: miraculous birth, circumcision, visit of the Magi, massacre of the in-nocents, flight into Egypt, retreat into the desert, acclamation of the multitude wishing to consecrate Jesus emperor, betrayal by Judas, trial before Pilate, Crucifixion, Resurrection, Ascension. The book ends with a critique of the principal sacraments—baptism, penance, and the Eucharist—and a mention of the Last Judgment.

Nowhere in the book is a glimmer of self-revelation to be found. George Elison thinks one may be perceived in the passage concerning the chosen and the reprobates. Ferreira refers to the former as *predestinados* (predestined ones) and expresses surprise that they have been "chosen by Deus for all eternity" (p. 300) to be saved, while the *reprobos* (reprobates) are condemned to hell. He adds, "And, moreover, the *predestinados* are saved no matter what evil they commit; and the *reprobos* fall down into hell no matter how they strive toward good. . . . But there is no distinction between good and evil in this; this is not the wellspring of universal law. . . . Yet to express doubt at this and to question the doctors of this religion is but to obtain the answer: 'In Deus' scriptures is the intent to save all.' This is a duplicitous rejoinder, spoken with a forked tongue" (p. 301). In fact, he explains further on, human beings, although endowed with free will, are not able to do good and avoid evil by themselves. They can only do good if they receive *graça*, that is, the assistance of God. No one knows why it is that not everyone receives this assistance.

Elison glimpsed behind this argument the grievance of the reprobate Ferreira thought himself to be, after his apostasy. One might also discern echoes of the anti-Lutheran diatribes he had surely heard during the course of his instruction. But why, here, would he impute to the Jesuits a doctrine that was well known not to be theirs? It might have been a comprehensible insinuation in a debate between Christians. It was lost on Japanese readers who did not even know Luther's name. It is more likely that in falsely imputing to his former colleagues the doctrine of salvation through faith alone, Ferreira was trying to persuade his Japanese masters that, on this point, the Jesuits were no different from the partisans of Amida Buddha, the central figure in certain of the more democratic forms of Buddhism, especially the True Pure Land sect. It had not been forgotten in 1636 that Oda Nobunaga had had to wage a merciless campaign against this sect to crush its political power. That is probably why the passage in *Deception Unmasked* about grace and free will is accompanied by a sober political warning. Immediately after citing the Scriptures in regard to universal salvation, in fact, Ferreira writes: "In everything they but deceive the people; using religion, they plot to usurp the country." The accusation is reinforced after the passage on the particular grace granted to Mary: "They make fabrication their teachings' base; their plot is to spread disturbance throughout the land and to pervert society" (p. 302). The insurrection in Shimabara showed that the seeds of egalitarianism the Jesuits sowed, despite themselves, were as dangerous for the state as the doctrine of the True Pure Land.

Ferreira often returns to this theme, but it is in addressing the First and Fourth Commandments that he develops it most thoroughly: "You shall worship no other Buddhas beside the one Deus" (p. 302). "You shall observe filial piety to your parents" (p. 303). In distorting as he does the First Commandment and associating it with the Fourth, Ferreira cleverly sets them in opposition to each other. Indeed, he says,

In all the countries where the Five Constant Virtues are preserved, where the Five Commandments kept, where the people pray for peace and tranquillity in the present world and beseech repose in the good place, for the afterlife therefore does the subject look up to the ruler and the child is filial to his father and mother, the aged are esteemed and the young are loved, and the ruler treats his subjects with sympathy and bestows compassion upon the people. There indeed the families prosper, the country flourishes, and all under heaven is regulated. . . . To treat the Buddhas with ceremony and the gods with esteem, and to offer prayers to the ancestors, is to practice humanity and propriety and to accumulate merit for the afterlife. (p. 303)

The society of reciprocal obligations described here is obviously the ideal society, from the dual viewpoint of Buddhism and of Confucianism. To replace it, in a country where this ideal has been achieved, with a "law" created for Jews and Christians is necessarily to preach "rebellion"; it is "the inception of reign's overthrow" (p. 303). In Japan, this translated as disrespect of the Buddhas and the gods, the destruction of temples and pagodas, and disobedience to the will of the sovereign and the military authorities. As for the Fourth Commandment, it is fatally flouted by its own community when anyone who wishes to become a monk may do so against his parents' wishes, even at the risk of condemning his family name to die out. The problem clearly lies in the missionaries' distinction between the secular sphere and the religious one. This distinction is unthinkable for the Japanese of the seventeenth century; for them, the two spheres are one.

This is also the reason the Third Commandment is unacceptable. In principle, all it does is sanctify the first day (*domingo*). But in Ferreira's commentary, keeping Sunday as a day of rest, as prescribed by the Scriptures, and doing the same for feast days, as prescribed by the Tradition, are merged. And now the total number of days on which the Christian is not supposed to work is considerable, at least eighty per year, more than a well-ordered society can tolerate: "If on these days the governor does not attend to the management of public affairs and in the Four Classes men and women alike do not perform their allotted duties, then neither the interests of the sovereign nor the individual will be served" (p. 304).

In other cases the commandment is acceptable, but the daily practice of Christians themselves cruelly undermines it. One must not "take the name of the Lord in vain"? One must not "make false charges against another"? But it is well known that Christians, "when they find themselves in a personal perplexity, they twist their words in all sorts of ways to escape the difficulty" (p. 304). It is also well known that in the eyes of the fathers, upright intention can justify the basest lie.

The Fifth Commandment outlaws murder? But by persisting in their preachings, though they be forbidden, the fathers are responsible for the deaths of thousands of people. The Sixth Commandment forbids adultery and the last prohibits coveting one's neighbor's wife? But the ancient Hebrews practiced polygamy, and priests sometimes have wives and children despite their vows of celibacy. Some have relations with prostitutes and dancers, others seduce widows and have children by them. One must not steal, but the Spanish, good Christians, have appropriated entire countries: New Spain, for example, and Luzon in the Philippines. The former Jesuit recalls the Treaty of Tordesillas, sanctioned by the pope as the representative of Jesus Christus, in which he said in substance to the kings of Castilla and Portugal: "Your plans, of course, are of great benefit to the wealth and reputation of your countries, and to the spread of the faith. However, it appertains to my position to determine the directions to which those who spread the faith are dispatched. The emperor of Portugal to the east, the emperor of Castela to the west: thus dispatch your men and spread the faith! And if at any time you should tear away and take over some lands, any place, treat them as you please" (pp. 305–6).

If the Seventh Commandment is broken by the Catholic states and by the pope himself, the Ninth is similarly violated in the private sphere, when the Church appropriates for any use it wishes the goods of those who enter the religion, because it needs them for the upkeep of its places of worship or for its charitable works. In the treatment of this commandment the chiefly political aim of *Deception Unmasked* is discerned: it is also an appropriation of one's neighbors' goods for one's own ends when a Christian nobleman levies a tithe on the production of his serfs' lands and remands the amount collected to the Church.

In the same chapter Ferreira addresses on a par with the Ten Commandments what he calls "the laws established by the pope" in his role as "representative of Jesus Christus." He purposely belabors the supranational nature of his function and the extension of his power over the whole earth. He well knew the feelings that would be induced in his Japanese partners by a statement like "Men of the highest families prostrate themselves in front of him; even emperors kiss his feet" (p. 307).

What follows is not surprising to anyone acquainted with the origins of the Reformation but must have been shocking to those who, to build modern Japan, had had to destroy the power of the feudal lords and the largest Buddhist sects. Ferreira takes obvious pleasure in enumerating the various domains in which the Church of Rome was an easy target for accusations of greed. Prayers for the dead could be bought; pardons required permission from the pope; even excommunication, which could befall the whole population of a country, could be used as a bargaining chip or a bribe. The conclusion is implicit but clear: the pope had no need to conquer new lands the way the kings of Spain and Portugal did; through his missionary representatives in far-off lands, he could drain little by little the states where they were established.

Ferreira mounts a three-pronged argument based on Christian preaching and catechism. Since these claim to have their basis in natural reasoning, it is easy to turn the weapon of reason back on them. Since they consider the teachings of theology to have universal validity, he has only to support his logic with theology to bring them down. And then there are the Scriptures, whose letter and spirit are often in contradiction to what the missionaries preach.

Ferreira takes on the first point much as Voltaire would, minus the wit and style. When those who call on natural reasoning nonetheless follow their biblical texts to the letter and at face value, it is not difficult to refute them with commonsense arguments. You say, for example, that the Hebrews have handed down through the ages the story of Creation. And by adding up the ages of the patriarchs to the beginning of the Christian era, you date it at six thousand years ago. But how is it that the chronicles of India, China, or Japan preserve no trace of such an event and that the Chinese count more than twenty thousand years between the invention of their script by Fu Hi and the end of the Shang dynasty? You say there is no salvation for humanity outside of your religion; you say, too, that humans are distinct from animals because they are endowed by God with an immortal soul. But what of the people who walked the earth before what you term "Creation"? Had they no souls? And if they had them, who had given them these souls? Are people of those times, and those who have never heard of your religion, eternally damned? You say that God has allowed humans free will, but you also say that they are incapable of performing good works of their own accord; they can only do this with the help of God. But God does not grant his grace to all, as we see in the case of the *predestinados*. And again: Are we to believe that all humankind is stained with original sin because the first man ate a forbidden fruit? Are we to believe that Jesus had no terrestrial father? Why had Jesus to be baptized, if he was without sin? Are we to take the Resurrection and the Ascension as historical fact? On all these points Ferreira's judgment is final: "Not one of these teachings satisfies the dictates of reason. . . . At its most profound this religion has no bearing on reason. . . . These are matters of sixteen hundred years' antiquity, without trustworthy evidence. They are but tales composed by the disciples of Jesus Christus, that is all" (p. 313).

Ferreira has a wonderful time bringing his critical mind to bear on the missionaries' naively realistic conception of the sacraments. If the soul is spiritual, and so too is grace, how can water, a material substance, cleanse away sin? How can the sacramental words pronounced by the priest, which are only words, produce a spiritual effect? In the sacrament of the Eucharist it is impossible to believe that bread and wine are actually transformed into flesh and blood because the priest says so. "Not one thing in all this teaching is reasonable" (p. 314).

Ferreira is less sure of himself when he attempts to undermine the philosophical bases of the priests' preachings by means of scholasticism itself. It is true that he is addressing readers unfamiliar with Western philosophy. His critique would have been more effective if he had grounded it in the philosophies of the Far East, as had Fabian in *The God of the Christians Confuted.* But by all indications, Ferreira, despite his official conversion to Buddhism, knew little about it. He knew enough to seek out in Aristotle the notion of the eternity of the world, common to Buddhism, Confucianism, and Taoism. Thus he borrows from Aristotle his arguments against the Christian conception of Creation: "Before the birth of Jesus Christus . . . there lived in South Barbary a great scholar named Aristoteles, who in discussing the beginning of heaven and earth correctly noted that heaven and earth have no beginning" (p. 298). This is followed by a brief discussion of the theory of the *mixed* (things composed out of the four elements) and the *simple* (the elements themselves), which allows him to say in scholastic words what the Orientals say in their own: "Earth, water, fire, air, and heaven are not created things and therefore have neither beginning nor end: they are the mysterious effects of the conjunction of Yin and Yang" (p. 298).

Aristotle makes another appearance in the treatment of the theory of the soul. Ferreira knows the three classes of this function, but Aristotle has taught him that it is not a reality separate from the body: it is the formal and final cause of the life of the body, the motor of the body, thus it is not immortal. Only the divine genius of the intellect has the privilege of immortality, but this immortality does not pertain to the individual personally. He writes:

> The Five Parts of the human body do not differ from those of birds and beasts, being compounded of the Four Basic Elements; their processes of origination and dissolution are the same. But within the human body is contained a soul called anima. This soul is spiritus and indestructible. Though the Five Parts be destroyed, the *anima* remains and is not destroyed. . . . The soul of birds and beasts, being contingent upon the Five Parts, originates together with them and is destroyed with them. . . . This thing called anima by definition is substance of spiritus, cannot be taken in the hand or seen by the eye, and is without material shape. Then what is there to be grasped and named indestructible substance? The soul of birds and beasts also is without material shape and cannot be taken in the hand or seen by the eye, and therefore in the same manner, be spiritus. But according to the doctrines of the Kirishi-tan religion it is not spiritus, and is destroyed together with the body." (pp. 299–300)

Ferreira's line of reasoning has become an academic argument, and not a terribly clear one, but its thrust comes through: if the souls of animals are not spiritual, then human souls are no more so; if human souls have the privilege of immortality, so must those of animals. In both cases, "philosophy" proves religion wrong.

When Ferreira finds no weapons in the stockpiles of common sense and scholasticism, he has recourse to the Bible, considered as authoritative as Aristotle or the pope and always taken in the most literal sense. He had cited the Scriptures in affirming the notion of universal salvation as opposed to the more restrictive conception held by the Church. He cites them again, rather audaciously, in regard to the miraculous birth of Jesus. It is not common sense alone that causes him to reject Tradition on this point but the words of Mary herself when she says to Jesus, in reference to Joseph, "This is your father." This is not found anywhere in the Gospels; Ferreira is undoubtedly thinking of Luke 2:48 (child Jesus and the teachers in the temple): "Behold, your father and I have been looking for you anxiously."

Ferreira cites the Bible a third time concerning the sacrament of penance. This man, who over the course of twenty-three years has risked his life a thousand times to hear confession and administer the sacraments, now wonders, in light of the shabby commerce in indulgences conducted by his former Church, if the fathers indeed have the power to pardon even the gravest sins with the sacramental words *Ego te absolvo*. The Bible states, "The sins of anyone whom you pardon will be pardoned also before God," but that does not justify the practice of confession, which was invented by the Church headed by the pope and allows the institution to have an abusive influence on consciences.

That Ferreira, ably or not, uses the Bible to oppose the teachings of the Church may indicate that at some point he was tinged, if not with "Lutheranism" (from which he is quite distant), at least with a pinch of Erasmianism. It is unimaginable that he would have read Erasmus, either at the novitiate in Lisbon or at the College of Macao. But the odor of Erasmianism was everywhere in the air, even in the convents and colleges, and it is obvious that part of *Deception Unmasked* derives from that sort of Erasmianism.

The passage on the *predestinados* and the *reprobos*, for example, may be compared to the famous diatribe on free will *(Diatribè sive Collatio de libero arbitrio)* that Erasmus issued in 1524 and in which, solidly supported by the Scriptures, the philosopher from Rotterdam disagrees with Luther's opinions on justification by faith alone. Luther responded the following year with publication of *Bondage of the Will*, and it is not at all impossible that the quarrel might have been mentioned in the philosophy courses Ferreira took in Macao. Indeed, in Portugal and Spain the debate had had aftereffects and repercussions in the late sixteenth century centering on Molina, the former professor of theology at the University of Évora, and his *Concordia liberi arbitrii cum gratia* (Concordat on Free Will and Grace).

His critique of the Fourth Commandment of the Decalogue seems to echo a letter by Erasmus published in 1529 in his correspondence

(Opus epistolarum). Addressing himself to a fictitious member of the Roman Curia by the name of Lambert Gracinius, Erasmus criticized hasty or forced entry into the orders, saying, "But what inspiration propels a man into monasticism, that very man who is drawn to it does not know for certain. . . . No worse misfortune can befall brilliant minds than to be drawn by trickery or precipitated by violence into this or that mode of life, from which they cannot then extricate themselves."[33]

Regarding the sanctification of Sunday, two texts by Erasmus parallel Ferreira's. One is found in the *Epistola apologetica de interdicto esu carnium* (On Eating Meat): "Just as Christ teaches that it is the Sabbath that has been created for humanity and not humanity for the Sabbath, in the same way I am inclined to think that our institutions, too, should stand aside whenever the needs of one's fellow require charitable intervention."[34] The other text is in the treatise *De amabili concordia ecclesiae* (On the Kindly Harmony of the Church), published in 1533: "As for the plethora of feast days the bishops have introduced to cater to popular religiosity, or the Roman pontiffs have instituted for no vital reason, it would be easy to permit their abrogation. . . . A smaller number of feast days would be well accepted, if those remaining were celebrated with greater respect. There is not a day left on which one is permitted to labor, without falling into sin, to procure nourishment for wife and children or the means to lighten one's neighbor's misery."[35]

On the subject of clergy who had wives and children despite their vows of celibacy, Erasmus said: "[Among priests], how rare are those who live in chastity, if we take into account the number who, on their premises, openly keep concubines who take the place of wives for them."[36]

Ferreira again joins Erasmus when he reviles the Roman custom of payment for prayers for the dead and all manner of dispensations. On fasting and abstention from eating meat on certain days of the week: "If one is oppressed by these laws, we are told, there is a means of relief. What means? One may purchase from the Roman pontiff the right to eat. It is a matter of his pronouncing a few words, but not everyone has the time, not everyone has the money necessary to purchase this right."[37] This question is similar to the matter of Indulgences in general, which Erasmus and Luther condemned with equal force.

These indications are too scant to permit the assertion that Ferreira was an Erasmian in the narrower sense, that is, a reader of Erasmus. But he was surely one in the broad sense. Had he been one in Macao? Had he become one progressively? Were there other Jesuits in the same situation? This is unknown. But it may be speculated that with such doubts in his mind, Father Ferreira was perhaps unwilling to make the supreme sacrifice when forced to make the choice.[38]

———

Nothing indicates that Sawano Chuan, the "new Buddhist," became a fervent follower of the religion (or philosophy) to which he supposedly converted. It is known, however, that after his apostasy he followed the path of many of his contemporaries, even in Europe, whether "old" or "new" Christians: he turned toward the sciences, especially medicine. In Europe he would have abandoned the habit and gone to Italy, Holland, or the University of Montpellier. In Japan he married, had children, and went to study with the physicians of the Dutch East India Company who were posted in Nagasaki beginning in 1640. From this experience he gathered the material for a book titled *Nambanryu geka hidensho* (The Secret Book of Southern Barbarian Surgery). In it he explains Galen's theory of humors and gives a few recipes for plasters and unguents.[39] He trained several disciples, including Sugimoto Chukei (1618–89).[40] Three of them went on to found their own schools.

Sawano Chuan had two daughters. One of them married Sugimoto Chukei, who was later physician to the shogun Tokugawa Yoshimune. Through her, the former Jesuit became the founder of an extensive Japanese family. A monument to this family stands in the Zuirinji cemetery in Tokyo. The first name inscribed on it is Chuan.[41] His name means "House of Faithfulness."

Chapter Three

Consulting Dr. Vázquez

Es del todo necesario que nos acomodemos.

A. Valignano, Sumario de las cosas de Japón, 1583

The Society of Jesus did everything possible to contact the apostate priest Cristóvão Ferreira and to gather information on his exact situation, material as well as moral. On November 1, 1636, three years after his apostasy, the Jesuits of Macao were called together by Father Manuel Díaz, Visitor to Japan, to pass judgment on his case. They decided first, in light of the seriousness of the matter and the impossibility of consulting with Rome in a reasonable amount of time, to judge it in good conscience according to the principle of *epikie.* The principle allows one "to interpret the thinking of the legislator as leaning toward a positive exemption of subjects from the observation of the law in exceptional circumstances that have not been foreseen." It is not an interpretation of the law itself but a conscious disposition to apply it in the most benevolent way, taking into account special circumstances.[1]

It was then suggested that Ferreira be excluded from the Society. Four Jesuits requested additional information before agreeing to this. Two priests were dispatched at once to the port to question Portuguese sailors and merchants returning from Japan. They confirmed the matter: Ferreira had apostatized. The congregation was reconvoked and settled on his exclusion, more than anything to put behind them a scandalous situation that could damage the reputation of the order.[2]

Ferreira had done serious damage to his case by writing *Deception Unmasked*, and above all by placing himself at the service of the Japanese Inquisitors as an interpreter between them and the Christians they captured, both priests and laity. But had he repented, as the Jesuits never ceased to hope? Could he have been pardoned and returned to a state of grace? A question for casuistry: specialized literature of the time refers to numerous cases as astonishing as his. The heart of the matter would no doubt have been the question of the relationship between civil and religious law, which indeed played a central role in the apostate's written refutation of Christianity. But Ferreira poses the question in regard to the *Japanese*. At the time he abjured his faith he was not Japanese but Portuguese, a subject of the king of Spain; he became Japanese only afterward. Perhaps, if he had read the *Opuscula moralia* of Father Gabriel Vázquez, he could have had recourse to the famous casuist's opinion. Very rare is the case in which the common good demands that the individual suffer death, according to him; it is only, Vázquez said, in cases of extreme necessity that one must sacrifice one's life, when the very existence of society would be endangered.[3] But to what society did Ferreira belong in 1633, when he was suspended over the pit? He had spent twenty years of his life in Portugal, ten in the Indies and China, and twenty-three in Japan in close symbiosis with a frightened, hunted, progressively decimated minority, in much the same situation as the "new Christians" in his native land. The Catholic novelist Endo Shusaku was perhaps not off the mark in imagining, in his novel based on Ferreira's story, that the priest had finally had to choose between two *fidelities*. The preface to his book states: "The tree of Hellenized Christianity cannot simply be uprooted from Europe and transplanted, as is, to the marshland of Japan with its completely different cultural tradition."[4]

JAPANESE PASTORALE

The first library created by the Jesuits in Japan contained, among other books, manuals for confessors. All of them came more or less directly from the *Summa theologica* of Thomas Aquinas. One found, for example, the *Suma silvestrina*, that is, the *Summa summarum* of the Piedmontese Dominican Silvestre Mazolini, alias Prierias, which was published in Rome in the early sixteenth century and reprinted more than fifty times, and the *Summa virtutum ac vitiorum* of Guillermo Peraldo, a thirteenth-century Dominican. The chief minister of morality was Martin de Azpilcueta (1491–1586), known as "Doctor Navarro." His *Manual for Confessors and Penitents* appeared in Spanish at Coimbra in 1553 and at Valladolid in 1565. It was a practical, rather than speculative, work. All these teachers took for granted the principles set out by Aristotle in the *Nicomachean Ethics;* in their eyes, these principles were the basis of "natural morals" and were universal in value and scope.[5]

But in the practice of guiding the conscience and of confession, the missionaries soon learned that this point of view was not easily accepted by converts belonging to a civilization so ancient and so foreign to Judeo-Hellenic tradition. Father Luís Fróis, who stayed in Japan from 1563 to 1597, left valuable testimony concerning the main contradictions he encountered there.

Fróis was a sixteen-year-old novice when he arrived in Goa in 1548. There he met Japanese Christians whom Francis Xavier had brought to Goa from Malacca. He also associated with Francis Xavier before and after the latter's voyage to Japan. In 1561 he was ordained a priest and the following year was sent to Macao, then Japan. He began his missionary activity on the island of Takeshima, northwest of Kyushu, and set about learning Japanese at once. Later he had occasion to visit the imperial capital and the Osaka region. He returned to Kyushu in 1576 and remained there as superior of the Bungo region. In 1581 and 1582 he accompanied Alessandro Valignano on his tour of inspection and served as his interpreter. He next worked with Gaspar Coelho, vice provincial of Japan. He returned with him to Miyako in 1586 before retiring to Takeshima. In 1592 he accompanied Valignano to Goa and then went back to Japan, where he died in 1597 in Nagasaki.

Throughout his career as a missionary, which lasted more than thirty years, Fróis wrote numerous letters, as all Jesuits were supposed to do. Many of these letters were published and helped to make known in Europe the Jesuits' work overseas. He also wrote, between 1584 and

1594, the monumental *History of Japan*, which he never finished and which, for obscure reasons, was not published in its entirety until 1976.[6] Yet Fróis had undertaken this work at the express request of Father General Aquaviva, transmitted via Valignano and Coelho.

The *Tratado em que se contem muito suscinta e breviademente algumas contradições e diferenças de costumes antre a gente de Europa e esta provincia de Japão* (Treatise Containing in Very Succinct and Abbreviated Form Some Contradictions and Differences in Customs between the Europeans and the Inhabitants of the Province of Japan) also remained in manuscript form for an extended period. It was probably written as an appendix to the long *History of Japan*, and rather early in the course of its preparation. The text was not rediscovered until 1946, in the Royal Library of the Madrid Academy of History, by Father Schütte.[7]

The *Treatise* is composed of fourteen disparate chapters concerning, successively, "men, their persons and clothing; women, their persons and customs; children and their customs; temples, images, and things having to do with the practice of religion; how the Japanese eat and drink; Japanese offensive and defensive weapons, warfare; horses; illnesses, doctors, and medicines; the writing of the Japanese, their books, paper, ink, and missives; houses, workshops, gardens, and fruits; vessels, their usage and . . . armaments; plays, farces, dances, songs, and musical instruments of Japan, miscellaneous unusual things that cannot be categorized in the preceding chapters." Father Fróis's observations are indeed rough notes; he has made no attempt to rank them in importance or to arrange them so that general observations may be made. He seems to place on the same level the fact that in Japan horses are shod with a straw covering over their shoes, that men strike their gunflints with the left hand, and that women kill their children by placing a foot on their necks.

There is, however, one strong guiding notion in the *Treatise:* in general and even in specifics, the Japanese think and act in a manner opposite to whatever Europeans would do and say in the same circumstances. Thus if there is consistency in European culture and civilization, there is just as much in Japan's.

Moreover, Fróis does not judge, or does so rarely. For example, he does not explicitly condemn the Japanese practice of infanticide and does not say that rejection of infanticide denotes the superiority of Europeans over the Japanese. He only notes, "In Europe, after a birth, killing the child is a rare practice that is almost never done; Japanese women place a foot on the neck of the child and kill nearly all they believe they cannot feed." The only chapter in which he gives full vent to his distaste is the one on "Buddhist monks and their customs." He cannot find words harsh enough to reprove their avarice, lasciviousness, insubordination, taste for pleasure and luxury, ambition, hypocrisy, immodesty, incredulity, and piggishness. Naturally, the European clergy (such as the Franciscans) are models of virtue and selflessness by comparison. It is not hard to imagine the questions that might arise for Catholic priests regarding some of the practices described in Fróis's *Treatise.*

The most delicate subjects concerned women, marriage, and children. At the start of chapter 2, Fróis notes that in Japan the virginity of girls is not prized as it is in Europe: girls who have lost it are not dishonored, and their condition does not prevent them from marrying. They are also permitted to come and go as they wish, without answering to their parents. Divorce is effected at will. The man may repudiate his wife without dishonoring her; the woman may also repudiate her husband. In either case, each remains the owner of his or her own property. The same freedom exists in regard to children: women often abort a pregnancy or kill their newborns without compunction when they believe they cannot raise them.

Another delicate question, indeed, is that of homicide, which is taken up in chapter 14. "In Japan," says Fróis, "any man may kill in his own manor." Each one works his own justice, and a mere theft may be punished with death. Killing in self-defense is also commonly permitted, with the consequence that "the one who has killed must die in turn," and if the killer manages to flee, someone else must be executed in the killer's stead.[8]

The first Japanese whom Francis Xavier met was named Yajiro or Anjiro; the encounter took place in Malacca in 1547. He brought him back to Goa, baptized him, had him learn Portuguese, and tried to draw out of him as much information as possible about Japan, where he was planning to travel. An Italian Jesuit, Father Lanzillotto, set down the content of several of his interviews with Yajiro in a letter that has been preserved.

On the subject of marriage, Lanzillotto noted that Japanese men were not all monogamous, although they "ordinarily" were. He also noted that in cases of flagrant adultery, it was the deceived husband's duty to kill his wife and her lover. If he killed only one, the justice system would pursue the other, and he was dishonored if he killed neither of them. If a wife gave cause for suspicion and rumor, without being caught in the act, the husband was to send her back to her parents and could remarry. The woman thus returned, however, was dishonored and could not marry again.[9]

There are many gaps in Anjiro's remarks as recorded by Lanzillotto and cited by Fróis; they do not address all aspects of Japanese social life and are not always consistent. They all have one point in common, however: they emphasize the predominance of custom over law and the capital importance of honor in Japanese society. Fróis does not, however, relate this observation to what he mentions, as though in passing, about voluntary death: "The Japanese at war, when they cannot go on, slit their own bellies, and this is a mark of great courage."[10]

In any case, it was often difficult for the missionaries, wishing to transmit the Christian message in everyday life, to counter the dominant mores. Their task would have been easier, paradoxically, if the religious laws they brought with them had encountered only the barrier of civil law.

The inspection report Valignano produced at the end of his tour of Japan from 1579 to 1582, partly in the company of Father Fróis, owes much to the remarks made by his faithful interpreter during their travels. Indeed, there are striking similarities between certain passages of the *Sumario de las cosas de Japón*, sent to the father general in 1583, and Fróis's *Treatise*, written later. These can only have come about from their conversations and from deep reflection performed jointly.

Valignano, like Fróis, was struck by the radical alterity of the Japanese. They were neither better nor worse than the Europeans but truly other: "They have rites and customs so different from all other nations that it appears as though they have done everything possible expressly to resemble no other." "Japan's distinctive features and way of life are contrary in every way, not merely to our customs and ways of doing things, but to our nature." Here Valignano goes further than Fróis, in that the differences are not just of custom but truly of *nature*. He repeats this elsewhere: "The very great difference [that exists] between the one and the other . . . does not seem accidental to us, but intrinsic and based in nature, for these differences in judgment and sensibility are so striking that what appears good to the one is displeasing to the other." The Visitor grasps the fact that all the information gathered in the field by himself and his companion form a whole that is complex but coherent; with no personal knowledge of the Japanese language and having stayed in the country only a few years, he does not feel able to formulate the intelligible principle of this whole, to rank and structure his observations, but holds the intimate conviction that this foreign civilization is no less ordered and regulated than that of Europe: "To behold that everything is the reverse of Europe, and that they have organized their rites and customs in such a rational system of civilization for those who knew how to understand it, is not inconsiderable cause for admiration."[11]

For those who knew how to understand it: this is the crux of the matter. One of the self-imposed rules of the Society of Jesus was not to think or speak ill of the customs and way of life in nations other than one's own. But to observe this rule scrupulously was not enough. Adopting a purely sympathetic attitude toward Japanese alterity did not allow one to "understand." One had to go further, to live with the Japanese, as the Japanese lived, to attempt, however difficult it was, to think and to feel as they did. It is significant that in chapter 16 of the *Sumario* ("Means of preserving unity between the Japanese Brothers and *dogicos*,[12] and our own, from Europe"), Valignano ranks the need to learn the Japanese language only in fourth place, after familiarization with Japanese *sensibility* and the study of *self-control* and *politeness*. So true was it that to be Japanese, or European, was above all a way of being in the world.

Valignano has sometimes been misjudged in regard to his obsession with avoiding at all costs the entrance of other religious orders into Japan. At the time he wrote his report, the Jesuits had been there for more than thirty years and could not affirm that they understood their interlocutors. The preamble to the *Sumario* speaks to this with exemplary humility: "I shall do all I can to express myself as best as possible, so that if one cannot understand all of what takes place in Japan, one may understand at least what one can."[13] He repeats this in chapter 19: "Whatever our experience may be, it is . . . impossible for us to be fully informed about the temperament, customs, and procedures of the Japanese; thus the superior and other fathers should always, when the occasion requires it, take counsel with the Japanese."[14]

In asking the recipient of the *Sumario*, and beyond him the Holy See itself, to grant responsibility for the Japanese mission to the Jesuits alone, Valignano wishes above all to avoid any blunders resulting from insufficient knowledge of the terrain. The slightest error of judgment could indeed be most serious in the case of such a proud people ("the nation most sensitive to questions of honor in the world," he says at the beginning of the *Sumario*). For this reason he strongly advises against any authoritarian intervention from the outside. He writes at the close of the preamble, "When considering Japan from Rome, one must not be surprised at the things one hears; rather, understand that decisions on many of them should be reserved for those who govern it, and they should be considered well taken even if one understands nothing of them."[15]

In this case, the danger not only came from Rome, but it also came from Goa, seat of the Jesuit province, and even Macao, so near to those who viewed things from distant Europe. The problems posed by Chinese society are, in fact, completely different; this is why "it is inappropriate for a bishop to come to Japan, but most especially that the bishop of China in any way meddle in Japanese affairs, by giving orders or asking a priest to visit Japan."[16]

What Valignano speaks of with the vague, generic term "Japanese affairs" was continually troublesome for the missionaries. They were ready to undergo a near-total transformation of mind and sensibility to reach the tone struck by the Japanese but could not identify with them completely without being untrue to their evangelical mission. Or rather, from a Japanese Christian's viewpoint, one could not remain completely in the mold of Japanese identity and continue to observe all the customs of the country without being untrue at some place or time to one's new identity as a baptized Christian.

The Visitor to Japan enumerates throughout the course of the *Sumario* several of these areas of conflict: for example, the freedom to dispense justice in one's own domain, even by homicide; the questions of suicide, abortion, infanticide; de facto polygamy; divorce.[17] In many cases, the difficulty is not simply reconciling Christian morality with the customs of the country; it is also, and primarily, a matter of whether to exercise its customary law. Valignano gives a typical example, that of Japanese lords who must mete out justice in the territories placed under their authority. Nine times out of ten, custom demands the death of the guilty party: "Anyone may kill his children and subjects, even if there is another lord above him, for such matters do not fall under that authority. And he may not only kill them but also deprive them at will of their property."[18] But if the lord is a Christian, may he in good conscience continue to behave as though he were not? Certainly the Christian princes of Europe and the tribunals of the Holy Office were constantly contravening the Sixth Commandment of the Decalogue; they did so in the application of customary or written law, after a trial conducted in due form. As the missionaries did not have the power to change customary law in Japan, and the Japanese Christian lords were very much in the minority in their country, what should one say and do? The question applied not only to the lord who was to render justice but also to his spiritual director. If a priest disapproved of homicide, he was forcing the lord to abdicate his authority and bring dishonor upon himself; if he approved, he himself became, willingly or unwillingly, the accomplice to murder and was in turn condemned. He became "irregular," and his irregularity could be dissolved only by a higher authority. In this specific case, Valignano suggested, "One must give special entitlement and permission to the superior of Japan, and also to those to whom he sees fit to communicate them, to give their opinions and counsel to Christian lords when they are called upon to condemn someone to death, and not only in general, but very specifically, even regarding particular cases, for one cannot live in Japan without this, since killing and vengeance cannot be carried out following the laws of Europe. When in doubt, the Christian lords have no one else to turn to in Japan for advice on this subject, and often it is necessary to give sentences of death, for otherwise these lords place the Christians and themselves in danger."[19]

More generally, the Jesuits in Japan were required at every moment to decide to what point the great principles they had learned from Aristotle, from Saint Thomas, and in their studies of philosophy at

Coimbra, Goa, or Macao were applicable to the Japanese context. The same held true for the canons of the Council of Trent as they learned of them, on the average two years after their creation. Valignano admits that out of caution, while waiting for Rome to make a definitive pronouncement, the missionaries in Japan decided to postpone communicating them and not to apply them until order was received to do so: "Christianity here is creating itself anew and is heavily intermingled with the non-Christian. For this reason, in this period of free development, so as not to have the law of God weigh too harshly on those who are making an effort to receive it, we have published nothing thus far, and should publish nothing of positive law, at least until there are kingdoms within Japan that are entirely Christian."[20] The ideal, however, would be for Rome to abstain from judgment and leave it to the local religious authorities: "In a Christendom so young, so free, and so ill accustomed to the yoke of divine and human precepts and to their observance, in a Christendom scattered through non-Christian masses and mingling with them, a great deal of prudence, experience, and tact is required in teaching our sacred doctrine and imposing human precepts; there must be a high level of consistency in the opinions and decisions given in each case, in preaching on various subjects, in dispensations granted or refused, in punishments and penances imposed, as well as in the refusal of sacraments or exclusion from the community and from religious burial, for we have no other jurisdiction from which we can guide them."[21]

The Appeal to Father Vázquez

When Valignano completed the *Sumario*, he certainly did not envision having to extricate his colleagues and himself from their predicaments by appealing to one of the famous casuists who in Portugal, Spain, and elsewhere were the last resort of spiritual directors. He even ruled out this eventuality quite specifically: "The customs, laws, and problems specific to Japan are so far removed from ours, and so new, that to make decisions in Japanese affairs, one may have no recourse to the opinions of Cajetan, Navarro, or other European au-

EUROPE THROUGH THE PRISM OF JAPAN

66

thorities. Beyond wisdom, in Japan one must have a great capacity for reflection, caution in making judgments, and a good knowledge of its customs, government, and modes of procedure. These achieved, the universal rules of natural law will be applied to specific cases in Japan to determine appropriate behavior in these cases, so difficult and new to us."[22]

Despite the difficulties and dangers Valignano foresaw, the first Provincial Congregation of Jesuits in Japan, which met in 1592, decided to submit to Rome a series of particularly thorny problems of conscience. It was Valignano, it seems, whose duty it was to draw up the list; this was delivered to Father Procurator Gil de la Mata, who was to take them personally to Rome. The procurator's mission was to submit litigious cases to the leading European universities—to gather their opinions, no doubt, but also to force them to confront directly, for once, the nearly insurmountable difficulties faced by the Jesuits in Japan on a daily basis.

Once in Europe, Father Gil de la Mata did not immediately hasten to Rome. He lingered in Spain and consulted at the University of Alcalá one of the most famous casuists of the times, Father Gabriel Vázquez. It seems that he also submitted the Japanese problem to other universities on the peninsula—at Évora, Coimbra, Salamanca—and received their replies. It also appears that the procedure ran afoul of other religious orders, especially the Spanish Dominicans and Franciscans, who had begun to make inroads into Japan despite Valignano's wishes.

Father Vázquez's replies, communicated to the father general, to a committee of experts, and finally to the pope, were approved by these authorities but went unpublicized and unprinted, and the text was not retrieved until 1955 when a Spanish scholar discovered them in the National Historical Archives in Madrid.[23] The discretion is understandable: the Jesuits, faithful to the position expressed by Valignano in the *Sumario*, did not desire publicity. Nor, perhaps, did they wish to further antagonize those who had become their rivals, if not their enemies, on Japanese soil.

The handwritten manuscript of questions posed and Vázquez's responses is found in a large collection of his works titled *Opera theologica*, in the section of the Madrid archives dealing with universities and colleges. After Vázquez's death, the rector of the College of Alcalá briefly considered publishing the complete collection. In the end, only parts of it were printed, in 1614 and 1616, but the Japanese dossier was absent. This was published for the first time in 1960–61, in Latin with a Spanish translation by Father Jesús López Gay.[24]

Gabriel Vázquez was born in 1549 in New Castile. He studied humanities with the Jesuits at Belmonte and philosophy at the University of Alcalá. He entered the novitiate at Alcalá when he was in his fourth year of philosophy. He performed his novitiate successively in Alcalá, Toledo, and Sigüenza and his theology studies at Alcalá, partly at the Jesuit college and partly at the university. During his final year of study (1574–75), he also learned Hebrew. In his second year of theology, he began serving as instructor to his younger comrades, guiding them in the study of Aristotle's *De anima*.

His theology studies completed, Vázquez taught ethics at Ocaña (1575–77), then scholastic theology, first at Madrid (1577–79) and later at Alcalá (1580–83). His work consisted principally of reading and explicating the *Summa theologica* of Saint Thomas. In 1585 he was called to Rome to replace Father Suárez. He taught at the Collegio Romano for four and a half years, then returned to Alcalá, where he dedicated two years to writing. He returned to teaching at Alcalá in 1593. He died in 1604, leaving a body of work in the process of being published, the first portion having been printed in 1598. The full publication, ten folio volumes, was completed only long after his death, in 1617.

It would seem that nothing in his career had prepared Vázquez to reply to the questions the missionaries posed. He was a man of studies, a pure product of traditional scholastic theology. Moreover, he had hardly traveled at all, apart from one excursion to Rome that entailed no departure from the narrow circle of his customary preoccupations. His method could not have been more stolidly traditional: he sought authority first in the Scriptures, then in the decrees of the Church and the decisions of its councils, and last with the Greek and Latin fathers of the Church.

Two or three of Vázquez's personal qualities might explain why Father Gil de la Mata, who was his contemporary, would address the missionaries' appeal to him. He was a good philologist: he knew Hebrew and enough Greek to correct a bad translation of Aristotle here and there. He shared this quality, and perhaps others, with many of the humanists of the preceding generation. He also had a historical sense that was rare for his era, and his interminable disputes with his colleague and rival Suárez had honed his talents as a dialectician.[25]

One of Vázquez's chief preoccupations was to determine to what degree human laws held sway over Catholics of good conscience. And he had a reputation for never resolving a case submitted to him solely by weighing the authorities invoked to shed light on it but always taking into account the context and historical circumstances. He was inclined to think that because humans were by nature social creatures, the obligation to obey civil laws was part of their essence.

Difficulty arises for the casuist when divine law and religious law come into conflict with civil law. The Church has the right to set up laws, but so does the state, *and its laws are also compelling to the conscience*, at least insofar as they are in accord with the exigencies of human nature. These are necessarily few in number: an unjust law, one contrary to the exigencies of human nature—which is to say, natural law—is not a true law, and no one can be obliged in good conscience to obey it.

The question becomes crucial when it is a matter of life and death, as we have seen in the illustrative "case study" of Father Ferreira. The distinction Vázquez made between the very few cases in which an individual must agree to sacrifice his or her life for the common good and the much more frequent ones in which this is not an obligation implies that as a last resort a person may decide whether or not the obligation accords with natural law on the basis of reason alone. In no case may the obligation be imposed from outside, as a constraint. From this stance, the work of Father Vázquez may be called humanist. God is not, of course, absent from his reasoning, but it is not divine intelligence that is expressed in natural law, as it is for Saint Thomas; rather, "it is the very essence of God that constitutes the basis of moral obligation and natural law." Since human nature owes to God its essence as well as its existence, everything that affronts human nature is also an offense against the Divine Being.[26]

The questions submitted to Vázquez by de la Mata are grouped into six chapters: marriage, usury, homicide, treatment of captives and laws of warfare, pagan and idolatrous practices, and hearing confession for the sick. The cases number, respectively, eleven, six, four, ten, seven, and seven. This comes to a total of forty-five questions, with replies—in a relatively limpid, if not always elegant, Latin—that are terse but always extremely precise. Only the most sensitive will be addressed here, ones that either touch on a very special area of Japanese custom or require complex juridical elaboration, marshaling all the means scholastic theology had at its disposal.

In the chapter on marriage, the document submitted to Vázquez naturally speaks primarily about marriage and divorce as practiced in Japan. For there to be divorce, there must be marriage, but is a Japanese marriage really a marriage? This is more or less the substance of the first three questions. The fourth is more subtle: "A Christian has repudiated in good faith his first wife. He had married her before the publication of the works of the Council. Now he has asked to marry another woman before the Church. He has not concealed in confession that he has repudiated his first wife. He is admonished to return to this first spouse. He does not do so and will not do so. Question: Should one in confession tell the truth to a Christian of this sort, and above all, should one administer to him before the Church the sacrament of marriage? Assume, by hypothesis, that if the sacrament is administered to some and refused to others it will result in discredit to the religion."

The Council of Trent evoked here had dealt exhaustively with marriage as a sacrament in session 24 in November 1536. There also existed a code called the *Taiho*, promulgated in Japan early in the eighth century, which allowed seven causes for divorce at the husband's initiative: if the woman reached the age of fifty without having borne a son, if she committed adultery, if she mistreated her in-laws, if she talked too much, if she robbed, if she was jealous, or if she had a serious contagious disease such as leprosy. The code also restricted divorce under three conditions: if the woman had always been faithful and obedient, if her social situation had changed a great deal over the duration of the marriage, or if she had nowhere to take refuge in the event of repudiation. But with time the custom had grown lax, and repudiation often occurred for frivolous reasons.[27]

Vázquez was unaware of the existence of the *Taiho* but knew its modern ramifications. He also knew the canons of Trent on the sacrament of marriage. He answered generally:

As to the difficulties put forth regarding marriage, it is necessary first, it seems to me, to advance as a probable opinion that the Japanese form of marriage is not valid, either when final or when contracted with the sole intention of testing the wife's behavior, only to repudiate her if she is not found suitable. In the second hypothesis, I see no reason for the slightest doubt, since the express intention runs counter to the perpetuity of marriage, which is itself postulated on the perpetuity of the bond and the obligation. It is like the case of a man who would buy a horse with the sole intent to try it out and later return it to its owner if it does not suit him, and take back the purchase price: no perpetual obligation results from such a transaction; the property is not removed. That is why, if the Japanese take wives by performing certain ceremonies but understand it as a marriage according to the custom of their land, for the sole purpose of testing the wife's behavior, they do not contract a perpetual union and it is not an authentic marriage.

Moreover, even when they contract a final union, it would seem that there is still no marriage, because they conduct themselves as though such unions were sealed under the express condition that they may repudiate their wives for whatever reasons and at whatever time they find convenient. Anyone who contracts a union of this sort concludes a marriage that is null; this would be to place upon it in effect a condition counter to the essence and nature of marriage, which presupposes perpetuity. In the same way, a person selling a piece of property on the condition that he will be able to buy it back whenever he pleases does not guarantee to the buyer, by this transaction, perpetual possession. This is why, when the Japanese marry according to the custom of their country, they evidently do so as though a condition were imposed thereon. In effect, if ancestral tradition were to hold that no sale of land can be made without reserving the right to buy back the property, even those who contract without this reserve are not held to have contracted any differently than those who do reserve it. Therefore, due to the fact that all Japanese men are accustomed to repudiating their wives at will, that neither the relatives nor even the wife herself objects to this, and that no dishonor to her ensues, it is seen that for them no contract is given to be perpetual.

The solution to the fourth case of conscience is thus obvious: the first marriage was not valid, so there is nothing to oppose the wishes of anyone who would now marry in the Church. This reveals the spirit in which Father Vázquez read the questions put to him: as a canonist, a jurist, rather than as a pastor. As it happened, however, his reminder concerning the unwavering position of the magisterium in regard to marriage eased the missionaries' work. If Japanese marriages were to be considered null and void, the separations were equally meaningless. There were no marriages in Japan except those contracted between two Catholic spouses who were adequately trained, instructed in the nature and scope of the sacrament, and sincerely determined to respect their vows unto death. This is why the missionaries celebrated relatively few of them: they were not sure that all of the baptized were capable of appraising what was at stake in their vows.

In the chapter on usury, the most interesting question is number 12: "Should those who practiced usury before their baptism be required to make restitution of the fruits of their practices as soon as possible, or may such restitution be postponed until they request the sacrament of penance when it appears that the admonition would have no effect prior to baptism? May one also apply here the dispositions on 'uncertain property' included in session 19 of the Council of Basel?" Vázquez's reply is terse: "One may wait until baptism to demand restitution, because it is permitted to wait for the opportune moment to do so; one may also apply in such a case the decree of the Council of Basel."

Usury had long been condemned by the Church. The Council of Latran, in 1139, had decreed in its canon 13 that "the insatiable rapacity of usurers" was "hateful and scandalous" to divine law as well as human law and had thus prohibited usurers from receiving the sacraments. They were even to be "held in infamy all their lives and refused religious burial," unless, of course, "they were to see the error of their ways."[28]

The Council of Basel, in session 19 on September 7, 1434, did not go back on this condemnation in principle but updated it to take into account the special situation of Jews "and other infidels" who practiced usury and later happened to convert to Christianity. After listing all the discriminatory measures designed to set Jews apart from civil society, such as making them wear special clothing and live in certain areas, Basel obliged any converts among them to restore to the victims of their practice their ill-gotten gains. If the victims had died or were un-known, the goods or money acquired through usury was to be "di-verted by the hands of the Church to pious ends."[29] It is to this clause that the author of the questionnaire submitted to Vázquez was alluding when he spoke of "uncertain property" *(bona incerta)*. Thus Vázquez, with his affirmative reply to question 12, was applying to the Japanese of his time—grouping them with all other "infidels"—a decree handed down one hundred sixty years earlier in the context of fifteenth-century Europe and chiefly concerning Jews, whose treatment by sixteenth-century Spain is a matter of record. This could not be further from the spirit motivating the author of the *Sumario* ten years earlier.

The chapter on homicide consists of four questions, at least two of them significant to the customs described by Fróis and Valignano. The first of these appears in the questionnaire as number 18:

It is generally the custom in Japan for temporal lords and fathers of families to have the authority to kill their subjects and the members of their household when they are caught committing a theft, even a minor one, but also when they have been insolent or disobedient. The same right accrues to anyone who has been the victim of a theft, even a trivial one; that person may in effect kill the thief. There is never a thorough investigation of these acts: if the fact is judged to be indubitable, the guilty party is executed on the spot. Question: Will the Fathers attempt to do something to change an ancestral custom? The hypothesis is that admonition is likely to have no effect. The same question applies to the relatives of the person killed, who assume the right to kill the murderer, and do so. In these cases the temporal lords do not intervene to prevent the murder but on the contrary spare the relatives: what they have done is legal.

Vázquez's reply is consistent with his position mentioned earlier on the authority of law in any society. But it assumes that there exists a Japanese state, and at its head a king under whose authority the law is applied, which at the time he was writing was still far from the case. His judgment is nonetheless cautious, and he refrains from inciting the missionaries to attack the custom head-on: "At this time, it is permitted to dissemble [your feelings] and not to try to introduce new practices, since this would be of no use. Perhaps the custom imposed in this country implies that whoever kills in this manner is acting not by individual authority but by that of the sovereign prince, since it seems to be acceptable to all, given the nature of the country and its people."

Question 20 is also quite weighty:

> It is common among the pagans that when a murderer flees, the family of the victim or the governor of the victim's country will capture the murderer, or if they cannot, then someone from the same country as the murderer. This is done because if no one is caught, the inhabitants of the dead person's country would be permitted to kill on their own authority any inhabitant whatsoever of the murderer's country. Question: When a pagan governor asks a Christian governor to hand over this sort of hostage, what shall he do, given that if the murderer is not discovered, by not delivering the innocent who is demanded, he risks his own life, not to mention the numerous other problems that would ensue?

Vázquez replied: "If the harm would come only to the [Christian] governor if he did not hand over the innocent [being demanded], he is not permitted to surrender the person; however, if a threat to the country itself would be incurred, then it would be permissible. Indeed anyone must accept with equanimity exposure to the danger of certain death in order to save the country from a like fate."

Of all the questions faced by the missionaries from the incessant warfare waged by the Japanese feudal lords among themselves, the thorniest was how to treat the Christian lords, since they took part in it like all the rest and did not conceal their adherence to the new religion. This is how it is formulated at the beginning of the chapter in the questionnaire titled "On Warfare and Captives" (question 22):

It has been a continuous custom in Japan since ancient times for the mightier lord to attempt to subdue by force of arms the less powerful one, and to bring his lands under his own domination. There are in Japan only a very few authentic and natural lords. . . . Question: May those who have acquired domains by means of this sort of warfare keep them in good conscience, at least after they have possessed them for some time in peace? In a dubious case, the possessor is in the better situation. In addition it appears to be impossible to find the true possessor, or, if he exists, to return to him his domains. In such a case, should one dissemble [what one really thinks], knowing that despite all admonitions one may make regarding restitution [of the domains], they will not restore them and will keep them with a clear conscience?

Vázquez again replies in classic form: "It seems that in this case the principle of prescription regarding sovereignty applies. It originated in natural law and appears legitimate: [there is prescription] whenever the holders of a realm, or their successors, even if they have acquired it by an unjust war, hold sovereignty in such a way that its exercise cannot be remanded to its legitimate holder without causing great harm. In effect the public interest must take precedence over the interest of the private person who was formerly the lord of the realm."

One chapter of the questionnaire in particular must have attracted Father Vázquez's attention: the one concerning superstition and the worship of idols. One of the major subjects of debate in which he opposed Francisco Suárez was the veneration of images. The Lutheran and Calvinist reform movements had both risen up against the cult of saints in the Roman church and against the place in Catholic worship of statues and pious images. In several places, there was even an outpouring of iconoclastic rage against all such representations.

There were also polemics on this subject within the Catholic church. The position of the humanists on this point was not very far from that of the Lutherans and reformists. In a famous chapter of *The Praise of Folly*, Erasmus speaks ironically, to great effect, about the popular cults of Saint Christopher, Saint Barbara, Saint Erasmus, Saint Hippolyta, and Saint George, "whose horse, piously decked out with trappings and bosses, they all but worship."[30] The fathers of the Council of Trent thought to put an end to this sort of dispute in their session of December 3, 1563: no virtue was to be imputed to images, and nothing was to be asked of them, but they could be honored, for the honor redounded to those whom they represented.

Father Vázquez had attracted attention while quite young for publishing a book on the adoration of images *(De cultu adorationis)* that incurred the lasting wrath of Suárez. More traditionalist than the fathers of the Council would prove to be later on, he affirmed that worship of the cross, of images, and of relics was addressed as much to the representation as to the person represented but in a different way, the sentiment expressed being directed to the person, and the external signs of reverence to the image, and only indirectly to the person.

The question of "images" was quite different in Japan, because the spheres of the secular and the religious were not separate, as they increasingly were in Europe. What could a Japanese Christian do or not do in the many cases in which, as a subject, he or she was involved, however unwillingly, in pagan ceremonies?

Questions 32 through 38 must be read together, one after the other, because Vázquez read them as a whole. He answered them, in fact, in one continuous stream, linking them in such a way that the answer to one dictated the answer to the next. His reply is entirely typical of a man enclosed in a hierarchical system of thought, accustomed to considering hypothetical-deductive reasoning as the crowning achievement of the human mind.

Question 32: When a pagan lord erects a temple in honor of his idol, is it licit for a Christian servant to carve the wood or place the carved objects in the temple, to make tiles and roof the temple with them, to spread clay on the walls or do any work inside the edifice during the time that it is not yet a temple? Assume that all of this is not imposed to show contempt for our faith, but that Christians who refuse to do the work as ordered will probably lose their lives, along with their family patrimony.

Question 33: When a pagan goes to a temple to worship idols and says to a servant who is Christian, "Bring my beads . . . , bring aromatic plants and everything necessary to sacrifice to the idols," is it permitted for the Christian servant to obey the pagan master in this matter? And when the pagan master kneels, is it permitted for the servant to kneel as well—not, however, showing any signs of veneration—without giving scandal? It goes without saying that if the servant remained standing while the master knelt, this would be the height of insolence. Likewise the case in which a pagan master says to a Christian servant, "Put burning coals on the altar and burn incense, and so on." It should be assumed that the pagan master is not giving these orders out of contempt for divine law, nor does this even occur to him; he gives such orders as he would demand any other service. It should also be assumed that if the servant does not obey, it is as though the master has been scorned, and the servant will be killed on the spot. Is it licit in such cases to obey pagan masters?

Question 34: It is a custom in Japan that when celebrating the feast of an idol, all the inhabitants tidy the villages and squares, decorate their houses with branches, construct carts, give various dramatic presentations on the carts, hold dances, and bear the idol in great pomp upon one cart while the multitude gathers around to witness the spectacle.[31] Question: May the Christians who live in these villages and amid the pagans tidy up around their homes and decorate the doors to their houses with branches? In effect, when the cart bearing the idol passes through the village, if one of the Christians' houses is not so decorated, this will be noticed and the Christians' lives will be gravely imperiled; they will be taken to be rebels, for they will have gravely offended their pagan master. It is assumed, of course, that there is no scandal and that the Christians do not perform these acts by way of adoring the idols but to participate along with the others in the general festivity.

Question 35: May Christians, during the solemnities for the idols, participate in the dances and presentations mentioned above, assuming that they do not intend to render worship to the idol but to contribute to the general festivity, that the Christians make no sign of veneration when passing before the idol, and that they give no scandal? Assume also that none of this is imposed to show contempt for divine law and that if the Christians refuse to contribute and serve as their masters request, their lives will be gravely imperiled.

Question 36: It is a custom among the Japanese that when pagan masters demand an oath from their servants, they trace certain pagan figures on a paper with these words: "We the undersigned say that if we do not speak the truth, or if we betray our oath, may the wrath of the idols by whom we swear befall us." Witnesses sign beneath these figures and words. Question: May Christians declare themselves openly as such and pledge their oath not to the idols but to God and to the cross on which they will swear? They would draw a cross, announce their intention to swear upon it, and put their names beneath it, on the same paper, without giving scandal. Assume that nothing in this is imposed to show contempt for divine law but that Christians who did not sign at the place indicated would clearly imperil their lives or risk, at the least, the loss of all their property.

Question 37: The Japanese pagans celebrate each year the feast of souls. They believe that souls return to earth; they prepare food for them and light the windows with lanterns so the souls will not go astray.[32] Question: May Christians who live in the pagans' midst light lanterns at their windows, assuming that they place no credence in this superstition and that no scandal occurs? They would do this to share in the general festivity and so as not to cross their masters, in fear of the extreme danger to which the Japanese are exposed when they are not submissive to their masters.

Question 38: The Japanese pagans, when they have doubts about the conduct of their servants or wives, to uncover the truth often ask them to hold a red-hot stone in their hands, or to plunge one hand into boiling water; if the suspected parties are unharmed, they are held to be innocent; if they are burned, however, the wives are either repudiated or put to death as adulterers; servants, too, may be condemned to death. It does happen sometimes that the wives or servants who undergo the trial of the heated stone or of boiling water feel nothing. If the wives and servants refuse to take the risk, they are held to be guilty and are punished as such. Question: May a Christian woman or a Christian servant, especially if they are innocent, to avoid death undergo either of these trials at the order of the husband or master?

This chapter, one notes, poses concrete questions that are nearly always a matter of life or death for the interested party. But it poses them, as do the other chapters, in an extremely narrow juridical framework, shaped by scholastic thought. Whatever Valignano may have thought, if it is indeed he who formulated these questions—and his underlying opinions are known from the *Sumario*—when officially consulting a casuist he had no choice but to speak in the language appropriate to this sort of communication. The result of his efforts surpassed his worst fears. This is what Vázquez replied to question 32:

It is licit to do what is mentioned here, as it is licit to sell a goat to a Jew, even when one knows that it is bought for sacrifice. Carving wood, placing it in constructions, and so on, in itself is work that anyone may use for good or for ill, as one wishes. Thus one must follow the rule of Thomas 2:2, question 43, articles 7 and 8: passive scandal cannot befall one whose work is at the origin of the scandal, if another has caused the scandal by malice. In effect, no one is asked to count as nothing his own interest, even a temporal one, on account of this sort of scandal, out of fear that another will give scandal through malice. Whoever sins by *habitus* gives scandal through malice, for sin by *habitus* is one which is done through malice, according to Saint Thomas 1:2, question 78, article 2. [In this case it concerns] those who ill use, for idolatrous ends, edifices built by Christians.

This reply is entirely typical of a casuist's intellectual procedure. It consists of implicitly defining *scandal* as the fact of consecrating to idols a building constructed by Christians (even if this is only said at the end), then distinguishing (and everything lies in the *distinguo*) between *active scandal* and *passive scandal*. The first mention of Saint Thomas refers to two articles whose titles are in question form. Article 7: "Whether spiritual goods should be forgone on account of scandal?" Article 8: "Whether temporal goods should be forgone on account of scandal?" After stating each question, the author of the *Summa theologica* first lists a number of "objections," adds one "on the contrary," then formulates a general "response," followed by a certain number of "replies" (one "reply" per "objection"). The distinction between "active scandal" and "passive scandal" is in the "response" to article 7; one must distinguish, it says, because the question put forth can only be posed in regard to "passive scandal," and not "active": "[W]e have to see what ought to be forgone in order to avoid scandal." Next there appears a new distinction, between "spiritual goods" and "temporal goods." In the case under consideration, what the Japanese Christian stands to "forgo" is not spiritual in nature but temporal: his or her life and goods. In the "response" to article 8, it is said that the temporal goods "of which we have the dominion" may or may not be given up "on account of scandal," depending on the circumstances. They must be given up, partially or totally, if the scandal is brought about "through the ignorance or weakness of others." But they need not be if "scandal arises from malice": "We ought not to forgo temporal goods for the sake of those who stir up scandals of this kind."[33]

The second reference to Saint Thomas directs us to an article titled "Whether everyone who sins through *habitus* sins through certain malice?" The "objections" show that some have hesitated on this point. The "response" seems to complicate things by making a new distinction: "There is a difference between a sin committed by one who has the *habitus* and a sin committed by *habitus*." Someone who has a *habitus* that is a vice does not inevitably sin in all things because of it: the person may at times commit "a virtuous act." But one who does sin through *habitus* "must needs sin through certain malice." This is true of those who have a temple built to dedicate to idols, causing a scandal in which the Christian worker is but the passive agent.

It is doubtful that even with their excellent theological training the missionaries would have been able, in Japan, to enter into such subtleties for each case brought to them. It is particularly doubtful that they could have made these fine points understood by the members of their flock, in the highly unlikely case that they had asked for explanations of the directives given.

Vázquez's subsequent responses flow naturally from these premises. To question 33: "For the same reason, it is licit for a Christian servant to bring beads to his or her master, even in the full knowledge that they will be used in the worship of idols. One may also bring aromatic plants. But the servant may not kneel, bring coals, or place aromatic preparations on the fire, for these are manifest signs of idolatry, constituting the act of worship itself.[34] This is not permitted, even if done without the intention to ostensibly worship false gods, for it is not permitted under any pretext to profess idolatry, even externally. I refer to cases when the external act appears to those present as an act of worship. For if the right intention [not to worship idols] be known to all, then it would not be a sin because it would not then constitute professing a false religion."

To question 34: "Same response as to 33."

To question 35: "The same. In all three cases, what is to be feared is that one will be taken for a worshiper of idols, that one will seem to make a public profession of a false religion. This is why one must take into account not so much scandal [itself] as opinion, the external appearance of professing faith. In effect, even if one did not by such occasion sin, which would constitute true scandal,[35] it would suffice that an act appears externally to others as worship rendered to idols. For this reason alone it would not be permitted, for in such case it would indeed be profession of a false religion. Naaman, in 2 Kings, chapter 5, does not demand that Elisha allow him to worship in the temple of Rimmon, and the prophet does not permit this, when he tells him, 'Go in peace.' But Naaman asks the prophet to pray to God for him, beseeching that he pardon him, in case he should enter the temple of Rimmon with his master when he is worshiping, and the prophet assures him that he will pray for him by saying, 'Go in peace.'"[36]

To questions 36 and 37: "Same as the preceding."

To question 38: "It shall be permitted that a servant submit to said trial, and a wife also, to avoid a greater harm, unless such an act is tainted with some sort of superstition, in which case they would seem in the eyes of the master to be professing a false religion."

Readers of Pascal are familiar with his lambasting of Father Vázquez in the fifth and even more intensely in the twelfth of his *Provincial Letters*, written a good half-century later. One cannot help imagining the perverse pleasure he would have taken in skewering the next-to-last question in the document Father de la Mata had brought to the master from Alcalá: "Is it possible in Japan to perform the sacrament with wine made from wild grapes? Although the leaves and seeds are tiny and the wine they produce somewhat weak *[aliquantulum debile]*, and although the wine does not keep long if it is not mixed with Portuguese wine, it is nonetheless of the same color and taste, and the wild grapevines seem to bear more abundantly than they do in Europe. [If this is not possible] may one at least, when the arrival of the ship [from Macao] is uncertain, mix the wine from wild grapes with Portuguese wine, even if the mixture contains more of the former than the latter?"

The question had importance, for the quantity of Portuguese wine delivered with each boatload of goods from Macao was small, and the risks of navigation in the China seas enormous. How to celebrate Mass without sacramental wine? Vázquez took the question seriously. But a glimmer of the humanist appeared at times beneath the casuist. His terse reply would have delighted Erasmus and fanned the flames of Pascal's wrath: "As long as it isn't vinegar, why not?"

Chapter Four

The Theater of Faith, Civility, and Glory

The European visit of Valignano's four "ambassadors" was organized in the manner of a triumphal sweep in days of antiquity, a nearly uninterrupted succession of ceremonies in which nothing was left to chance. This monumental stagecraft had two aims: to demonstrate to all of Europe that the mission established in Japan was a complete success and to present to the envoys Christian Europe in its best light. The first objective was achieved by means of a judicious choice of stages in the trip, from Lisbon to Rome and back, passing through the cities where the Japanese would be seen by the largest crowds, the highest civil and religious authorities, and the ambassadors of all the nations on diplomatic terms with them. The news of this welcome was spread via pamphlets distributed with stunning rapidity in all the European languages and countries: there were forty-nine of them in the years 1585 and 1586 alone.[1] The organizers of the trip achieved their second objective through numerous presents, often quite lavish, that the envoys brought back to their country, and also through the narrative in dialogue form *De missione legatorum*, published in Macao in 1590 for use as a reader in Jesuit establishments in Japan. The effect of the presents and the text was then augmented by a wealth of new artistic production in Japan, of which only a fragmentary idea can be gleaned today, as it was destroyed in part by the Japanese Inquisition. The report of the envoys' reception in Venice alone conveys the tone of what was one of the most astounding spectacles of the century.

The young men and their retinue arrived in the territory of the republic on June 26, 1585, coming from Ferrara. They were met three miles from Chioggia by the *podestà*, escorted by three brigantines and several galeasses. The bishop of Chioggia, leading his clergy, joined them. Two miles from Venice, a group of forty senators in ceremonial garb awaited them. From there the procession sailed into Venice on three sumptuously decorated vessels wreathed by a cloud of gondolas; these boats were ordinarily reserved for royal receptions. They paraded down the Grand Canal and the Canal de la Giudecca between two banks of curious onlookers packed onto the quays and behind windows. That evening, a Te Deum was sung in the Jesuit church. The "ambassadors" received a visit from the papal nuncio the same evening and the next day met with the patriarch and several ambassadors. The visit with the doge, Niccolò da Ponte, who was over ninety years old *(un amabile vecchietto di novantacinque anni)*, was the highlight. Then the young men were shown the Arsenal, the fortress of Lido, and the glassworks of Murano. Tintoretto was asked to paint a group portrait of them, but perhaps he did not have the time, or the piece has been lost. Precious gifts were exchanged. The Japanese had brought a scimitar in a mother-of-pearl sheath, "its garnishments notched with inlaid gold," two knives, a dagger, and three silken garments "in the Japanese style." They went back to Japan on July 6 with ten lengths of rare cloth, two trunks of Venetian glassware, eight mirrors in magnificent frames, and four ivory crucifixes.[2]

De missione legatorum dedicates nearly three chapters, interviews 27 through 29, to the recounting of these ten memorable days and the description of all the wonders the travelers saw. It reads like an explication of an exquisite painting from the Museum of the Academy, perhaps *The Procession before Saint Marc* by Gentile Bellini (1429–1507).

At several points, there was theater within theater. The Jesuits, always great innovators in education, had decided that to instruct their pupils in good literature as well as good morals, nothing was better than an excellent play, mounted by the pupils themselves before their peers. And these were not patronage pieces. Among the still vivid successes of Jesuit theater in the mid-sixteenth century was *Acolastus*, performed at the College of Saint Anthony in Lisbon with beautiful sets and musical accompaniment both vocal and instrumental, as well as *Saül*, performed in 1559 on the occasion of the opening of the University of Évora. The subjects of these plays were most often taken from the Scriptures or from Christian hagiography. The *Ratio studiorum* specifies that they must be written and performed in Latin and must include no female roles, even if played by men.[3] The missionaries had introduced this form of expression into Japan, too, and the "ambassadors" were surely not surprised to find it practiced to equally good effect at both ends of the world.

Beginning in the 1560s, the fathers had made a custom, on the great Christian feast days, of mounting as pedagogical theater pieces the most meaningful episodes of the story of Christianity. The high point of this veritable theater season, which paradoxically coincided with the Lenten period, occurred at Easter. In Funai, beginning on Palm Sunday, the chapel was decorated with "Roman arches" in black paper, on which were painted the emblems of the Passion: cross, crown of thorns, nails, shroud, sepulcher, and so on. These emblems were accompanied by inscriptions in Portuguese and Japanese explaining the images or indicating the biblical texts that referred to them. On Wednesday evening, the candles were extinguished one by one, and as the darkness grew, the congregation sang the Lamentations of Jeremy. On Thursday, a cenotaph was set up amid green branches and glowing candles; posted around it were guards costumed as Roman soldiers, armed with lances and wearing breastplates, helmets, and greaves. Friday morning the account of the Passion was sung in call and response, and in the afternoon the faithful worshiped the cross before a Crucifixion scene hung with long black drapes as a sign of mourning. The choir and altar were also veiled in black for the night of Friday to Saturday, and the ceremonies of the day, such as the benediction of the holy water and the Pascal candle, were held before a portable altar. In the evening, after the Kyrie, the black veils fell, and to the chant of Gloria an image of the resurrected Christ appeared, surrounded with candles, at the back of the choir loft, now hung with white. The faithful then passed, we are told, "from the bleakest dejection to the most exuberant joy."[4]

Other testimonies recount a typical Easter Sunday at Funai, with the church opening two hours before dawn, children dressed in white and crowned with roses bearing gilt-paper representations of the symbols of the Passion, angels seated at both ends of the tomb, the procession leaving the church after the Mass to walk the stations of the cross to the strains of *Victimae paschali laudes*, from the 116th Psalm, and the Alleluia. A dialogue was sung between Mary Magdalene and the apostles. Mary pointed to the empty tomb, the shroud. The children explained the meaning of the symbols they carried.[5]

Christmas, too, was an occasion for sacred spectacle, as it often was in Europe. In 1560 at Funai, a drama was presented in two acts with an interval piece. In the first act Lucifer tempted Eve before a tree laden with golden apples that had been set up in the middle of the church. They were driven from Paradise after the Fall, then returned to hear an angel announce the Redemption. In the second act Noah boarded the ark to escape the flood; Lot, captive and in chains, was delivered by Abraham; a prophet announced the mystery of the Incarnation; an angel told shepherds that the Child was born and invited them to come and worship Him. All that has survived of the interval piece is the theme: the judgment of Solomon. It is not known whether it was enacted in a style and tone different from those of the main drama, but the record shows that its intent was to demonstrate to the pagan women, still tempted to kill their newborns, the powerful natural love of a true mother.[6]

De missione legatorum contains a detailed account of the spectacles the "ambassadors" attended at Coimbra in 1586 when they visited the college there. They first saw a sacred drama whose protagonists were the respective guardian angels of Asia and Europe, who discussed the marvelous successes of the missionaries in Japan. It ended with wishes for the safe return of the "ambassadors" to the land of their birth. It was performed, we are told, with rare elegance in both the acting and the speeches (*quae omnia cum summa personarum venustate, sermonisque elegantia peracta sunt*). Another dialogue brought the students of the college on stage. They spoke of the arrival of the Japanese delegation, of the joy it brought them, of the guests' privilege in meeting the Holy Father in Rome. In a third and more ambitious sacred drama, spectators saw Asia herself, then Oceanus, Europa, Lusitania, Castella, and

Italia. Asia bemoaned the fact that her children were so far away. Oceanus assured her he had brought them to a safe port with gentle benevolence *(molliter indulgenterque)*. To convince her that they were safe and sound in her keeping, Europa called in her daughters, Lusitania, Castella, and Italia. All three confirmed what their mother had said. It ended with Asia and Europa swearing a pact of eternal friendship and Oceanus promising to be just as benign in bringing the young people back home.

These three plays were presented consecutively within the walls of the college. The entourage then went out to attend another spectacle, this one public, given in honor of a prelate who had recently come from the province of Algarve to Coimbra. Its topic was the life and death of John the Baptist. The play was in five acts. The first showed the saint at the age of five leaving his family to go to the desert. In the second act he was thirty years old. His fame had spread, and all the Jews came to him to be baptized in the river Jordan. In the third act, John traveled to Jerusalem to admonish Herod and convince him to renounce his dissolute life. In the fourth act, he was in prison. In the fifth, he was beheaded. This scene was performed so vividly that the audience believed they were seeing the real thing, right before their eyes *(ut non in scena agi, sed re ipsa evenire videretur)*. Adding to the beauty of the spectacle was the choral chanting presented between acts. The Japanese were particularly impressed with the beautiful chants to the glory of the saint in the third act, and in the fourth by the entry of the Furies, issued from Hell to harden Herod's heart.

On December 25 they attended a Christmas pageant. It was a sort of eclogue *(quaedam Aegloga)* that brought to the stage the angels, the shepherds, and the Magi around the grotto and crèche.[7]

The Art of the Japanese Counter-Reformation

The Jesuits were convinced of the value of images as a supplement to preaching and a prop to the act of faith. And with all the more reason in Japan, since the Buddhist temples and Shinto sanctuaries, like the Hindu temples they had seen in India, were often heavily laden with images.

The place and function of images was very much in debate in Europe by the different currents of the Reformation as well as by humanists. The moderate position taken by the fathers of the Council of Trent in 1563 was simply adjusted by the various regional religious authorities; thus the art of the Counter-Reformation cannot be said to reflect a rigorous and universal application of a preestablished program.[8] There are, however, in the period following the council during the late sixteenth and early seventeenth centuries, a certain number of convergences in artistic expression that are due to more than chance, at least in the Catholic countries.

The religious art of this period is characterized first and foremost by the primacy of the subject over all other considerations: nothing in a religious depiction was to distract the mind from what was being represented. And the Jesuits were most mindful of this in the commissions they gave to artists. They saw in art, accessorily, a useful weapon in controversy. And since the Protestants were hostile to the worship of the Virgin and the saints, contested the real presence of Christ in the Eucharist, and rejected the primacy of Peter, everything in Catholic art was obliged on the contrary to exalt these themes. Although the dogma of the Immaculate Conception had not yet been proclaimed (and would not be until 1854, by Pius IX), favorite depictions showed Mary crowned with stars, her feet resting on a crescent moon, as she had existed since the beginning of the world, before the Fall. It was also popular to show Saint Peter with the Bible in his right hand and keys in his left, as though to underline the importance of Matthew 16:18–19: "And I tell you, you are Peter, and on this rock I will build my church. . . . I will give you the keys of the kingdom of heaven; and whatever you bind on earth shall be bound in heaven, and whatever you loose on earth shall be loosed in heaven." Finally, to underscore even more strongly their differences with the Protestants, they found numerous ways to represent the holy sacrament, often as a host surrounded by an aureole, sometimes above a chalice.[9]

In Japan, however, the Jesuits had to make an important concession to the sensibility of their hosts: they could not represent the Crucifixion as realistically as was customary in Europe in the late sixteenth century. The Japanese inflicted the torture of the cross on highway robbers; thus it was an ignoble torture unbefitting the Son of God. In addition, the Japanese were repulsed by suffering bodies, not only the contact with them but also even their depiction. This was not from oversensitivity—on the contrary, all indications are that the Japanese of the sixteenth century could be extremely cruel—but out of the hatred for impurity that is so important in Shintoism. Thus the Jesuits broached the topic of the Crucifixion with extreme caution: they used the symbol of the Greek cross rather than the Latin one, preferred to evoke metonymically the emblems of the Passion rather than the Passion itself, and, most important, refrained from translating the word *cross* by its Japanese equivalent. They instead created a Japanese form of the Portuguese word *cruz*, transcribed as *kurusu*.

To adorn the numerous churches and chapels the missionaries built during the second half of the sixteenth century, it was necessary to import a great number of images and objects of worship. These they had sent from Lisbon and Goa. Numerous altarpieces were dispatched from Europe to Japan. They showed the Visitation, the Nativity, the Virgin holding the Infant Jesus in her arms, or "the triumph and glory of the Resurrection of Our Lord Jesus Christ." Some of these pieces were copied by Japanese artists, who did quite a good job if we may believe the witnesses of the time.[10]

The return of the "ambassadors" in 1590 marked a decisive step toward implanting permanently European Christian art on Japanese soil. They brought back with them many works of art that had been given to them in Europe, especially in Italy. They brought from Macao a press with movable metal type and all the material necessary to produce copperplate engravings. And it happened that during their absence, in 1583, a consummate artist had arrived from Europe, an Italian brother named Giovanni Niccolò. Niccolò was born in Naples in 1558. He entered the Society of Jesus at the age of twenty and shortly thereafter was sent to Japan, precisely because of his artistic talents. He first studied philosophy and theology without much success, having no doubt more of a taste for fine arts. The material brought from Europe allowed him to open a school of painting at Shiki, on the Amakusa archipelago. The school was moved in 1601 to Arima and in 1603 to Nagasaki. It was there that he trained the majority of his students. He remained until 1614, when the fathers reassigned him to Macao to rescue him from the persecution. He continued to work for a few more years until his death. The Jesuit school in Nagasaki produced oil paintings, watercolors, and engravings in great number. Part of its production was even exported to China.[11]

The copperplate engravings that have survived are most often illustrations for books printed in Japan after 1590. There is a bearded Saint Peter, holding a huge key, on the title page of a book printed in 1591 containing a compilation of the lives of the saints; a resurrected Christ on the title page of the *Fides no dôxi* printed in Amakusa in 1592;[12] a Virgin holding the Child on her lap, with a woman reading a book to her right.[13]

The title page of *Dochirina kirishitan* published in romanized Japanese in 1592 was illustrated with a copperplate engraving of a haloed Christ holding in his left hand a globe of the earth topped by a cross. His right hand is raised, with two fingers extended in a gesture of blessing. He is dressed in a robe and cloaked in a mantle. In the distance is a city, most likely Jerusalem; above it an inscription reads: *Ego sum via et veritas et vita* (I am the Way, the Truth, and the Life).[14]

The most curious of these engravings is beyond a doubt a Madonna and Child that shows the mother being crowned by angels, she wears a richly embroidered robe and stands within a highly decorated frame. The painting it is modeled on is known: it is *Nuestra Señora de l'Antigua*, a mural painting found in the cathedral of Seville. Numerous prints of it had been made and distributed throughout the Spanish-speaking world. The Japanese engraving was copied from one of them, probably Flemish, in 1597. The caption, in Latin, goes back to the beginning of the thirteenth century when Ferdinand, king of León and Castilla, attacked the Muslim kingdom in southern Spain, conquered Córdoba, Seville (in 1248), and Jaén, and vanquished the king of Granada.[15] He founded a Christian community in Seville and died a few years later. A cathedral was erected after his death on the previous site of the mosque, of which all that remained was the minaret. The Madonna painted on the wall of a chapel built where the mosque's *mihrab* had been is supposed to be a reproduction of one found in an ancient Visigoth chapel that predated the mosque. The significance of these details will emerge in due course.[16]

The paintings that have been preserved in Japan from the late sixteenth and early seventeenth century were produced in various media.

Some are copper panels painted in oil, a technique that had been used in Italy since the early sixteenth century and had come into widespread use. The Madonna and Child preserved in the National Museum in Tokyo is of this type. It is a small painting (14.7 × 11.3 cm) of a very young woman seen from the waist up. She holds in her arms a child, his cheek pressed to her own. The child's gesture recalls an Italian model from the fourteenth century, itself inspired by a Byzantine icon. It is likely that this painting was not done in Japan but was imported along with similar works before the great persecution of 1614.[17]

These painted metal panels should not be confused with the unpainted bas-relief plaques in hammered tin that were used, beginning in the second half of the seventeenth century, in the trial of *fumi-e*. This test was imposed at the start of each year on populations suspected of remaining secretly aligned with Christianity; people were told to trample holy images, and those who refused or hesitated were arrested and sentenced. The subjects shown on these plaques (19 × 13.6 cm) were relatively diverse: Passion of Christ, Crucifixion, Descent from the Cross, Virgin and Child, Mater Dolorosa. Some were nailed onto small boards, others were not. Several dozen remain in Japanese museums, their relief often blunted by the trampling of countless feet.

During the thick of the persecution, from 1620 to 1640, the Japanese Inquisition used images confiscated from the Christians themselves to force Christians into apostasy. They had originally been struck by the Madrid Mint. Later, in 1669, when they needed to refresh their store, the Inquisition had them turned out by an artisan from Nagasaki, Hagiwara Yusuke, who specialized in making objects of worship for Buddhist temples. His imitations were perfect. Two of them, preserved in the National Museum of Tokyo, are particularly noteworthy. One is an *Ecce homo* image of Christ crowned with thorns, hands tied, head bent, clasping a reed to his naked torso. The original model for it is a Byzantine mosaic. The image was widespread in Italy in the second half of the fifteenth century and was often copied by Spanish and Portuguese artists in the time of Charles V.[18]

On another plaque issued from Yusuke's workshop the Virgin, seated on a throne in the sky above mountains representing the earth, receives homage from Saint Dominic and Catherine of Siena, accompanied by priests and nuns of their order, kneeling to the right and left of the central figure. The frame of the image is a rosary. The cross of the rosary, at bottom center, holds the frame together, its image superimposed on the earthly landscape. The image taken in its entirety evokes the invention of the Rosary, attributed to Saint Dominic (1170–1221), and indirectly the naval battle of Lepanto in which Christian fleets fought the Ottomans in 1571. Pope Pius V had in fact attributed this victory over the infidels to the recitation of the Rosary. Post-Tridentine religious art strongly links the three themes: the cult of Immaculate Mary, the recitation of the Rosary, and victory over the infidels.[19]

Oil painting on canvas in the European style seems to have been little used in the Jesuit mission in Japan. Hardly any examples of it remain in any case. The most noteworthy of them is a painting of Saint Peter that has a colorful history. The 119 × 69 cm painting was found in a Buddhist temple in Funabashi. It was long believed to be the Sakyamuni Buddha descending from his mountain. But there is no doubt about the identity of the figure, with its long bearded face, very straight nose, Franciscan-style frock, and crimson mantle, a bound book held open in the right hand, two large keys dangling from the left. The saint, his weight slightly shifted onto one foot, walks barefoot amid flowers in a mountainous landscape. His head is encircled with a halo that stands out against an azure sky with faint golden clouds. The painting is European not only in content but also in technique: bold shadows carve out the folds of the garments and, with a somewhat lighter touch, the features of the face. Yet it seems certain that the hand behind the paintbrush was Japanese: the general style of the painting and several details, such as the clouds and flowers, link it to contemporary works of the Kano school.[20]

In the realm of sacred art, the exchange between Japan and Europe was not unilateral. It was also in the missionaries' interest to convince Europeans that images of worship would be even more precious in forms that evoked their endless dreams of the Orient. Many precious objects were fashioned to satisfy this endless thirst, dating back to Marco Polo: chests, boxes, tables, writing boxes, secretaries, kettles, and washbowls are found everywhere in Europe today, at London's Victoria and Albert Museum, Warsaw's Wilanów Palace, in Krakow, the Hague, Porto, Braunschweig, Saint Petersburg, Paris's Musée Guimet. These objects are usually made of precious wood, lacquered in black and elaborately decorated with inlaid gold, silver, and mother-of-pearl in arabesques or geometric motifs. The exuberant ornamentation makes lavish use of animal and floral figures. Made expressly for export, these objects are in no way representative of Japanese art of the times but rather reflect the idea wealthy Europeans must have had of Japanese art. They were shaped to the function they would have in Europe. Their overload of ornamentation corresponded to Europe's taste for the baroque, at the opposite pole from the predominant Japanese taste, in which simplicity, stylization, and soberness prevailed. The materials and choice of decorative motifs, on the other hand, had to evoke the inexhaustible riches of the distant Orient: despite their functional forms, they were made not to be used but to be shown in ceremonial salons amid other collectors' items.[21]

The Suntory Museum in Tokyo holds a very lovely reredos of the Virgin and Child that beautifully illustrates the marriage of Western religious art of the Counter-Reformation and Japanese-style ornamentation. The painting itself is done in oil on a sheet of copper. It is of a type often found in work by Spain's Luis de Morales, as seen, for example, in the Prado Museum or the National Gallery.[22] The young woman, her eyes downcast, has her head tilted slightly to the right above the child she holds in her arms. With her right hand she supports his head as she holds him to her with her left arm. The child, his head resting on the right shoulder, looks up at his mother's face, his left hand slipped into the folds of her robe as though seeking the breast. The frame and wings of the reredos (37.5 × 27 cm) are in black lacquered wood inlaid with gold, silver, and mother-of-pearl. The frames of the main painting and the wings are decorated with rectangular or triangular patterns that contrast with the floral patterns of the cartouches on the interior of the wings. At the bottom of one of these ornamental enclosures, a few sprigs of bamboo suggest that the whole is meant to be "typically" Asian in decoration. Although this reredos is now in Japan, it is certain that the painting was done in Europe, for Europeans, and that the frame and wings were commissioned and produced in Japan.[23]

The "ambassadors" who traversed Portugal, Spain, and Italy at the end of the sixteenth century discovered with wonder some of the most beautiful cities in Europe. They describe them in their journals in lavish detail, as shown in the description of Venice. They had already referred in chapter 15 to the grandeur of European cities in general and the magnificence of their civil and religious establishments; in chapter 16 to Lisbon; in chapter 17, to Évora, Vila Viçosa, and Toledo; in chapter 19, to the great works of Philip II, including the Escorial; in chapter 21, to the Duke of Tuscany's villa at Pratolino; and finally in chapters 22 and 26, to Rome.

They were also given books to aid their recall and to proffer as gifts to Japanese notables on their return, as *De missione legatorum* notes in the beginning of chapter 15. The University of Padua bestowed on them the *Theatrum orbis terrarum* by Ortelius and the three volumes of Georg Braun and Franz Hogenbergh's *Civitates orbis terrarum* published from 1572 to 1581.[24]

Abraham Ortels, or Oertel, known as Ortelius (1527–98), is considered the founder of modern cartography. He was born in Anvers to wealthy Bavarian parents. He was a friend of Plantin and Mercator. He traveled a great deal, to the Netherlands, Germany, England, Ireland, France, Italy, and Spain, and was the first to conceive of compiling all the maps published up to that point by different mapmakers. His *Theatrum*, published in Anvers in 1570, was an immediate success and was quickly translated into Italian, Spanish, and French; in 1575 he was named geographer to Philip II. His chief collaborator was Franz Hogenbergh (1540–90/92) of Mechlin, who produced the engravings.[25] The work opens with a planisphere *(Typus orbis terrarum)* that soon became famous. His maps are enlivened with all sorts of ornaments (caravels, monsters, tritons, heraldry), aerial views of cities (Salzburg, for example), animals (bears, camels, elephants, depending on the country), and even little scenes, such as one of the Duke of Moscow at the entrance to his tent.

Hogenbergh, a Protestant, was banished from the Netherlands by the Duke of Alba and from 1570 to his death worked principally in Germany. There he encountered Georg Braun, archdeacon of Dortmund and later dean of the collegiate church of Cologne, with whom he collaborated as etcher in preparing the *Civitates* up to the fourth volume. A large number of the maps used by Braun and etched by Hogenbergh were drawn by Georg (or Joris) Hoefnagel (or Hufnagel), an artist of miniatures and drawings who was born in Anvers in 1542 and died in 1600 in Vienna. Hoefnagel was also a Protestant. He traveled to France, Spain, England, Italy, and Germany, making numerous drawings of landscapes and cities, always trying to be as faithful as possible to "nature" *(natura sola magistra)*.[26]

The work of Braun, Hogenbergh, and Hoefnagel is typical of both Flemish and German cartography at the end of the sixteenth century and of the spirit of humanist concord that Braun, the Catholic priest, and his two Protestant collaborators obviously shared. The title page of the first volume of the *Civitates* is highly symbolic of this. It brings together Minerva, standing at left, and Samson, standing at right, as well as the City, symbolized by a building scene on Minerva's pedestal, and the Countryside, symbolized by a rustic scene on Samson's pedestal. Inscribed in a cartouche border below the central tableau is the title *Consociat(i) humani gen(eris) origo: The Origin of Human Society.* The preface, written by Braun, recounts the genesis of society according to Vitruvius, Cicero, and Plato, and although he cites in passing the stories of Enoch and Cain, he lends them no more weight than he grants to Pallas, the founder of cities in Greek mythology.

The cities represented in the three volumes brought back from Europe by the "ambassadors" are seen in aerial view. Each one occupies from one-half page to two pages. All the important sites are labeled, and each map is adorned with figures wearing the local dress and going about their everyday occupations, as well as by cartouches that may frame texts, coats of arms, or various ornaments.

A pair of eight-panel screens preserved in the Municipal Museum of Kobe attests to the success of these maps in Japan. This is a top-quality work, painted in the Japanese style on paper with India ink, traditional colored pigments, and gilt. Each screen measures 158.7 × 477.7 cm. Unfortunately, they are not signed. One of the screens is a planisphere in vivid colors, the drafting highly approximate, with picturesque decorations of caravels in full sail and marine divinities inspired by Greco-Latin mythology. The other represents four great

"Occidental" cities: Lisbon, Seville, Rome, and, oddly, Constantinople. Running above the cities, each of which occupies two panels, is a frieze of figures in the dress of the various countries, both men and women, some on foot and some on horseback. It is thought that the two screens come from the workshop of Giovanni Niccolò. The models used to represent Lisbon and Constantinople are found in the first volume of Braun's *Civitates*. The view of Seville appears in the fifth volume, published in 1598, but was already in circulation as a separate sheet as early as 1593. The map of Rome comes from the *Vita Beati Patris Ignatii Loyolae*, published in 1610. The original engraving was by Cornelius Galle (1576–1612). The figures in the frieze above it probably are taken from other cartographic works or from late-sixteenth-century engravings. The relief technique is definitely Western, as is the garb, but despite the Mannerist treatment of certain shapes (the horses' tails, the riders' scarves, the swaying posture of the Portuguese woman, who seems to be dancing), they all appear rather stiff. They are outlined like cardboard cutouts against a continuous background of rounded hills and a uniformly golden sky very similar to that seen in other contemporary screens of the Kano school.[27]

De missione legatorum does more than exalt the grandeur of the Western cities. It also paints an idyllic picture of the life led there. The pleasures of urban life are moreover indissociable from those to be had in the country, among select company in a setting of tranquillity. These were, of course, pleasures offered to those at once young, rich, and cultured: common folk enter the picture only as extras; they are the onlookers by the side of the road or leaning from their windows to applaud the passing "ambassadors" and the dignitaries garbed in crimson and gold who greet and escort them. This is no doubt the way the travelers experienced things. And it is no doubt the image the editors of the interviews, Valignano and Sande, wished to communicate to all who would read them.

Chapter 8, titled "De monarchia profana," gives the reasons put forth by the Society of Jesus to "explain" this state of affairs. Long ago Rome had brought a reign of order on the whole of the inhabited earth—Europe, Asia, and Africa—with its power and wisdom. The Barbarians had conquered it, but the Holy Roman Empire and the papacy had brought it back to life from the ashes, the former by temporal power, the latter by spiritual power, miraculously united for the good of humanity. Moreover, if the Holy Roman Emperor (*rex Romanorum* in the text) is chosen by election, it is the pope who confirms him and makes him truly emperor. The hereditary or chosen monarchs have no formal need for this confirmation, but two common practices reveal that in the final analysis they owe their crowns to the pope: "In some cases they receive the royal insignia with great pomp and circumstance from the hands of the Sovereign Pontiff himself," and in all cases they quickly dispatch ambassadors to the pope, "recognizing him as the supreme head of Christendom." When a pope dies, they swiftly send new delegations to his successor. Indeed, says *De missione*, the pope can make or break kings and emperors, if it is in the interests of the "Christian Republic." The visible sign of this temporal and spiritual allegiance is that all the princes bow down on one knee three times before they reach the pontiff's throne and kiss his slipper on the third genuflection.

In the "Christian Republic" formed by all the European nations together, all are governed, of course, according to Christian principles. Violence and deception have no place there, and all conflicts are resolved by law and arbitration. Thus Europe lives in perpetual peace and knows no poverty. In the cities, the buildings are well proportioned and adorned with porticos and peristyles. The citizens have lovely villas in the country where they retire for relaxation. The interiors of palaces and villas are richly decorated with hangings and tapestries, which are changed according to the season. They are of wool and silk in the winter, interwoven with gold and silver thread, and represent "various figures of people, animals, forests, mountains, and rivers." The beds are of rare wood, inlaid with gold and painted in rich colors. The cushions and pillows are soft, covered in silk, warm or less so depending on the season. The seats are inlaid with ivory, upholstered in fur, silk, and velvet. Those who live in this enchanting setting wear sumptuous clothing and change their outfits frequently. The garments are of wool, silk, or velvet, often with golden clasps, and have sable linings for winter. Even the valets are well dressed: their cleanliness and elegance heighten their masters' glory.

There are often parties in Europe, and festive occasions such as weddings or hunting excursions. At such times, people garb themselves in special clothing adorned with precious stones and pearls; they wear gold and silver jewelry, necklaces and bracelets, finely worked rings. In certain circumstances the men dress in Roman style: greaves, tunics, breastplates, helmets, and other pieces of armor filigreed with gold and silver. The elegance and richness of the women's attire is in every respect equal to that of the men.

Chapter 9, on which this description is based, begins by recalling the Queen of Sheba's visit to Solomon, in chapter 10 of the first Book of Kings. This evocation delivers the implicit moral of the story. The Queen says, in the Bible: "Blessed be the Lord your God who has delighted in you. . . . Because the Lord loved Israel forever, he has made you king, that you may execute justice and righteousness." The interpretation of this "moral" is clear: if the "ambassadors" are analogous to the Queen, Japan to her kingdom, and the supreme head of all Christianity to the king of Israel, what can one do but bow before him and worship Eternal God?

Chapters 9 and 10 brilliantly complete the fresco. In them the "ambassadors" describe the sumptuous feasts, the fine china, the silverware, the African servants. They describe the stables full of purebred horses, elegant, swift, docile, perfectly trained, their harnesses in which gold and silk compete with the trappings to make the animal as dazzling as its rider, the riding schools where the marvelous creatures learn to perform amazing exercises.

Young people of noble families receive more than just a good Christian education. They also practice the use of arms, learn horsemanship, play music, sing, and dance. They test their bravery and skill in tournaments. The hunt is an exercise inseparable from the exercise of arms. They hunt all sorts of birds, as well as wolves, stags, deer, rabbits, hares. The "ambassadors" brought back from Europe several books dealing with all types of hunting, with engravings showing men and animals in action in real-life poses.

The travelers report that in Europe men and women dance together. This is a delicate point for the well-bred Japanese, schooled by priests. They justify this practice, however, by noting that in Europe men and women live side by side in society and that there is nothing dishonest or lascivious in their dancing.

Although many of the religious paintings that came out of Giovanni Niccolò's workshop have been destroyed or lost, there is a much higher survival rate for the secular ones, created in the same workshop for purposes of edification, or as we would say today, propaganda. These works appear to be designed to demonstrate to those who purchased and exhibited them the most seductive side of European civilization. The painted pieces augmented the effect of *De missione legatorum* on the imagination of Japanese high society and added luster to the popular rumors it inspired.

The Jesuits orchestrated the return of the "ambassadors" in such a way that the trip, their report, and all the wonders they brought back with them would have the strongest possible impact. The high point of this seduction scheme was their reception by Toyotomi Hideyoshi on March 3, 1591. Many in his entourage had strongly discouraged the man who was then the most powerful figure in Japan from receiving this delegation led by foreign priests. But Hideyoshi, yielding to curiosity as much as to greed, ignored them.

The "ambassadors" had arrived in Nagasaki in October 1590. They had left the city in December with their escorts and had taken a route through Kyushu to Shimonoseki and from there sailed across the inland sea to Muro. They remained there for quite some time: it was a necessary way station for many great lords traveling to the court at Miyako, and the lords were so curious that they simply had to be accommodated. The travelers recounted their voyage, showed them maps, and displayed clocks brought back from Europe. The fathers were assured, by the time they left Muro, that their arrival in the capital would be preceded by a buzz of the most laudatory gossip. They arrived in Osaka at the end of February, then proceeded to a small town about a mile outside of Miyako.

Finally, on March 3, came the official entrance. It was organized to resemble a Roman triumphal procession. First came chariots bearing the presents sent from India and Europe. The last of these carried a campaign tent to be given to Hideyoshi. There followed at a distance a superb Arabian stallion outfitted with a velvet saddle blanket and silver bridle. The horse was led by two Indians in turbans and brightly colored silk clothing. Then came the delegation itself, on horseback or carried in litters: the four "ambassadors" in gold-trimmed uniforms, thirteen Portuguese dressed in velvet and silk, seven smartly attired pages. Behind them came the two interpreters, Fathers Rodrigues and Fernández, and Valignano's two closest companions, Father Diogo de Mesquita, who had escorted the "ambassadors" to Europe, and Father António López, who spoke Japanese fluently. Last came the Visitor, Valignano. He represented the Society of Jesus, the pope, and the viceroy of India all in one. He was dressed in the strict habit of his order: long black robe, mantelet, and biretta. The reception was opulent. The message from the viceroy of India was read, the gifts for Hideyoshi were unveiled, a great feast was held. The "ambassadors" played the organ and instrumental music before their enchanted host.[28]

The marvelous life led by Europeans in the "Christian Republic" is illustrated on beautiful screens that have been preserved to this day. Several of these screens are similar in composition, which is generally quite loose, and have several motifs in common, as though certain groups of characters had been transported whole from one painting to the next with only a few alterations in detail. The division of the screens into panels of equal width partly explains the lack of compositional unity, causing one group of characters or objects, as the case may be, to be clustered on one panel or another.

The best-preserved pair of screens is found in the Eisei collection in Tokyo. Each of the screens is 93 × 302.5 cm. The base (paper), the use of traditional pigments, the vast gilt sky strewn with light clouds in horizontal strata, an obvious unfamiliarity with the laws of perspective, all suggest contemporary Kano school works describing the life of the "Southern Barbarians" in the western and southern provinces of Japan. The similarity is certainly not fortuitous: items from the West were in fashion, screens of the "Southern Barbarians," or *nambans*, were highly sought after, and it was in the Jesuits' interests to cooperate with this fashion to help impose on the Japanese aristocracy the European "model" whose broad outlines had been sketched in *De missione legatorum*.

The background in the two screens consists of low mountains with the blue cast lent by distance. In the center of the first screen, coming from the horizon line in the middle distance, is an inlet of the sea that

Johannes Stradanus, Adrianus Collaert, and Philippus Galle,
The Triumph of Caesar. © *Montpellier Municipal Library*

Twelve European Princes, early seventeenth century, pair of screens with six panels (132.8 × 308.4 cm). © *Museum of the Prefecture of Nagasaki*

Our Lady of Antigua, sixteenth-century Japanese engraving, Catholic church of Ohura, Nagasaki

Saint Peter, early seventeenth century, oil on canvas (119 × 69 cm).
© *Museum of Namban Culture, Osaka*

Paul Bril and Raphaël Sadeler, *The Months: May, June.*
© *Bibliothèque nationale de France, Paris*

Pastoral Symphony among the Europeans, early seventeenth century.
Pair of screens with six panels (93 × 302.4 cm). © *Eisei Collection, Tokyo*

Cornelius Cort, *Battle of Zama.* © *Bibliothèque nationale de France, Paris*

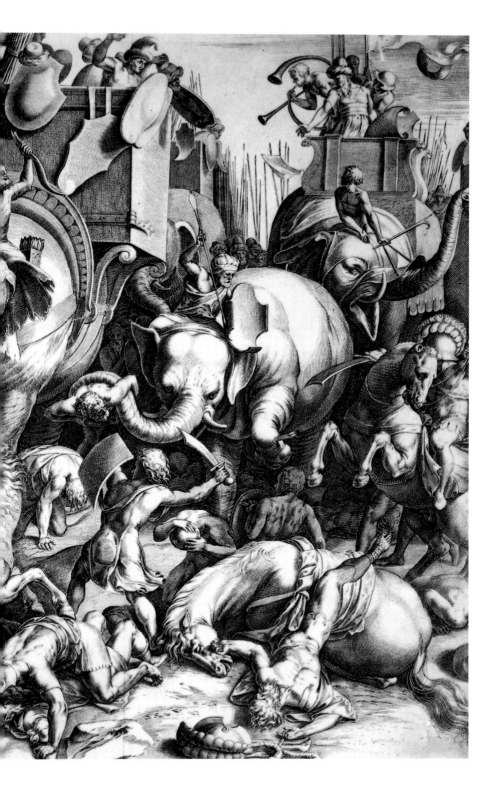

Pastoral Symphony among the Europeans, early seventeenth century.
© *Eisei Collection, Tokyo*

Marten de Vos and Raphaël Sadeler, *Paternus.*
© *Bibliothèque nationale de France, Paris*

Martinus Heemskerck and Philippus Galle, *Pyramus and Thisbe.*
© *Bibliothèque nationale de France, Paris*

extends to the right and into the foreground. The sea is deep blue in the center, lighter toward the background, where caravels sail. The mountains that intervene at midrange resemble the wings of a theater. Between two of the "wings," at left and right, are the walls, houses, and towers of what appears to be a port. The pink walls of the city, on the left, seem to be lit by the setting sun, but nothing else in the painting indicates that the light is coming from any specific direction. At the right in midrange, on an esplanade before a small grove, we see a hexagonal temple topped with cupola, turret, spire, and weathervane. In the middle of the temple, standing on a pedestal, is a statue of a half-naked figure reminiscent more of Eros or some mythological demigod than of anything in Christian art. On either side of the temple stand two figures in long robes of yellow and red, playing the trumpet. In front of the temple, five figures seated on the grass appear to be viewing some sort of performance. A man and a woman, both standing, also gaze toward the statue. On the road leading from the temple and grove toward the mountains, a woman in red carries fruit in a basket on her head. Farther off, appearing smaller due to distance, are two horsemen, one of whom seems to be waiting for the other.

The left side of the scene is symmetrical with the right: In midrange is a winepress under a steeply sloping roof; four men with baskets on their backs and staffs in their hands hasten toward it. A man tramples grapes inside the vat. Two fat jugs with handles stand on the ground before the vat, awaiting the new wine. In the background the houses of a village can be glimpsed through the trees. Their steep roofs and stepped pediments recall northern Europe more than Italy. A road partially bordered by trees passes diagonally before the winepress. On it one sees two horsemen side by side, with a white dog farther on, and still farther a man and a woman walking along. They all seem to be heading toward the town with its low pink wall.

The foreground is occupied by figures grouped in twos or threes. On the right are three men wearing ruffs and swords. One is seated, bareheaded, with his back turned toward the viewer. He is raising his hand as though speaking to someone who is out of sight. The two others are standing and talking to each other. One of them wears his hat on his head; the other holds his hat in his hand. Their doublets are of gold brocade, their mantles bordered with gold.

In the center of the tableau are two symmetrical groups. One consists of a standing man and woman. The man, with hat in hand, has his head tilted toward the woman, his eyes fixed on her. The woman's head is tilted toward him, her eyes downcast. She is playing the harp. He wears a deep red doublet and knee breeches brocaded with gold, a dark-colored mantle, and a gold chain; her hair falls loose down her back, and her bright red jacket and dress are trimmed with gold. The other group consists of two women seated on stones. One plays the lute, the other tilts her head to listen. Their garments, predominantly red, are richly brocaded with gold, and the listening figure wears a gold necklace. Last, to the left we see another group of men, sitting on the ground. One of them, his head turned toward the ships and the port, seems to be pointing out something to the other two. In the close foreground is a bush with red flowers, cut off by the frames of the first and second panels. This is the only Japanese touch in this bizarre assembly of *namban* figures and objects.

The second screen in the Eisei collection is stranger still. Its six panels are actually grouped in twos. The left-hand third of the scene is occupied by a fantastical castle, built over the water, standing before a town with whimsical domes and ramparts. The town lies at the foot of some mountains, along a shoreline that stretches back to the horizon at left. The walls of the castle are pale blue, the town white and blue, the sky pink where seen through the blue-tinged mountains that mask the horizon, golden above them. The architecture of the castle is improbable, but the towers, pinnacle turrets, terraces, balustrades, friezes, peristyles, stairways, pavilions, and porticos bespeak an intent to make it somehow the essence of all castles. In the foreground is a glorious spray of flashy red flowers with two men on either side of it. The man standing is a gray-bearded pilgrim leaning on his staff, a wide-brimmed hat on his head; the seated one, with sword at his side and hat hanging at his back, appears to be speaking to him.

The two central panels show a hilly, compartmented landscape where various groups of figures engage in indefinable activities: here two dogs are waiting, for what we cannot tell, next to a bush bearing huge pink flowers; there two well-dressed men converse, wrapped in their mantles and sitting on the ground; elsewhere two men walk along the road that leads toward the castle and the town; farther on a horseman presents himself at the gate of the town where he is met by a figure dressed in green. In a grotto resembling a Mongol yurt, near the gate, a tall white statue stands on a pedestal. On a hillock in the middle distance, above two seated men, a group of men and women gathers around a woman playing the guitar. Near her a young girl or child appears to be dancing.

The two right-hand panels are roughly organized around a sort of lake into which a waterfall is flowing. In the foreground to the right, a bearded man crouches, reading a book. A younger man, leaning against a rock or stump, his head raised skyward, seems to be listening to him read, or dreaming. Farther left a man in a red jacket trimmed with gold, with staff in hand and a dog at his feet, appears to be looking after some unseen sheep. Behind him at some distance a man with a gun lies in wait.

Everything in these two screens would seem to be imaginary, yet none of it is. They form a veritable puzzle, a few pieces of which have been identified. The blue castle is definitely copied from an engraving by Philip Galle (1537–1612), after a drawing by Maarten van Heemskerck (1498–1574) titled *Pyramus and Thisbe*. The Temple of Love in the first screen and the pilgrim in the second come from an engraving by Raphaël Sadeler (1551–1628), after a drawing by Marten de Vos (1532–1603) titled *Paternus.*[29]

With Galle, Heemskerck, Sadeler, and de Vos we enter the universe of Flemish artists who left the strongest mark on western Europe in the second half of the sixteenth century. It is the world of the publisher Plantin and that of the artists and engravers known as the Fiamminghi because many of them worked for so long in Italy.[30] Jesuits from all over Europe preferred to have their works printed in Anvers, and it was there, too, that they sought engravings to illustrate them. This attraction, already well-developed before the fall of Anvers, was even stronger after 1585, when the city fully capitulated to the Spanish.

Through Anvers, all of late Renaissance Italy, the Italy of Niccolò, arrived on Japan's doorstep. And not just in engraving and painting. A whole current of sensibility, embracing literature and music as well, came into play, as the Japanese "ambassadors" sensed during the course of their travel and as Valignano, born and educated in Italy, well knew. This was the current of the pastorale, which irrigated all of Europe at that time, especially the Latin countries. The humanists were, of course, not averse to this resurgence of their own themes, which went back to Virgil's *Georgics*, to Theocritus, to the myth of Orpheus. A brilliant example of the genre in Italy at the beginning of the century was *Arcadia*, by Jacopo Sannazaro (1458–1530). This work, first printed in Venice in 1502, was quickly translated into all the known languages.

The pastoral genre was all the more successful in that it could be put to an entirely secular use as entertainment but could also be given a moralistic, Platonic, even religious interpretation. As noted in chapter 1, the Jesuits taught humanities using Hieronymus Vida's *Christiad*, written in Virgilian hexameters, and excerpts from Jacopo Sannazaro's *De partu Virginis*. In the plastic arts, *Jacob and Rachel* by Palma il Vecchio (ca. 1480–1528), painted in the first quarter of the sixteenth century and now found in Dresden's Old Masters Museum, exemplifies the successful marriage of the pastoral genre and the Bible. Against an imaginary landscape fenced off in the distance by bluish mountains and framed by large trees, two shepherds, Jacob and Rachel, chastely embrace. In the distance, on a hill, the rooftops and towers of a somewhat fanciful town stand out, light against a dark background. In the middle distance, behind the young couple, sheep and cows are grazing. A shepherd sits at left, looking on at the young lovers. Another gives the animals water.[31]

Of course, one does not demand realism in this arena. Secular or Platonic, pastoral art is a worldly diversion like the dance and music, both instrumental and vocal, from which it is inseparable. Because of its distant origins, it often makes all sorts of allusions to ancient art or literature, with no concern for plausibility. Such is the case with Titian's *Pastoral Symphony*, now at the Louvre. The two seated men in the center of the painting, one of them playing the lute, could be young Venetian noblemen from the artist's own times. The shepherd seen farther off and to the right amid his sheep is also of that era. But the unclothed young woman who is facing the musicians, her back to the viewer, and another one drawing water at the left can only be nymphs.

The model engravings from which Niccolò's students worked, whatever they may have been, were surely not images that pushed the taste for the mythological to such an extreme. *De missione legatorum* describes in detail, however, the animated mythological tableaus the "ambassadors" saw in the Duke of Tuscany's garden in Prato. Their commentary is found in interview 21, "De amoenitate, ac deliciis Pratolinae villae ducis Hetruriae" (Of the Pleasures and Delights of the Duke of Tuscany's Villa at Prato). In these gardens they saw streams, ponds, waterfalls, and on every hand statues animated by hidden mechanisms that were set in motion by hydraulics. Here was Neptune, there Galatea, Apollo, or the Muses, here tritons, sea monsters, nymphs, a satyr (*hominem quemdam silvestrem*), a faun (*ab Ethnicis ita dictus:* "this is what the pagans call it").

Niccolò could not decently convoke all these pagan deities in the paintings he had his students execute. Nor could he introduce naked nymphs into his groupings of conversing figures. Yet significant traces of this pagan universe are to be found in the screens of the Eisei collection: the Temple of Love, the statue in the grotto, for example.

Three themes predominate in these two "pastorales": the outdoor concert (pastoral symphony), fantasy architecture, and the hunt. They are supremely Italian. Titian's painting has been mentioned in regard to the first screen, and numerous lesser-known examples demonstrate the fecundity of the theme. It was also widely used among the Fiamminghi because the Flemish masters of polyphony were extremely popular in Italy in the fifteenth and early sixteenth centuries. The sovereign instrument of the day was the lute. It was usually a precious object inlaid with rare woods and encrusted with stones and diamonds. The harp, zither, guitar, and viola were also in vogue. The theme of the pastoral symphony, often associated with the seasons or the months, is well represented in sixteenth-century Flemish art. For example, Adriaen Collaert (1560–1618), son-in-law of Philip Galle, left a series of twelve engravings titled *The Months*, based on the drawings of the Belgian Hans Bol (1534–93). The one for the month of May shows several groups of men and women in an imaginary rustic landscape. Some converse tranquilly. In one group composed of five people, a woman standing to the left plays the lute. Another woman is seated before her; a man sits on the ground, leaning back with his head on her lap. Two other women sit to the right, leaning over him.[32] In the first screen in the Eisei collection, the theme of the months is also associated with that of the pastoral symphony: the grape-harvesting scene is a common allegory for the month of September. It must have seemed totally exotic in Japan, where the domestication of grapes was still unknown, as revealed in the question put to Father Vázquez.

A wonderful engraving by Raphaël Sadeler (1560/61–1628/32), after a drawing by Paul Bril (1553/54–1626), seems to embody all that the Italian experience contributed to the Flemish artists and all in these artists' work that enchanted Niccolò's generation of Italian artists. The tableau symbolizes the months of May and June together and is set on the grounds of an Italian villa at the edge of a river, with countryside seen in the background. In the center of the piece, overlooking the lower part of the grounds and the river, is a low hill with trees and a temple or kiosk with two people inside it. One is seated, the other walking toward him, and a third is starting up the steps of the structure. Pairs of men and women are walking, talking, or resting on the grounds. By the side of a reflecting pool at bottom left are two larger groups, one listening to a lute player and a guitar player, the other to a storyteller. Another lute player is sitting in a boat next to a woman holding an open book. A couple approaches to join them for a boat ride. In the countryside, peasants shear their sheep in front of the fold. Farther off a horseman with a pack of dogs and a group of beaters runs a stag to ground. In the far distance, at the foot of some hills dominated by a fort, one can make out the towers of a town.

The theme of fantasy architecture also came into fashion thanks to Flemish artists, whether they had stayed in Italy for a long time, lived in its palaces, and dreamed amid its ruins or had only imagined it from the depths of the northern mists. Maarten-Jacobsz van Veen, known as Heemskerck, spent three years in Rome before settling in Haarlem. He studied the work of Michelangelo, made drawings of the Roman ruins, and played a significant role, thanks to his collaboration with Galle, in the diffusion of Italian taste. A good example of this dream architecture is his imaginary reconstitution of the *Lighthouse at Alexandria*, which Galle engraved in 1567. It is remarkable not only for its wildly hypothetical reconstitution of the lighthouse itself but even more so for the fantasy structures arranged in rows at the foot of the lighthouse by the seashore and in the background, toward the mountains at the right.[33] An extraordinary S-shaped bridge links the port to the town. Heemskerck has also given us a grand landscape whose pretext is to illustrate the ravishment of Helen. This scene, now in the Henry Walters collection in Baltimore, is undoubtedly the most vigorous effort ever made to resurrect the urbanism of antiquity. While the foreground is in vivid colors, the background is an immense cameo in blue, in which nuances of white and pink form temples, arches, towers, triumphal columns, bridges, arcades, obelisks, rotundas, the Temple of Diana at Ephesus, and even the Colossus at Rhodes, covered in gold leaf.[34]

The theme of the hunt is only indirectly evoked in the second screen in the Eisei collection, by the man walking alone with a gun in his hand. It is central, however, in the pair of screens in the Museum of Namban Culture in Osaka. One of the two screens (84.6 × 268 cm) shows two richly attired riders at the center rushing toward a boar that has been flushed from the underbrush at left. Three large dogs dash toward it; five men on foot, holding their guns, also close in on the animal from different directions. In the background of the scene, amid a lyrical landscape of mountains and water and beneath a broad golden sky, stand the domes and towers of a white city. The engraving that inspired this vision of the scene is unknown, but its theme is not. It has been wonderfully illustrated by Hans Bol in *La Grande Chasse de Marguerite*, an etching in the Plantin-Moretus Museum of Anvers.[35]

"OF THE POWER OF PHILIP, KING OF SPAIN . . ."

When the "ambassadors" left for Europe in 1582, Portugal had been joined to the crown of Spain for two years. Philip II also ruled Naples and Sicily. His empire extended to New Spain and the Philippines. He was, says *De missione legatorum*, the greatest king in Europe with the exception of the Holy Roman Emperor. Philip II was also the son of Charles V; he was thus still bathed in the aureole of his father's glory, and the Jesuits made certain its rays reached Japan.

Two screens that are unsigned but clearly produced by Niccolò's students splendidly fulfill their design. They are six-panel screens, 132.8 × 308.4 cm, with each of the twelve panels representing the majestic figure of one of the kings of the Occident. The series, now in the Museum of the Prefecture of Nagasaki, is comparable in its conception to that of the *Twelve Caesars* engraved by Adriaen Collaert based on the drawings of Jan van der Straet, known as Johannes Stradanus or Giovanni Stradano (1523–1605). Stradanus, born in Bruges, worked primarily in Venice, Rome, Naples, and Florence, where he died. His twelve Caesars are those of Suetonius, but the series is dedicated to Philip III of Austria, and a thirteenth plate showing his coat of arms indicates that the glory of the Roman emperors of old was evoked chiefly to heighten that of its chief honoree: the four figures kneeling beneath the coat of arms symbolize the four continents. Two of these pieces engraved by Collaert obviously inspired the screen panels meant to represent Philip II's son-in-law, Albert VII (1559–1621), regent of the Spanish Netherlands, and Julius Caesar. The first of these engravings shows Caesar's triumph, the second the emperor Vespasian. Such errors demonstrate that the identity of the figures had little importance; what counted was the insignia of their rank. The Albert VII seen in Nagasaki is not borne like an idol on a chariot with four horses, as is Stradanus's Caesar, but is seated on a raised throne, wearing Roman-style boots and breastplate and wrapped in a crimson mantle. Two pages at his feet flank a cartouche that frames his coat of arms. The Julius Caesar in Nagasaki, unlike the Vespasian on which it is modeled, is not on horseback but has the same medallion-like profile, raised index finger, mantle flowing over his shoulders, and laurel wreath on his brow. The other kings are unidentifiable except for David, because he is playing the harp. The harp is a modern one, as is the crown on his head; moreover, he is dressed in Roman style. Like Philip II's son-in-law, he is placed before a triumphal arch. The other kings, alone or accompanied by pages, are attired and armed in the Roman style and placed in a common urban or rustic setting comparable to those seen in the pastoral concerts. The artist, however, did not neglect to recall to whom all these powers owed respect: the shield of one of the kings, casually placed on a table next to his plumed helmet, bears the distinguishable monogram of the Society of Jesus, the letters *IHS* printed in gold letters on a scarlet field and surrounded by an aureole.[36]

In the course of this story, a few signs have discreetly connoted the presence of Islam: Constantinople seen from above in the "four cities" series, *Nuestra Señora de l'Antigua* as a model for a Japanese Madonna and Child. The missionaries who arrived in Japan with Francis Xavier and after him were not short on memory, or experience. They remembered unpardonable wars that, up until the end of the preceding century, had pitted Christianity against Islam on the Iberian Peninsula. Portugal still faced Muslim princes in Morocco and Ethiopia. The pressure of Islam was also felt in India, where the capital of the Jesuits' Far East province was located, and a part of Southeast Asia, including Malacca.

And Islam is omnipresent in *De missione legatorum*. Beginning in chapter 4, concerning the arrival of the Portuguese in India, the Muslims are presented as "enemies of the name of Christianity"; they are treacherous and greedy, because they worship false gods. But Christ forever battles them by means of his defenders. In India, the king of Cochin (now Kerala, on the coast of Malabar) welcomed the Portuguese at once. But the evil king (or *zamorin*) of Calcutta attacked the king of Cochin because he was a friend to the Christians. The Portuguese built a fortress to help him defend himself, and soon all the other kings demanded the same service. It was thus that step by step the Saracens had to bow to the yoke of the Portuguese.

The fourteenth interview, "De navalibus certaminibus" (Of Sea Battles), returns to the topic of Islam in describing the Battle of Lepanto, during which twenty years earlier (October 7, 1571) the Christian fleet headed by Don John of Austria had fought the Ottoman fleet. In those times, says the narrator,

[T]he Christian princes, King Philip of Spain, and the Republic of Venice formed a solemn alliance with the Sovereign Pontiff to attack the Saracens, the most odious enemies to the name of Christianity. They equipped 210 triremes. Under the treaty, the illustrious Don John of Austria, brother of King Philip, was placed at the head of the entire fleet. Under him were the illustrious Marco Antonio Colonna, who commanded the Sovereign Pontiff's triremes, and the nobleman Sebastianus Venerius, who led the Venetian fleet. . . . The Saracen triremes were far more numerous, but under the banner of Christ, who comes always to our aid if our sins do not preclude it, the Christians won a memorable victory. They captured 170 enemy triremes along with 20 corsairs, sank 40 more triremes, killed 30,000 Saracens, took nearly 4,000 prisoners, freed 15,000 Christians held by the enemy in various regions, and returned to their lands laden with superb booty.[37]

This narrative, dictated by Valignano, was obviously not created for the sheer pleasure of competing with Titus Livius or Polybius: it was meant to demonstrate to the Japanese the advantages they, too, could gain by rallying under "the banner of Christ." It was also meant to put them on guard against a threat that was already quite strong in all of Southeast Asia.

One of the most astonishing paintings to come out of the workshop of Giovanni Niccolò is in fact a scene of this narrative and its "explication." It is a six-panel screen (153.5 × 362.5 cm), now in the Nagataka Murayama collection in Kobe. It is painted in the manner of the Kano school, on paper with traditional pigments and gilt. Its companion piece is a planisphere, a clear indication of the importance of the stakes: nothing less than the conquest of the world. Unlike the pastoral scenes already described, the Kobe screen contains a profusion of people, animals, and actions in a furious melee that seems to push on toward the right and left, foreground and background, to unimaginable limits. Since the Japanese did not know what a naval battle was, the combat is shown taking place primarily on land. Ships in full sail are seen, however, in the background, and beyond them is a town depicted "à la Heemskerck." On the left-hand panel a young man dressed in Roman style, wearing a laurel wreath and seated in a victory chariot, overlooks the battlefield. He is surrounded by a tight cohort of soldiers bearing lances; above them flies a crimson standard with the letters *SPQR* (*Senatus PopulusQue Romanus:* The Senate and the Roman People). Since this illustrious insignia might not have been understood by the Japanese, a gilt cartouche above the young man contains the inscription "Roman King" in Japanese.

In front of this compact group, a detachment of cavalry and torch-bearing foot soldiers furiously charges toward the center of the scene, which is occupied by enemy combatants, some on horseback, others grouped inside structures resembling square towers borne by elephants. The Roman horsemen brandish more standards with the insignia *SPQR*. The Turks also carry standards but without distinguishing marks. The ships in the background fly the Roman flag and are clearly headed toward the town at right. Above the town is another gilt cartouche, with the Japanese inscription "Turk."

Among the very surprising motifs seen in this painting, the elephants inevitably catch the eye. The two most frightening ones face the

Roman cavalry, looming over them with their enormous bulk augmented by the massive towers on their backs.

The main source for this strange *Battle of Lepanto* has been identified. It is an engraving by Cornelius Cort (1533–78), and its real subject is the Battle of Zama: the cavalry charge, the standards with the legend *SPQR*, the foot soldiers bearing torches, and the two large battle elephants come from that work. Several figures of horsemen that stand out in the crowd are based instead on equestrian statues of Nero, Othon, and Domitian in the *Twelve Caesars* series by Stradanus and Collaert. The same is true of the image of Caesar sitting in majesty in his victory chariot at the far left of the scene.[38]

This reinterpretation of the Battle of Lepanto through the canonical narrative of the Battle of Zama is clearly no caprice of Master Niccolò, nor is it a Machiavellian invention of Jesuit propaganda. The Battle of Zama in 202 B.C.E., in which the Roman legions of Scipio of Africa fought the battle elephants of Hannibal's army, resulted in the defeat of the Carthaginians and ended the second Punic War. It was the topic of several accounts by Polybius, Silius Italicus, and Titus Livius. These texts, read over and over during the era of Humanism, were frequently reprinted in all parts of sixteenth-century Europe. They became classics and charmed many a prince who identified with Scipio. The princes, wishing to manifest their own glory in exalting that of the African, commissioned great artists to paint the scene, and soon the subject was all the rage.

In 1532 Francis I commissioned in Brussels a silk and gilt hanging depicting the story of Scipio. Produced from 1532 to 1535, it was composed of two suites, one dealing with Scipio's great deeds, the other with his triumph at Rome after the victory. The painter on whose work the weaving was based was Jules Romain (1499–1546). Some of the preparatory studies and small patterns have been preserved, including a wash drawing attributed to Giovanni Francesco Penni (ca. 1488–1528), in the Louvre. Francis I's hanging was destroyed during the Revolution, but had become so famous throughout Europe that several imitations had been produced in the sixteenth and seventeenth centuries. The oldest of these imitations is a seven-part suite that belonged to Marie of Hungary, who governed the Netherlands and was the younger sister of Charles V. These seven pieces illustrate five episodes in the life of Scipio and include the *Battle of Zama*, now at Madrid's Royal Palace.[39] Several details make it clear that well before the Battle of Lepanto (Marie of Hungary's tapestry was woven in about 1544), artists and kings had already merged the Carthaginian army with the Saracens in their imagination: several of the warriors seen in the towers on the elephants' backs are wearing fine turbans, and scimitars are seen among the weapons wielded by the "Carthaginians."[40]

————————

The lesson the Jesuits hoped to impart to the Japanese through these images of Romans brought together in time and space to combat the infidels was a modest one, it would seem, and a moral one to boot. Valignano put it in the mouth of one of the participants in the dialogue reported in *De missione legatorum*. "May it please Heaven," he cries, after hearing the account of the wonders worked by the Christian people, "may it please Heaven that in our land, Japan, the Christian religion may flourish as it does in Europe, so that the hearts of the Japanese, inclined toward treachery and rebellion, may be more easily checked; in such wise might we put an end to all our warfare and enjoy at last the peace and tranquillity of which you speak."[41] The missionaries no doubt sincerely believed that a Japan converted to Christianity and practicing its virtues would peaceably and of its own accord join what they called the "Christian Republic."

Despite his attraction to the beautiful objects they had brought him from the West, Hideyoshi understood the lesson differently. Not having studied humanities in a Jesuit college, he did not fathom the reasoning that would identify Philip II and the pope with Caesar, who himself was merged with Scipion. The Tokugawas who came after him had no better grasp of it. The devil must have whispered to them that perhaps they were as easily merged with the Turks and the Carthaginians. The notion did not please them, and they made a firm resolution not to allow history to repeat itself on their soil.

Chapter Five

The History of Beginnings

D espite their bias against Erasmianism and their hostility to the Reformation, the fathers of the Council of Trent never dreamed of questioning the authority of the Scriptures. It is true that they also recognized as expressions of their faith the apostolic tradition, the Fathers of the Church, the decrees of previous councils, the Constitutions, and the decrees of the popes. But reading the Bible, enlightened by the Holy Spirit, remained for them, as for their adversaries, the foundation of Revelation. In the face of the numerous translations of the Bible into popular language, they decided out of caution that only Vulgate Latin would be considered "authentic in public lessons, in debates, preaching and explication."[1] But this was not a judgment on its exegetical value: it was simply the translation that could gather the widest consensus.

There was bitter dispute, in spring 1546, as to whether to authorize the distribution of translations of the Bible into popular tongues. The Spanish and French were opposed; the Germans, Italians, and Polish, in favor. In the end the Council did not declare itself. The decision was left to the regional authorities. But the Pontifical Indexes of 1564 and 1596 reined in this freedom: the Bible could be translated into popular languages, and the translations could be distributed, but their use by the laity was strictly controlled study, and interpretation of the Bible was for all practical purposes reserved for the clergy.

Among the clergy, however, it would have been difficult to pretend that the great humanist movement toward a return to the original Hebrew or Greek text had never existed. Study of biblical languages and of the Scriptures came fairly late in the training of a Jesuit, but it had its place: Valignano, Vázquéz, and Ferreira knew the Bible and could quote it if need be in support of an argument. Generally, exegesis by the Spanish Jesuits played no small role in "the immense and intense enterprise of spiritual and dogmatic reconstruction attempted by the Society of Jesus in the late sixteenth century."[2]

In Japan, as in Portugal and elsewhere in Europe, theatrical presentations were a favorite method for bringing to the people the foundational narratives of the Old and New Testaments. The Jesuits proved to be masters of this mode of expression, but they were not its inventors. The Middle Ages had had its mysteries; indeed, the *Mystery of the Passion* by Simon Gréban and Arnoul Gréban, which dates to the middle of the fifteenth century, was still being staged in Paris at the beginning of the sixteenth. As late as 1547, Marguerite de Navarre's *Drama of the Three Kings' Worship of Jesus-Christ* attested to the vitality of the genre.[3]

If the Jesuits had not had time to translate the Bible into Japanese by the time the great persecution began, they had often had occasion to translate rather large excerpts of it, for purposes of preaching or catechism. It seems that Anjiro, Francis Xavier's first catechumen, knew enough Portuguese to read the Gospel according to Saint Matthew in that language; he even translated it into Japanese.[4] Fróis, in his *History of Japan*, also mentioned Anjiro's activity as a translator but in regard to the story of the Creation, the coming of the Son of God, the Decalogue, and the Last Judgment.[5] No trace of this work remains, nor of that of Brother Juan Fernández, who furnished to preachers a convenient Japanese version of the Gospel texts they were to preach about on Sundays and feast days. Fróis declared that "over years . . . [Fernández] had translated all the Gospels and all the sermons for every Sunday of the year, plus explications of the Credo, the Paternoster, the Ave Maria, and the Decalogue."[6]

It is thought that numerous compilations of the life of Jesus must have circulated, all amalgamating for practical reasons the four narratives of Matthew, Mark, Luke, and John and reorganizing them around the major events commemorated during the course of the liturgical year, especially the Passion. There was no question of translating the entire Old Testament: the preachers retained only what could be related to the story of salvation. On the other hand, it lent itself well to the theater. Thus the stories of Adam and Eve, Noah, Abraham and Isaac, Joseph, the flight from Egypt, the handing down of the Ten Commandments to Moses, and King Solomon's judgment were performed as sacred dramas.[7]

The Vatican Library preserves a manuscript, once belonging to Christina of Sweden,[8] that casts a particularly revealing light on the way the Jesuits used the Bible in Japan. Its author is Father Manoel Barreto. It is made up of four hundred pages divided into four parts. Only the second part is pertinent here (fols. 4–111). It has three sections. The first is titled "Gospels for Sundays and Certain High Holy Days of the Year." The second contains the Gospels of the Fridays of Lent; they were probably meant to be read in the gatherings that were held each Friday evening during this period. Here, too, is a narrative of the Passion drawn from all four Gospels, and at the end, several "dialogues" of two kinds. Some take place between characters such as Mary, mother of Jesus, and Mary Magdalene; Mary, at the foot of the cross, gives poignant expression to her grief, and the two women, reflecting on the symbols of the Passion one by one, speak in turn of their compassion for the Crucified One. The other group of dialogues is an "explication" of the Passion; the supplicant meditates on each of the emblems, draws out its significance, and enumerates the personal favors the supplicant hopes it will bestow.

From a linguistic point of view, Father Barreto's manuscript is a strange hybrid. The subheadings are sometimes in Portuguese, sometimes in Japanese, but most often in Latin. The main body of the text is in Japanese, but all the specifically Christian concepts appear in Portuguese. A certain effort at "Japanization" can be detected: in the desert, Jesus is tempted by the *tengu* (devil); in Canaa, he changes the water into sake rather than wine; the miracle of the loaves takes place with rice cakes instead; and the Roman officer of Capernaum (Luke 7:2–10) becomes a samurai. Most of the excerpts referred to, excluding the composite narrative of the Passion, come from the first gospel, that of Matthew.[9]

But the Bible, quoted, paraphrased, sung, dramatized, or illustrated in statuary or paint, was not the sole item in the imaginary of Japanese Christians. The Jesuits had also made available to them a good portion of the hagiographic literature then in wide use throughout Catholic Europe. Among the works printed in Japan beginning in 1591 is a compendium of lives of the saints, illustrated by an engraving of Saint Peter surrounded by other saints. Fróis mentions somewhere a *Flos Sanctorum* (Flower of Saints) that had been translated by Father Vilela in 1566, as well as a *Life of the Glorious Saint Sebastian* rendered in "fine Japanese style" in 1577.[10]

One must return to the apologetic dialogue written by Brother Fabian in 1605, *Myôtei Mondô*, to fully comprehend why the biblical message delivered by the missionaries had to undergo a complete metamorphosis in the minds of the faithful once the fathers had been decimated by the persecution and forced to depart for Macao or the Philippines. In 1605 Fabian was still a Christian; he was Japanese and wrote in his own language. He had undergone a thorough philosophical and theological training; he knew Portuguese and a little Latin. Before his conversion he had also, it seems, received a good Buddhist education. Thus he was ideally suited as a conduit for the fathers' message. His version of the story of Christianity is found in the third book of *Myôtei Mondô*, when Yûtei says:

> When the Lord made heaven and earth, he created eleven levels of heaven. He assigned to the first ten the limits of their respective circles, and named the eleventh *paraiso*. He did not limit this final circle with any circumference. Here he placed the multitude of celestial beings called *anjo*, beings he had created in infinite number to be something like your trusted vassals. . . . The word paradise is equivalent to the Japanese term *gokuraku*. . . . To say that someone is saving his or her soul means that the person is going to this place to know the same joys as the angels. . . . Thus the Lord had created an innumerable multitude of these celestial beings called angels, which are analogous to your trusted vassals, and had placed them in heaven. In addition to the gifts of swiftness, freedom, and insight, he had also endowed them with beauty and rectitude, spiritual gifts that elude our fleshly eye. The Lord forbade them nothing, except

to covet the role of Sovereign. One of them, named Lucifer, nonetheless grew proud of his bounty of spiritual qualities; he forgot the kindness of heaven and conceived the proud thought of attaining the supreme honor; he disclosed his thoughts to his companion angels, and from among the innumerable multitude a few were found who welcomed his suggestions and attempted to revolt against the Lord. Then the Lord visited upon them his punishment: he cast down from heaven first Lucifer, and after him all the angels in his camp, sparing none, and established their prison in the center of the earth. Then they began to endure a mortal heat and cold which they continue to feel to this day. These beings doomed to eternal torment are called *tengu*. . . .

When the Lord had made heaven and earth, he made the ancestors of the human species, a male and female couple, to become the spiritual leaders of all existence. He called the man *Adam* and the woman *Eve* and put them in a place called *paraiso terreal* ["earthly paradise" in Portuguese], the first place of delights in this world. There all their desires were satisfied and they possessed, moreover, the privilege of escaping old age and death. God destined them to enter the celestial paradise bodily when the time came, there to know endless happiness. To increase their merit, he made them one prohibition. Now the demon mentioned earlier flew into transports of rage to think that humans were to be raised to the honors of which he had been stripped. He secretly entered the earthly paradise, tricked Adam and Eve, the ancestors of all humankind, and lured them onto the path of vice by causing them to violate the prohibition. In punishment, they lost first their exemption from old age and death, then all their privileges: they were moreover expelled from earthly paradise and all their descendants were creatures in revolt against the order of heaven. Then their children and grandchildren multiplied and spread into all the countries and all the islands humanity now inhabits. Although all were direct descendants of Adam, they gradually lost the habit of invoking the name of the Lord; this is why all the people of this place [Japan] have come not to know Him anymore. . . .

Seeing all the pain and tribulation visited upon them and their descendants after they violated the prohibition, Adam and Eve realized the extent of their error in rebelling against the Lord. Raising their eyes to heaven or prostrating themselves on the ground, brokenhearted and seized with eight thousand pangs of remorse, they asked pardon for their offense. Deeply contrite, their beds soaked with tears, they implored the Lord to grant them salvation in a future life, for themselves and for their descendants to the last generation. Then, in his will toward goodness and mercy, and as a grace to end suffering and restore happiness, the Lord abided in the womb of a princess named Mary, a descendant of King David, a woman of great holiness who had remained chaste all her life; he abided in her womb without relations between husband and wife, but by virtue of the will of the Very High. He took on our humanity and came into this world as the Redeemer to extinguish error and have goodness appear. After having endured extreme pain, he died, then came back to life three days later in his original body, spent forty more days with his disciples, then ascended to heaven on the fortieth day after his resurrection and opened the path of salvation to humankind. *Jesus Cristo* is the name of this master. Among his disciples, the head preacher had the name *San Petro*, and those who have succeeded him throughout the ages took the general name *pappa*. Their main temple is in Rome, in Italy, the primary Christian country. From that Saint Peter to the current Pope Clement, two hundred thirty-five generations have transmitted the heritage without interruption. Thus what doubt can we have as to the truth of this doctrine?[11]

It is easy to see the direction in which the Holy Scriptures had begun to drift for Fabian. Never having read Genesis, he believed in good faith that the scholastic reduction of Aristotle's theory of spheres was an integral part of it. He also visualized and dramatized to an extreme the story of the Fall, perhaps from having seen it enacted in a sacred drama. He seems ignorant, however, of nearly all the Old Testament, although he is aware of the existence of King David. As though he were taking his history from the Nicean Creed, Fabian also seems not to know that between his miraculous conception and his Passion, the Christ of the Gospels lived, preached, healed, and taught. It is not certain that he fully realizes that Christ was crucified. But he definitely knows that Christ's successor was Saint Peter and that Peter's successor in the early seventeenth century was named Clement VII. In the end, despite Yûtei's precautions to distinguish the Christian notions from the corresponding Buddhist notions *(paraiso/gokuraku)*, one senses that the temptation toward syncretism is always present in the Japanese listener. As Myôshu has trouble seeing *paraiso* as distinct from *gokuraku*, Yûtei insists on their distinctness: "No, no, Myôshu, listen: the propositions in the canons of Shaka have nothing in common with this Christian doctrine. . . . You must understand that there is nothing more than an analogy of name between these madnesses and the Christian religion."[12]

In any case, since the Japanese did not have the Book itself, the collection of excerpts from the Bible and the lives of the saints, transmitted and inculcated through preaching, drama, and painting, would have left only dubious and confused traces in the memory of Japanese Christians, especially those who came after the great persecution, had the missionaries not bequeathed them in addition a framework by which their recollections could be ordered and ingrained. This framework had been laid out by Francis Xavier himself even before setting foot on the archipelago, during his time in India beginning in 1542. His preparations were inspired by two works, one written by Pedro de Alcalá in the late fifteenth century and intended for the Muslims of Granada, the other by Alonso de Molina, written in the sixteenth century for the people of Mexico. Bourdon summarizes Francis Xavier's "Christian doctrine" thus:

After the sign of the cross and homage to the Holy Trinity came three prayers for the mercy of the Father, the Son, and the Holy Ghost; then the Credo, followed by a declaration of faith in everything the Church teaches; then the Paternoster, Ave Maria, and Ten Commandments of God, followed by prayers to Christ and the Virgin to grant the strength to observe them and forgiveness when they were transgressed; then the five precepts of the Church, the Salve Regina, the Confiteor, the seven deadly sins and their opposite seven moral virtues, the three theological virtues, the four cardinal virtues, the fourteen works of mercy, the five senses, the three faculties of the soul and their three enemies; then the worship of the host, a prayer to the chalice, several invocations and exhortations, and last the Benedicite.[13]

The Council of Trent came to a close only after charging one of its members, Cardinal Borromeo, with the task of setting down the results of its work in a catechism. This was the *Catechismus romanus* published in 1566. It was summarized in Japanese in 1568 for use by preachers and coadjutors. It was finally printed in its entirety at Amakusa in 1596, but in Latin, which restricted its use to the clergy. However, its substance had already been communicated for use by the catechumens themselves in two works printed in Amakusa and Nagasaki in 1592 and 1600, the first in Japanese characters and the second in romanized Japanese.[14]

This is what the Nagasaki edition contained, according to a copy discovered at the end of the nineteenth century in a private collection: the meaning of the word "Christian"; the sign of the cross; the Paternoster; the Ave Maria (with the sections of the rosary detailed as the joyful, sorrowful, and glorious mysteries); the Salve Regina; the Credo; the Ten Commandments; the laws of the Holy Church; the seven deadly sins; the seven sacraments. The book ends with a series of lists (works of mercy, theological and cardinal virtues, gifts of the Holy Spirit), along with the Beatitudes and the Confiteor.[15]

All known copies of the *Christian Doctrine* (*Doctrina cristão* in Portuguese, *Dochirina kirishitan* in transliterated Japanese) are presented in dialogue form, with questions and answers; the answers were designed to be learned and recited by heart. All accounts concur on one point: well before the *Dochirina* was in print, it was transmitted orally in this form everywhere the mission had catechumens preparing for baptism. At times the text was even sung, to aid in memorization. Father Fróis recounts that one day he heard children singing the *Dochirina* in the street. It was in 1548 at Arima, as Mass was letting out. The children rang a little bell and sang by turns the *Dochirina*, a few psalms, and some litanies, inviting passersby and onlookers to join them.[16]

THE SECRET CHRISTIANS

When their last priests had been expelled, their churches destroyed, their images and books confiscated, Japanese Christians were not left entirely without resources. They had for such a long time contemplated the icons of Jesus, Mary, the angels, and the saints, so often recited or sung the prayers and professions of faith from the *Dochirina kirishitan*, so dutifully modeled their lives on the liturgical calendar, that they could follow by themselves the path forged by those they still called the Bateren (Fathers).

Japanese Christendom soon developed the means of doing so. Of its own accord it organized into groups and subgroups of villages and families and set up a hierarchy of laypeople who would be responsible for maintaining the framework.[17] Each group was headed by an elder, the *chokata*, whose duty was to keep alive the collective memory, especially that of the liturgical calendar, prayers, and basic teachings of the missionaries. The office of the *chokata* was passed down from father to son, and women were forbidden to exercise the function.

Within each group were smaller groups set up under the direction of a *mitzukata*, or baptizer. His principal function was to baptize, and the post was held for a term of ten years. Since baptism was the only sacrament in the Catholic church that a layperson could dispense, it became the only one that survived for a time after the departure of the Bateren. Given Japanese customs in regard to marriage, for the most part the missionaries had remained reserved on the subject. They promoted monogamy and publicly reproved adultery and divorce, but they did not press their flock into religious marriage: this was only for "those who had shown in confession undeniable proof of their mutual attachment and sincere desire to observe the commandments in all conscience." The secret Christians continued, thus, like the majority of Christians when the mission had been present, to practice concubinage.

If the sacramental life of these Christians was reduced to its simplest level (without priests, they could not even take communion), their life of prayer was intense. Each village had an "auditor" *(kikikata)*, whose task was to transmit the content of the "doctrine" to families, and a "catechist" *(oshiekata)*, in charge of leading prayers *(orasho)*.

The secret Christians had no books; their tradition was purely oral. It remained so until the time, probably rather late, when it was deemed necessary and possible to set down in writing the various versions of the tale the *Beginnings of Heaven and Earth*. Also transcribed were certain fragments of the liturgy and the Credo; such documents were seized in 1822 at Urakami.

Above and beyond what was sayable, the collective memory of the secret Christians was laden with more poignant and more intimate memories: recollections of suffering undergone, of tortures feared and sometimes sought, of clandestinity, flight, and death. The Jesuits who evangelized Japan in the sixteenth century had brought with them, consciously or not, all the characteristics of the baroque piety predominating at the time in the countries of western Europe. They were nonetheless taken aback by the zeal with which the neophytes flung themselves into the most excessive and spectacular penitential practices. Father Valignano was so moved by it that he wrote in his inspection report of 1583: "It is not good . . . to oblige the Japanese by force to mortify themselves and to think that, in order to mortify them and make spiritual men of them, they must be urged with many mortifications; rather, experience and even rationality show the errors of these ideas."[18]

The problem came from far away. Valignano also mentions it in his narrative, without explicitly making the connection between the two things: the Japanese were irrationally fond of mortifications, and this well before the arrival of Christianity on the archipelago. "There are some," he says, "who in order to win sainthood and go to a certain paradise of their imagining, walk into the sea amid great ceremony and drown; others have themselves buried alive. . . . Finally, they engage in many very rigorous penitential practices so that the *kami* and the *hotoke* will aid them."

Father Fróis had already noticed, as reported in his *History of Japan*, that members of the Yamabushi brotherhood, who lived in the mountains, engaged in particularly severe exercises. They made endless pilgrimages garbed in crude clothing, eating only a handful of rice in the morning and evening and drinking but a few swallows of water. Those who fell in exhaustion were left by the side of the road. The religious leaders who guided them visited horrible trials on them during the journey. One trial consisted of suspending a pilgrim over a cliff in a sort of unbalanced scale and forcing him to make a public confession. The scale would be made to go up if the confession appeared to be sincere, down if the sinner hesitated to accuse himself or sought to dissemble; if he persisted, he was dropped off the cliff.[19]

But confession and penitence were not practiced only in those purification rites. They also had their place in several Buddhist sects. Even in the Pure Land and True Pure Land sects, two varieties of the cult of Amida that assured their faithful salvation through grace, regardless of their merits, there was fasting, marching, and sometimes ritual suicide.

Thus the *Dochirina kirishitan* and the preaching of the fathers, wherever they emphasized the need for confession and contrition, the sacrament of penance, and its fulfillment through acts of mortification and charity, matched a preexisting taste in the Japanese. Lent and the period of the Passion became privileged times when the taste for mortification could be indulged. This inclination was only heightened by the recitation of the rosary before pious images and symbols of the sufferings of Christ and his mother, as well as the exemplary tales drawn from the lives of the confessors, for whom the worst sufferings were as nothing since they brought the joy of identifying thereby with Christ.

The dissemination among the faithful of paintings and engravings representing the fifteen mysteries of the rosary went hand in hand with the dissemination of flagellation instruments, which they used on themselves as a way to identify with the Crucified One. A significant number of these whips and scourges still exist in Takatsuki and Nagasaki, on the islands of Ikitsuki, and on the Goto archipelago. The neophytes' zeal went so far at times that the fathers had to intervene to prevent them from harming themselves or breaching the dignity of hallowed sites. Some, for example, had to be prevented from using iron whips inside a chapel.

The arrival of Spanish Dominicans and Franciscans from the Philippines at the very end of the sixteenth century, then the onset and rapid expansion of their persecution, precipitated in Japanese Christians a veritable collective delirium, which the Portuguese Jesuits, familiar with the mentality of the country, tried in vain to restrain before being swept up by it themselves. A Spanish merchant who lived in Nagasaki from 1594 to 1598 and from 1607 to 1619 described the penitential processions he witnessed there in 1614. On May 9 he saw three thousand people, many flagellating themselves bloody, traveling from church to church. Another procession was held on the tenth, and another on the twelfth. In this last he saw a man carrying a heavy cross to which his outstretched arms had been tied. Another bore on his back a huge stone. Yet another was weighed down with chains. Several were dressed in straw sacking tightly tied with heavy ropes. Others, their hands tied behind their backs, were being led with ropes around their necks.

On May 14 there were seven processions from morning to night, with more than ten thousand penitents in all. One man had had himself tied up and followed the procession with a saber protruding from his thigh, losing blood copiously, until a priest intervened to have the saber removed. The man died the following day. It all began anew on the fifteenth, sixteenth, seventeenth, nineteenth, and twentieth. The last procession, that of the Corpus Christi, was organized by the Jesuits. Among the images the marchers carried, alongside that of the infant Jesus, was a large flag with the chalice and host on one side and Abraham preparing to sacrifice his son Isaac on the other.

In fact, the germ of these extreme practices had been introduced very early in the history of the mission. The Jesuits had the custom of scourging themselves and had contributed to spreading the practice on the Iberian Peninsula. The Japanese Christians imitated them, at first with lashes made of untanned steerhide and then with balls of metal studded with spikes. Fathers Almeida, Fernandes, and Vilela attest that during the first years of the mission (1557, 1561), rivers of blood flowed during certain processions. Sometimes Father Torres would skip verses of the Miserere to shorten the ceremony and would have to use his authority to force the flagellants to lay down their whips. This example and the warning of Father Valignano in 1583 reveal that those responsible for the mission were torn between their desire to set a good example and their fear of seeing this example perverted.[20]

The sight of Christian martyrs being tortured by the Japanese Inquisition was tailor-made to inflame the imagination. There were various tortures: the stake, crucifixion, the pit torture, or immersion in the sulfurous boiling waters of Unzen northeast of Nagasaki.

The penitential processions that took place in the darkest days of the persecution induced and fulfilled in the faithful a dual desire for identification, first with the sufferings of Christ, evoked by the preachings and images, then with the sufferings of the martyrs they saw before them. Among the latter the most spectacular was the torture of the fifty victims during the Great Martyrdom of 1623. As they walked toward the stake to be burned, some of them raised crucifixes in their hands and all sang as they were being bound. Carlo Spinola, their leader, addressed an exhortation to the onlookers from the top of his stake, and the crowd chanted in unison with the martyrs. Most of the spectators had rosaries in their hands, and many women wore white veils on their heads.[21]

BEGINNINGS OF HEAVEN AND EARTH

The Japanese tale *Beginnings of Heaven and Earth* was transmitted orally for several generations in the communities of secret Christians that had managed to survive the persecutions of the early seventeenth century. Several versions that were committed to writing early in the nineteenth century have come down to us. The first came to light in 1865 in Urakami, near Nagasaki, even before the Meiji Restoration. It was given to a French priest but was destroyed in 1874 in a fire that demolished the headquarters of the Yokohama mission. A Japanese professor, Tagita Koya, was fortunate enough to discover nine more in the 1930s. One of them was immediately translated into German by a Bavarian Jesuit, Alfred Bohner. He published his translation in 1938 in *Monumenta nipponica*.[22] Tagita himself published several editions of another copy of the *Beginnings*. The first appeared in 1954 under the title *Showa-jidä no Sempuku-kirishitan* (The Crypto-Christians of the Showa Era). In 1966 it was published in *Nagoya joshi shoka tandai kiyo* (Journal of the Young Women's College of Nagoya). The last critical, annotated edition of the same manuscript of the *Beginnings* was included by Ebisawa Arimichi in a 1970 collection, *Kirishitan sho, Haiya sho* (Christian and Anti-Christian Writings).

Urakami, where the first known version of the *Beginnings* was found, and Kurosaki in the Nighi-Sonogi peninsula, where the version translated by Bohner was discovered, delimit rather well the geographic area in which the communities whose beliefs it summarizes and whose practices it illustrates held out for a great while, isolated from each other but very much alive. More such communities existed on the islands off Kyushu, such as Ikutsuki, to the northwest of

Hirado, and still farther offshore, on the islands of the Goto-retto archipelago.

It may seem strange that this tale is unknown in the communities that remain today. The explanation lies in their continual isolation, not only from the outer world, but from each other; in the progressive disappearance of those responsible for keeping the memory alive; and in the material and cultural poverty of this class of the population generally. Those who took care to set down in writing the tale of the *Beginnings* had presentiments, no doubt, of this evolution. But, as all preservers of folklore do, in their concern to rescue the tradition they unwittingly contributed to its demise. For the tale was kept alive only through its constant transmission by word of mouth, with the play of variations that makes a popular tale always the same and always different. It is perhaps not coincidental that the attempt at preservation occurred in the early nineteenth century, soon after the great "displacement" of Kyushu's secret Christians to the islands of Goto late in the eighteenth century. These secret Christians came from Kurosaki but also from Mie, in the Sotome district, and settled the islands of the archipelago in successive waves. For some time, they had successfully worked unproductive land in Kyushu belonging to the lord Omura Sumiyasu, but he had driven them off at the request of a lord from Goto who needed the workers to improve his own undercultivated and sparsely populated lands. Once on the islands, they found themselves cut off from the milieu in which they had managed to survive for generations and were met with instant hostility by the local people, who were settled on the best land. They were forced to retrench in the most desolate areas of Goto. There, at least, they were free to practice their religion in private. They would be persecuted again after the Meiji Restoration; in 1869 the heads of twelve families on the island of Kazurashima were arrested and horribly tortured at the behest of the central government.[23]

The *Beginnings of Heaven and Earth* could be seen as a moving yet amusing pastiche of the story of Christianity as taught by the Jesuits to the faithful, especially as understood by the latter. Composed of twelve progressively briefer chapters, the tale comes to a mere twenty-two pages in Bohner's translation. The narrative line is simple: Creation, Fall, wanderings of the children of Adam, Noah, the Annunciation, the

Visitation, the Nativity, baptism of Jesus, Circumcision, adoration of the Magi, flight to Egypt, Transfiguration, Jesus in the Temple, founding of the Church of Rome, massacre of the Innocents, betrayal by Judas, capture of Jesus by Herod, the Crucifixion, the Good Thief, Jesus' descent into Hell, the Resurrection and Ascension, the Assumption of Mary, the Last Judgment. Whole sections of the story are omitted, from the end of the Flood to the selection of Mary, and the traditional order of events is reversed in several places.

Overall, however, the narrative of the *Beginnings* is not unfaithful to its Christian sources. The secret Christians have retained the belief that there is one God, who has created all things, that for the salvation of humanity he went so far as to incarnate himself as a human being and to suffer the worst of deaths. They have lost the memory of the Eucharist but still know that God, in some mysterious fashion, "shared his body." One reads in chapter 3: "The angels . . . said: if God does not share his body, there is truly no means to salvation." And God, indeed, agrees to separate from the best part of himself by sending his son to earth.

These Catholics far from Rome also know that to benefit from the grace offered them, they must sincerely repent of their faults and ask forgiveness for them. Eve and Adam know this even before they have sinned: in chapter 1, they recite the Act of Contrition at the moment Jusuheru (Lucifer) determines to have himself worshiped as the equal of God. After the Fall, Adam, who repents, is pardoned. Eve does not repent and is condemned, but not for eternity: "until this world passes away," says the tale. Even Judatsu (Judas) could have been saved, despite his betrayal, if by his suicide he had not proven that he despaired of all possibility of divine forgiveness. The Good Thief, on the other hand, goes to paradise because he has the courage to admit that his crimes deserved punishment.

Baptism being the only sacrament preserved for a while in the tradition of the secret Christians (they still have "baptizers," but these no longer baptize), they still have a good sense of its meaning: it is the sign by which the child or adult is admitted into the community and becomes the beneficiary of the grace of salvation. Zezusu (Jesus) himself, although engendered by the Father, receives baptism at the hands of San Jiwan (John the Baptist), but it is the former who truly institutes the practice of baptism, in chapter 5: "'How pure and clear this water is,' he said. 'It must be shared for the salvation of those in the world to come. . . . All those to whom water has been administered on the banks of this river share in the happiness of *baräso* [paradise].'"

Although the missionaries celebrated relatively few religious marriages, and although the sacrament of marriage was unknown to the secret Christians, the tale of the *Beginnings* preserves traces of the recommendations and prohibitions that the fathers had not failed to emphasize to the faithful. Eve and Adam are united by God himself to form a "couple." Later their children, although brother and sister, swear the "oath of fidelity" as husband and wife. But in joining together, they commit incest and bear the shame of this. The most surprising part is the marriage of Maruya (Mary) to the king of Roson, San Chisenasu. Since he is the king, she cannot refuse to marry him. But as she has made a vow not to know man, she refuses to unite with him and flees. At the end of the tale, however, she does not forget that she is married. She prays the Lord to accord grace to San Chisenasu; God then makes them "a couple" and gives them a rank of honor.

There are nonetheless several points on which the *Beginnings* betrays a lack of comprehension that gravely contradicts dogma. This can be explained as an accentuation to the limit of the possible, even to the absurd, of certain tendencies in the missionaries' preaching. The Jesuits, for example, downplayed as much as they could the aspects of the Passion that were the least tolerable to Japanese sensibility. The secret Christians at last forgot, if they had ever known it, the significance of the cross. Apparently God, incarnating himself in the body of Zezusu, son of Mary, on the counsel of his angels, had no particular plan for the redemption of humanity. It is the massacre of the Innocents by Yorutetsu (Herod) that unleashes the process leading to salvation, and this undoubtedly explains the displacement of the episode in the sequence of the narrative. Zezusu, having reached adulthood, reproaches himself for having been involuntarily its cause and undertakes to expiate his guilt through "exercises" of an undisclosed nature. Then God intervenes to enjoin him to press his asceticism to the ultimate by sacrificing his own life: "Because this multitude of children died because of you, you must, in the interests of the life to come, take upon yourself the responsibility for it, go to your martyrdom, and cast your body from you." This is far closer to the practice of voluntary death in the Japan of yore than to the folly of the cross according to Saint Paul.[24]

One might also wonder whether it is not Maruya who is the true redeemer of the human species, rather than her son. This is undoubtedly due to the fact that Marian piety and the recitation of the rosary played an essential role in the missionaires' religious practice. Moreover, in the absence of the images with which they used to pray, the secret Christians, for convenience as well as from caution, often substituted for Mary Buddhist statuettes representing the goddess of mercy, Kannon Bosatsu, who appeared as a beautiful young woman, sometimes accompanied by a small child. It is probable that the dogma of the Trinity, formulated obscurely in the *Dochirina kirishitan*, underwent significant deviations to make it comprehensible and receivable. In chapter 11, the Holy Spirit as a *person* steps aside in favor of a *title* (Subiritosanto), so that Maruya may accede to the rank of third person in the Trinity: "The Mother received . . . the task of mediator, and the Very High [in this case the Son] gives her the role of savior. This means that the Very High became the Son, Hiriyo, and the Mother, Subiritosanto." It seems equally extraordinary from a theological point of view that Maruya then marries before God the conveniently resurrected king of Roson.

Although theologically the story of the *Beginnings of Heaven and Earth* is of dubious orthodoxy, it does a fine job of providing the justification and framework for the community's liturgical life. And indeed, this is its chief function.

Among the engravings that circulated in the parishes during the missionary days were calendars indicating month by month the feast days Christians were to celebrate. These were Western-style calendars, and it was indispensable for the faithful to be familiar with them, because the Japanese broke up the year in a completely different way. Thus the Purification of Mary was celebrated in January, the Circumcision in February, the Annunciation in March, the Resurrection in April, the Ascension in May, Pentecost in June, Mary's visit to Elizabeth in July, and so on until the Nativity.[25]

The *Beginnings* includes all of these feast days, with a single exception, Pentecost, a clear indicator of how much the person of the Holy Spirit had been eclipsed by the person of Mary. And it respects the order of their occurrence, which is complex because it intertwines two series of events, those centering around Mary (Purification, Annunciation, visit to Elizabeth, Assumption) and those centering on Jesus (Nativity, Circumcision, death and Resurrection, Ascension).

The week had its proper order as well. The *Beginnings* provides an extra reminder of this by using words transliterated from the Portuguese: *shiguda, terushiya, kuwaruta, kinta, sesuta, sabado, domingo*. The days thus designated, from Monday to Sunday, come into play first in chapter 1, to "date" the creation of the different parts of the human body: head, hands, long bones, testicles, feet, soul, eyes, breath. The same calendar also serves in chapter 5 to establish the fast day, *kuwaruta*, or Wednesday, the day when Deus removed one of his ribs to create the bones of Adam. Last, in chapter 11, *sesuta*, Friday, is the day when the Crucified One descends into limbo; he remains there during *sabado*, Saturday, before ascending for the first time into heaven on the third day after his death.

The day itself follows a very strict pattern of prayer in the morning, at noon, and at night. These are rosary prayers, associated with the three groups of mysteries—joyful, sorrowful, and glorious—each calling up sacred scenes that center, alternately or simultaneously, on Mary and on Christ for meditation. The narration here begins strangely to turn the table on itself: originally, the fifteen mysteries were fifteen memorable scenes cut from the fabric of the Gospels. And these fifteen scenes become a posteriori the material for contemplation and prayer. In this tale, however, everything occurs as though the institution of the different prayer times structured the narrative itself, which is in a sense itself confirmed by the institution it is supposed to justify.

The *Beginnings* again fulfill their anamnestic role by reproducing several texts, such as the Ave Maria and the Paternoster, at the end of chapter 4. These are precisely the two prayers that recur in the recitation of the rosary. The text reproduced is not identical to that in the *Dochirina kirishitan* but is clearly recognizable.

It was inevitable that once ties with the tale's Western sources were severed, it would become more or less Japanized, especially in the humble peasant world of the secret Christians. The effect is discrete, however. It is seen, for example, in details such as indications of measure: the Lord takes a *sho* of earth to make the clay from which he will shape the first human; lengths are measured in *cho, jo,* or *ken.* In such matters, which are not the transcendant domain of theology, it is better to be understood. The same holds true for the origin of the cultivation of rice, a food crop so essential in Asia that it cannot be spoken of in a borrowed language.

Throughout the reading, small details allow the reader or listener to believe in the reality of what is being recounted: Deus descending from heaven with his imperial retinue; the jet knife he carries, doubtless with his saber, like every good warrior; women who shave their eyebrows and blacken their teeth to distinguish themselves from men; the sedan chair into which the envoys of the king of Roson push Maruya when they carry her off; the damask and brocades from China laid out by the king to dazzle Maruya; the bamboo hats the Magi use to hide their faces when they embark on their journey.

The most original aspect of this Japanization is the tale's arrangement in space. The Christian sources on which it is based imposed certain names, such as Bethlehem, Mount Tabor, Jerusalem, and Rome. These indeed appear in the tale in easily recognizable form—Roma, Taboro—or slightly altered form—Jurusaren, Beren, from the Portuguese Belém (Bethlehem). But there are two Jurusaren: in chapter 5 it is the name of a river near Beren; in chapter 6 it is a town of undetermined location where there is a temple called Barunkata, in which a disciple of Shaka teaches. Other names are typically Japanese, even though their identification or locale is uncertain, such as the island of Arioshima at the end of chapter 3, or the Abe River late in chapter 4.

The geography of the *Beginnings* becomes outright fanciful with the appearance of the king of Roson. Roson is most likely Luzon, in the Philippines. But Maruya is also a native of this country, which is not far from Japan and from the Abe River, since in late chapter 4 she meets on its banks Isaberuna (Elizabeth) after a journey that is not very long.

In the story of the Magi, Beren, which might be in Japan or anywhere at all, becomes literally the center of the world, equidistant from New Spain, France, and the Ottoman Empire. But it is a world that might be imagined by a peasant bent over his rice in the paddy, delimited by the horizon visible on his land: when they meet, each of the three kings has traveled between thirty and fifty miles, and at their meeting point there is not far to go to reach Beren. Nor is it far from

Beren to Mount Taboro: forty days' march. On the other hand, it is impossible to say how much time it takes to go from Beren or Mount Taboro to the city of Jurusaren or to Roma. Thus, little by little, the tale leads us into an unreal world neither Japan nor Judea nor that of the late-sixteenth-century planispheres, but rather resembling the world of fairy tales.

Forced to register in Buddhist temples near their homes, living amid Buddhists and Shintoists, participating willingly or forcibly in Buddhist ceremonies (especially funeral services), adopting the image of the goddess Kannon to represent the Virgin—at times marked with a discreet cross—the secret Christians could not remain unmoved by the seductions of Buddhism, especially the Amida sects, so close to Christianity in some regards that the fathers saw them as their most formidable adversary. Indeed, Valignano was speaking of Amida influence—represented by the Pure Land sect (founded by Honen in the twelfth century) or the True Pure Land sect (founded by Shinran in the thirteenth century)—when he wrote in 1583: "The better to win over the Japanese and receive them more easily into their sects, they make salvation easy for them in this wise: they tout the mercy and the great charity of Amida and Shaka, and go so far as to say that even with all the sins it is possible to commit, when one invokes the names of Amida and Shaka with a firm hope in them and in their merits, one is purified and washed of all one's sins, with no need to make penance or perform other works, for this would be to misunderstand the penance and works that these gods themselves have performed for the salvation of humanity. It is Luther's doctrine all the way."[26]

The *Beginnings* would appear to have no indulgence at all for the Amida sects. The debate in the temple between Jesus and the teachers, as told in the Gospels, is transposed in chapter 6 into a confrontation between the Very High and Gakujuran, a disciple of Shaka. But the dispute, which remains eminently civil, deals not with fundamental matters (salvation through faith or salvation through works) but with accessory issues such as the locale of paradise. And when Gakujuran joins his adversary he is only asked to change masters: from then on the Very High takes the place of Shaka for him. The baptism he asks only seals a new pact between master and disciple, and before receiving it, he is not even required to burn the sacred books of Buddhism; he is saved by pure grace.

Moreover, except for the fact that the God of the *Beginnings of Heaven and Earth* created everything that exists, which would be unthinkable to a Buddhist, he is barely distinguishable from Buddha. The first chapter of the tale explicitly states that he is "a living, free, and self-sufficient buddha." This affirmation is repeated strongly and authoritatively by the Very High in the debate with Gakujuran: "The Lord of Heaven, Deus, who is venerated as Buddha, is the buddha who assures the salvation of human beings in the world to come." Two more times in the ensuing debate Deus is called the Hotoke, a title that in Japanese Buddhism refers equally to the historic Buddha (Gautama or Shaka) and to all the temporal manifestations of transcendental buddhaness (Tathagata).

In identifying the missionaries' "Deus" as "the Hotoke" of the Japanese Buddhist tradition, the secret Christians unknowingly reverted to the errors that characterized the early days of the mission in Japan, before the vigorous reaction of Father Gago. Francis Xavier, wishing not to do violence to either the language or the religious conscience of his interlocutors, spoke not only of the creation of the world by "Dainichi" but also of the incarnation and passion of "the Hotoke" and of the beatitudes of the "Pure Land," using the same terms as the followers of Amida sects.

The infiltration of Buddhism into the *Beginnings* is seen at several levels of the text. On the most elementary level, it simply produces "realistic details," such as the Magis' bamboo hats. For example, at the end of chapter 7 the Very High becomes "abbot" *(osho)* of the Santa Ekirenjiya *(ecclesia)*, and in chapter 10 one of the "confessors" who accompanies the Very High in his agony adopts the sitting position of Zen meditation in the branches of a pine tree.

Contamination of the biblical facts that lie at the distant origin of the tale by legends that actually concern the great figures of Japanese Buddhism, such as Kukai or Nichiren, pushes the amalagmation quite a bit further. At yet a deeper level is the tale's representation of supernatural beings and occurrences: the thirty-three forms of *anjo* created in the beginning by Deus and the thirty-three forms of Adam;

Jusuheru's frightening aspect after Adam's fall, with a long nose, broad mouth, claws on his hands and feet, and horns on his head; the metamorphosis undergone by Judatsu after his betrayal; the eternal flame kindled at the beginning of chapter 9 with the top of the tree Kurosu, from which the cross will be hewn.

So deep is the infiltration of Buddhism that it is detectable in the very sentiments the characters are said to feel. It is not terribly surprising when in chapter 3 the king of Roson tells Maruya to use a substitute to fulfill a vow: the king is not a Christian, and we may assume that his reasoning on the matter is like that of any other Japanese lord. It also seems natural, in chapter 6, that Gakujuran's students ask the Very High if they may become his disciples "to learn to know the causes and effects." But it is quite another thing for the *narrator*, at the end of chapter 9, to speak of the *karma* of the Good Thief whose fate was to hang on a cross in the company of the Very High.

The elements of the tale that come from Shinto legends have a different meaning, depending on whether they are only there to add folkloric color to a fantastic story or they translate a particular relation between humans and the divine. No doubt the story of the girl and boy tossing to each other a comb and needle in chapter 2, which recounts the misadventures of the children of Adam, has symbolic significance in Shintoism: the comb, planted in the hair, says something about the relationship of the one who wears it with the upper world; it links, in a sense, heaven and earth. But in the *Beginnings* this meaning is no longer perceptible. The same is true a little later of the Dragon's castle, built on the bottom of the sea and symbolizing in Shintoism the alliance of the celestial *kami* and the marine *kami*.

The place of purification rites in the tale is of greater significance. When in chapter 3 Maruya wishes to obtain from heaven the favor of a miracle, she does not simply turn toward heaven to pray, she first goes to rinse her mouth to purify herself, as she would at a Shinto shrine before praying to the *kami*. After the birth of the Lord in chapter 5, she purifies herself by going to bathe in the river, despite the snow and the cold. A little later San Jiwan in turn purifies the child by bathing him *before* going, on his request, to baptize him in the river of Jurusaren. The tale thus establishes a sort of equivalence between Shinto purification rites and Christian baptism. This is not heretical, for

Christian baptism is not only the symbol of a death and a resurrection in Christ but also a cleansing that washes away sin. This is in fact a good example of successful inculturation, given the importance of purification rites in Shintoism.

The secret Christians thus carried out themselves, in their way, the task of inculturation the Jesuits could not see through to completion. They did so out of the necessity to justify in their own eyes the fact that they were still authentically Japanese and yet deeply bound to the forms of piety the fathers had inculcated in them. Indeed, the tale the *Beginnings of Heaven and Earth* is in reality much better and much more than a distorted reflection of the teaching they had received. It is the story of the "beginning" of the community, a foundation myth to which the group can return for sustenance again and again.

Even the language in which the myth is set down, then transmitted, is itself a unique hybrid. When Francis Xavier and his first companions arrived in Japan, they did not know the native tongue: their sole conduit was Anjiro. Francis Xavier's first preachings in Japan and his first debates with the Buddhist monks were thus at a great disadvantage. The missionaries had honestly believed that they would be able to borrow from Japanese words and expressions that could immediately render concepts such as "God," "Trinity," "Demon," "Rational Soul," "Savior," "Path of Salvation," "Paradise," and "Hell." Unfortunately, these concepts were not directly transposable into Japanese, and the words borrowed from Japanese retained, despite all efforts, the meanings they had always had in their original context. *Dainichi*, for example, could not be used for God, because in Anjiro's religion it was the name of the buddha Mahavairocana, the dynamic force of perfect wisdom that illuminates the universe, and the choice of *Hotoke* to designate the Savior was especially infelicitous, as that was the title commonly given to the Buddha himself.[27]

The solution finally reached, thanks to Father Gago, was to insert into the Japanese language, in transliterated form, Portuguese or Latin words that would retain their original content in their new shape. Thus fifty or so words or expressions taken from Portuguese or Latin were introduced into written and spoken Japanese and have remained ever since, words such as *Deus, Trindade, Padre, Espírito Santo, Cruz,* and *Virgem.* But given the syllabic nature of Japanese, words containing groups of two or three consonants had to be modified in varying degrees to be put into written form. Thus "Deus" came to be be written in Latin characters *(romaji)* as *Deusu,* "Trindade" (the Trinity) as *Chirinidade,* "Padre" (Father) as *Bateren, Patere,* or even *Hatere,* "Espírito Santo" (the Holy Spirit) as *Esupiritosanto* or *Supirito Santo,* "cruz" (cross) as *kurusu,* "Virgem" (Virgin) as *Biruzen,* and so on.[28]

The result of the intrusion of a theological or ecclesiastical vocabulary into Japanese produced surprising results. What did the children of Bungo understand by the text they had learned by heart when they recited: *"Deus Pater, Filho et Spirito Santo,* mitsuna *perusona,* hitotsuna *sustancia"?* To the missionaries, it meant: "God the Father, the Son, and the Holy Spirit, three persons, one substance." But only two words in this text, those shown here in roman type, belonged to the Japanese language.

This sort of work was not entirely original to the Jesuits in Japan. The problems associated with acclimatizing Christianity to a cultural context initially foreign to it had also arisen in other lands with active missions. They had arisen in Europe itself, in a time when the language of the clerics was everywhere different from the vernacular tongue. The Reformation made the decision to say and write everything in these vernaculars, elevated to the dignity of literary and learned languages that could rival Latin in every domain, even philosophy and theology. The Catholic Reformation believed it had to take an opposing stance, and it was one that turned out to be a dead end.

This stance is very well illustrated in a work fortuitously rescued from oblivion a few years ago by an Austrian scholar, Wolfgang Meid. The work in question is the exact equivalent in content to the *Dochirina kirishitan* and was published around the same time, in 1602, at Vicenza, under the seal of the bishop of Padua. It is an adaptation of the *Dottrina christiana breve* published by Cardinal Bellarmin at Rome in 1597 and intended for children and humble folk. The problem in Vicenza was that part of the population of this northern Italian diocese did not speak Italian but used a dialect of German. Had they spoken High German, even better, had they been able to read and write it, Bellarmin's work would have been translated into that language easily enough. But these were simple, illiterate people in whom the fundamental truths of Christianity had to be inculcated orally, and if possible, in their own dialect. The dialogue form of the presentation, in a question-and-answer format, indicates that the answers were meant to be learned and recited by heart. The result was a linguistic artifact constructed much like the *Dochirina kirishitan:* the base of the edifice is the German "sentence," but all the theological and ecclesiastical vocabulary is in Italian or Latin.

One reads, for example, in the first chapter: "What is a Christian? One who professes the faith and the law of Christ." Which comes out: "*Baz bil koden* Christan? *Der da macht* profession *der* Fede, *und* Leze de Christo." Again, in the chapter on the sign of the cross: "Why are the three divine persons one single God? Because they have one essence, one power, one wisdom, and one goodness." The reply reads in Latino-Italo-German: "*Barome* si habent hona medema essenzia, hona medema *macht*, hona medema sapienza, *unt* hon medema bontà."

The big difference between the *Dochirina kirishitan* and the *Dottrina christiana* adapted to the German-speaking minority of the Padua diocese is that in about 1637 the users of the former abruptly ceased to have any contact with people, whether preachers or merchants, who spoke Portuguese or knew Latin, while the German-speaking Italian minority was continually immersed in a population of fluent Italian speakers and had priests who probably spoke both languages.

It came about naturally that as time went on some of the borrowed terms were no longer understood at all. Others were distorted by contamination from Japanese words having similar pronunciation. Others changed meaning. The astonishing thing, under these conditions, is not that meanings were lost and forms altered: it is rather the extreme ingenuity with which successive storytellers succeeded in *making sense out of non-sense*. Here are two examples.

The first is found in the narrative of the Visitation.

When the fourth month had gone by [the] body of Maruya had grown gradually heavier. Then she said to herself: "Isaberuna's months must be done by now; her pregnancy must surely cause her pain." And she set out to go and see Isaberuna. Isaberuna also gauged Maruya's pregnancy by her own body and said: "What pain pregnancy must have in store for her." And she set out to go and see Maruya. On the way, they both found themselves on the banks of the river Abe. Had it been a matter of the usual courtesy, the niece should have bowed to her aunt; but because the Lord had made the body of Maruya his abode, Isaberuna quickly drew back and said: "Maruya, full of *garassa*, I greet your person with reverence. The Lord dwells in your body, and among all women there is none more wondrous than you. And the life inside your body, Zesusu, is hallowed as well."

Maruya replies by reciting the Paternoster; later Isaberuna's salutation and Maruya's prayer will together become the prayer of Zesusu. And the narrator concludes the chapter by saying: "And because it was composed on the banks of the river Abe, this poem is also called the *Abe Maruya*. On the banks of this river the two women told each other long stories, then they took leave of each other and went back."

It is necessary to back up a little to appreciate the second example. It is found in the text of the Paternoster itself, as recited by Mary. She says, in effect: "Our Father in heaven, may your name be hallowed; you come in person; what you think in heaven, you also bring about on earth; you give us today our daily bread from heaven; as we forgive others, you forgive others, too, their faults." Nothing unusual so far. It might even be of interest from the evangelical point of view that the prayer is enunciated in declarative form, rather than the imperative to which we are accustomed. But with the next proposition, everything goes haywire: "Say nothing to Lord Tenta; from this day on you banish evil."

Who is this Tenta, found nowhere else? His name proceeds quite simply from the Portuguese word *tentação*, temptation ("lead us not into temptation"), introduced whole into the Japanese version of the Paternoster. The word was understood perfectly, no doubt, during the time the *Dochirina kirishitan* was being taught and explicated; then it ceased to be so, and the Japanese finally heard *Tentasan*, Lord Tenta or Mister Tenta. Little by little its environment was modified as well, to create a meaning as best as possible.

The result of all this work of imagination and language, and often of imagination on language, was in the end highly fulfilling for the community of secret Christians. And it is understandable that even after having forgotten the myth on which the community had been founded originally, its members stubbornly insisted on maintaining their own identity, first against the Buddhist and Shintoist environment and later, beginning in the late nineteenth century, against the repeated offers of the Roman church to bring it back into the fold.

The religion invented by the secret Christians is a sui generis creation that might be called Christianized Buddhism, in which Maruya and the figure called the Very High (he who is on earth, the Son) play the role of bodhisattvas in the Buddhist tradition, those beings—very human—on the path of sanctification who voluntarily postpone the moment of their own salvation to devote themselves to the salvation of others. Well before being chosen by Deus, Maruya wonders: "If I think earnestly about the state of the world, what can I do, I who have been born into the world of human beings, for the salvation of the world to come?" Deus himself, despite his rank (he has two hundred of them, and forty-two forms), is a very human character, a kindly king who asks the advice of his angels when he does not know what to do. He is not a jealous God, the God of armies, the frightening avenger often depicted by the Old Testament, but a God of forgiveness. From the start of the story, he allows his creatures, conditionally, to worship Jusuheru, even though Jusuheru wishes to usurp his place. Later, after the Fall, he says: "Since these are human beings whom I myself created, it seems a shame to cast them into Hell." Thus he is once again ready to forgive, if Adam and Eve accept the light penance he imposes. The couple's children, too, get a reprieve: if they do as the Lord recommends, he will show them one day "the path that leads to Heaven." Jusuheru himself, through whom all this evil came to pass, should in all justice be flung down into Hell. He is only demoted and condemned to the ridicule of being sent to live off the flesh of sparrows in the middle regions of heaven.

At the end of the story nearly everyone is saved, as the Good Thief was. In a context dominated by the figure of an all-merciful God, the majority of the tale's protagonists model their conduct on his: Maruya, from early childhood; the innkeeper's wife who welcomes her and her infant into the inn on Christmas morning; Beronike (Veronica), the water carrier in chapter 9. Yorutetsu himself is moved by the sight of Maruya weeping for her dead son. Then there is the stone dog guarding the entrance to the temple where Happamaruji (Noah) comes to pray, and the animals in the stable where the Very High is born. Here the piety of Japan's secret Christians reconverges with the popular piety of Old Europe as expressed in countless Christmas tales and canticles about the Lord's birth, "between the ox and the gray donkey." The missionaries' teachings had touched the same fiber here. It continued to vibrate, it seems, long after the departure of the Bateren.

Excerpts from *Beginnings of Heaven and Earth*

The Creation of Human Beings
When the multitude of the *anjo* had been created, it happened that they did not have children and did not multiply. Then the Creator said: "I wish to form human beings, have them multiply, and see that they observe virtue religiously." He descended from heaven into the lower world and took up in his hands a *sho* of earth.[29] He went back up to Koroteru, mixed the earth with water, put in some salt and oil, not too much and not too little, and with his buddha power kneaded it all together. On the day *shiguda* he shaped the head, on the day *terushiya*, the hands. Since in fashioning the body he lacked what was needed to make the long bones, he took out his left rib and formed them from it: that day was *kuwaruta*. On the day *kinta* he made the testicles, on the day *sesuta* he made the feet, and on the day *sabato* he completed his assemblage:[30] he took the moon and put it inside to serve as the soul, he took stars and made them into two eyes, and when the Lord Deus blew in his own breath through the head, the nine doors of the body opened. The man was wondrously wrought. . . . The following day, *domego*, the army of angels celebrated the completion of the creation.

Later, Deus took his right rib to create woman. He shaped her in as many days as it had taken him to shape Adam. He called her Eva Domêgasu.[31] He made them a couple and gave them as a dwelling place Koroteru.

The Gift of Rice
[The son and daughter of Adam] knew the way of carnal love, and the woman bore twins twelve times. This is why it is said: "The uniting of near relatives is not to be done."

Afterward, the children she had borne procreated; the children of their children in turn procreated, and they multiplied to the ends of the islands and the fords. There came a time when the lions and birds were no longer enough to feed them. Then it snowed nine cubits of deep snow. They turned toward heaven and prayed, saying: "Give us something to eat." As they were praying, Deus said to them from the heights of heaven: "Rub your palms together and taste." They rubbed the palms of their hands together, tasted, and found that they had a sweet taste in their mouths and no longer felt hungry.[32] One person of great virtue formed a little ball by rubbing his hands together and said: "Could this not be used as seed?" He planted the little ball in the nine cubits of deep snow, and when he came back to look after six months, the object had divided into four roots below and eight spikes above. And it bore fruit on eight sprigs. The following year it produced nine *koku* of grain.[33] Then they sang a song of joy and its text was this: "How good is the rice, the rice this year: on eight spikes it bears eight *koku*, and at the very tip more than nine *koku* of rice; it is the granary of the eight fruits.[34]

In this way they rejoiced. This rice they buried in the valley and in the heights, and when they came back to look at it the next year, what they had planted in the valley had produced rice, and what they had planted in the highlands had given barley, pearl and grain millet, buckwheat, and other grains. There was food in abundance.

The Flood

Afterward, humans became more and more numerous; they all began to steal; their greed was insatiable. They turned to evil, and evil acts multiplied and worsened without cease. Then Deus had pity on them and sent King Happamaruji the following message: "When the eyes of the temple dog[35] become red, this world will be destroyed by a tidal wave." The king went to the temple every day, and between these visits he built a hollow boat on a tall mountain.

The children of the temple school assembled and saw the way the king worshiped the temple dog. They asked him: "Why do you worship the temple dog?" The king replied: "When the dog's

eyes become red, this island will be destroyed by a tidal wave."
Then the children started to laugh. They said: "Ah, that is a joke. If
someone paints them, they will be red right away. It is unthinkable
that an island of two thousand miles could be destroyed." And they
painted the dog's eyes.

Happamaruji came to the temple as usual, he saw the red eyes
of the temple dog, he was afraid, and he had his six children get
into the hollow boat, which was all ready. With great regret, he left
the eldest behind, for his legs were not sound. Immediately, an immense wave overtook sky and earth, and in an instant all became a
vast sea. The temple dog whose eyes the children had painted
walked on the sea; it came bearing on its back the brother who had
been abandoned and put him on the boat. Then they rowed with
planks and spoons[36] as though they could see the island of ten
thousand miles which is Arioshima.[37] They rowed toward the island
to take refuge there. Even today the race called *peiron* is a replaying
of this episode.[38]

The Choosing of Maruya

There was in the country of Roson a king named San Chisenasu.
There was also in this country the daughter of a carpenter named
Kichié; her name was Maruya. At the age of three she was separated from her mother and lost her father. When she would play, as
a child, she would take the blame for the naughtiness of others, and
when she took the consequences it was said: "Maruya is a very
naughty child." But since this happened repeatedly, it was seen that
she had taken responsibility for the naughtiness of others; her in-
nocence was quite clear, and all at once she became venerated. Her
beauty was beyond compare. When she was seven years old she
began to study, and at twelve she had already made great progress.

One day she wondered: "If I think earnestly about the state of
the world, what can I do, I who have been born into the world of
human beings, for the salvation of the world to come?" No sooner
had she thought this than she received from heaven, oh miracle, the
following instruction: "If you remain a virgin all your life, to fulfill
the position of a *biruzen*, you will obtain salvation at once." Then
the young girl Maruya rejoiced; she fell to her knees and prayed. It

is then that she instituted the *orasho* repeated twelve times. The position of a *biruzen*, for a woman, consists of never in her life touching the body of her husband. She made her vow before the world and before heaven, and from that moment on she was the *biruzen* Maruya.

But it happened that the king of Roson was seeking a wife. And there was no one he found pleasing. Then someone came before him and said: "Maruya, the daughter of a carpenter of this country, is beyond doubt the daughter of a man of humble means, but to be the king's wife no other surpasses her." The king said: "And even if she is the daughter of a man of humble means, if she is beautiful, no more need be said." The king sent as envoys to Maruya's house the highest dignitaries of the court. Maruya's grandfather accepted with deference the proposals they put to him. He said: "For a daughter, there is no higher destiny than to become the wife of the king, and there is no greater joy for her relatives. I submit to your will." But Maruya said to the king's representatives: "I am not at all in agreement, and I cannot be content with this answer." The others, however, said: "Let us go, none of this prattle." And they pushed her into a sedan chair to bring her before the king.

When the king saw her, he was greatly pleased. He said: "You are even more beautiful than I had been told. From now on you must follow me." Maruya replied: "I respect your will, but since I have made an important vow regarding my person, I must not sully my body." The king said: "If you have made an important vow, it is well that you fulfill it first." "I cannot." "Then take a substitute." "That is not possible either." The king said: "However much you desire, I can satisfy you." Maruya answered: "The power of a king is nothing extraordinary; it partakes only of the greatness of this world. This world is only a temporary lodging; what is important is salvation in the world to come." The king said to her: "Then what is your rank? I hold the rank of king, and I am going to demonstrate it to you right now."

From his treasury he had brought forth gold, silver, rice money,[39] of course, but also damask brocaded with gold and silver, brocades from China, lengths of purple wool ten *ken*[40] square, coral, small incense boxes made of lapis lazuli, sculptures in agate and amber, flagons of perfumes based in essence of musk and aloe wood. The king's great hall, covered with gold and silver, was magnificent to see, and the treasures were stacked up as far as the eye could see. Maruya said to the king: "This has nothing to do with power. These are only treasures of this world; when one becomes used to them, they are no good any longer. Now I am going to show you my power."

Then she ran to the end of the veranda, purified herself by rinsing her mouth, turned toward heaven, made a vow, and prayed in her heart: "Let me now work a miracle." She prayed, heaven heard her, and after a moment fresh food appeared on four small tables.[41] Maruya bowed and said: "Do you mind?" and then calmly drew the meal toward her. Astonished, the king addressed Maruya and said to her: "Work more miracles." Maruya answered him: "I can work many more. What is your wish?" The king said: "Myself, I wish nothing in particular; do whatever you will." Maruya replied: "It is now the sixth month, the hottest time; what would you say if I made it snow?" "That would be wonderful," said the king with joy.

As Maruya prayed, turning toward heaven, to the north there formed a black cloud which unexpectedly spread out with great speed. Then, falling from the sky, snow piled up in the wink of an eye; its flakes were as fat as balls three inches wide. There was a great stir in the royal palace: "Kindle the hearth fires." "It is cold." "Fool, I am freezing in my light clothing." "Hie, bring out the quilted bedding and night clothing."

In the midst of the commotion, Maruya fled. A chariot of flowers descended from heaven, and she stepped into it and went up to heaven.

The Nativity

In the middle of the eleventh month, [Maruya] chanced to arrive in the country of Beren. A thick snow was falling without letup. She looked around for a place to shelter her body for a while, and behold, she saw a small stable for cows and horses. "What good fortune," she thought, and crouched down in a corner. She was in pain. In the middle of the day, as of the eighth hour, she observed *zejin*,[42] and around midnight she gave birth to a child: this was the Lord.

Since it was the cold season, the Lord, the Very High, was soon stiff with cold. Since they were in a stable, Maruya placed him in the manger, then went to purify her body in the river.[43] When she returned, she saw that the breath exhaled by the cows and the breath exhaled by the horses had warmed the infant. Thus the Mother, Santa Maruya, said: "Since cows and horses have shown such compassion on a being who is not a domestic animal, they must not be eaten on the day *kuwaruta.*" This is the reason one observes *zejin* on the day *kuwaruta:* this is the day one must eat neither beast nor fowl.

When the night gave way to dawn, the wife of the master of the house came out and saw Maruya: "On so cold a night, you have been happily delivered, but you must have suffered greatly. I beg you, come into our house right away." So saying, she had her come in and took care of her in every way. She broke the loom and the spinning wheel into pieces, threw them into the fire, and thus warmed the mother's body. Then she prepared a meal of buckwheat noodles and rice. While she served it to her, the infant came away from his mother's breast and held out his empty hand. From that moment on she took the name Santa Maruya the Mother.

The Magi

Some hours from there, the king of Turkey, Mancho, the king of Mexico, Gasubaru, and the king of France, Botuzaru, all three received a divine mission. They hid their faces under deep bamboo hats and set off, one from fifty miles, another from thirty miles away. Yet, by a miracle, it happened that they all met on their journey. When they compared and calculated, they found that all three had left on the same day. A happy coincidence, they thought, and they traveled on together. They made haste for the rest of the journey, their eyes fixed on the star that showed them which direction to follow, and they soon arrived in the country of Beren. Since that country was under the dominion of the emperor Yorutetsu,[44] they decided to go and see him and make inquiries of him. All three presented themselves before him, saying: "We have received a message saying that there has been born in this land a lord who has come from heaven, and this is the reason for our coming. Let us know, please, where he may be found." Yorutetsu answered: "This news has not yet reached my ears." The three kings said again: "Would it please Yorutetsu to come with us to worship him?" Yorutetsu said: "Oh no, I shall not go. You three go to him first." Then they said: "Good, that is what we shall do."

They went away together, but when they looked up, ah, what ill luck! Look! The star that they were to follow was no longer visible: "Ah, it must be because we went to present ourselves there. What a pity!" The three kings raised their hands to the sky and prayed. Suddenly the star reappeared, so near that one could have seized it in the hand. The words they spoke on this occasion became the prayer that is recited on one's knees. Then they followed the star that guided them, and as they made haste, they soon arrived.

When they had worshiped him, the infant, who was thirteen days old, said to them: "As the place where you stopped is the home of a wicked man, the road by which you came is also a road of the wicked. That is why it has disappeared; it is no more. That is why I intend to create a triple road that will depart from here and by which you will return." The child spoke, and in an instant the divine Floating Bridge spread in three directions, preparing three different paths for the three kings.[45] Each one followed it back to his country as it had been foretold.

The Arrest of Zezusu

Around this time some peasants in the country of Beren went out to hunt lions. They took a sheep, placed a rope around its neck, and when they pulled it along in that fashion the sheep was in great fear. "Let us do likewise," said the pursuers. They knotted a cord around the neck of the Very High and pulled him along as though he were a sheep:[46] "Haste, haste, haste! Go on!" they said, and at the same time beat him from behind with a stick: "Slower, you rogue!" Amid such curses they led him on farther and farther with brutal force, without regard for his pitiable, lamentable state. They pulled him as one pulls a sheep. Soon they dragged him before King Yorutetsu.

Yorutetsu looked at the pursuers and said to them: "I thank you for your trouble. You must be very careful with that man, for I have heard that he performs wicked deeds, at his pleasure. Tie him to that pillar of stone." The others said: "At your orders!" and tied him as they had been ordered.

"Break his bones[47] as well," they said, and they began to strike him so hard that the bamboo staffs broke to pieces. They made him drink a bitter and biting potion,[48] and on his head they placed a crown made of a ring of iron. The flow of blood that streamed down his body was like a waterfall. Yorutetsu was in a rage. He said: "Because it is his fault that the lives of tens of thousands of children were taken, make a scaffold of thirty-three *ken*, drag him to the top of Karuwaryu,[49] and nail him to the cross." Then they dragged him outside.

Money Blinds

Yorutetsu said over and over: "Soldiers, kill him quickly." The soldiers obeyed him; they took their unsheathed swords in hand and tried with all their might to run him through. But their bodies were paralyzed, their hands and feet failed them, and they could not manage it.[50]

A blind man was passing by just then. They said to him: "You there, blind man, there is a crucified man here. If you give him the final blow, we will give you money. Well? Will you?" The blind man said: "If you show me the way to do it, I will give him the final blow." Then the samurai of the guard showed him exactly what he was to do. "I understand," said the man. He did as he had been shown and ran the crucified man through in one stroke, from the left flank to the right shoulder.[51] A rush of blood spurted forth and reached the eyes of the blind man. And behold, oh miracle, both his eyes suddenly opened. "Wondrous! Wondrous! The world has now become bright.[52] Had I given the final blow to the criminal a little faster, my eyes would have opened even sooner," he said.

Then the Very High said: "The blind will not be saved in the world to come." Since this blind man felt joy at giving the final blow, and received money in recompense, his eyes failed again and became as before. This is the source of the saying that money makes one blind.

The Last Judgment

Since the tens of thousands of children who had been killed in the preceding years by King Yorutetsu were wandering in Koroteru, the Very High gave them names and had them rise with him to Baräso. He also made rise into heaven, all together, the innkeeper who had sheltered him at the moment of his birth, the three kings who had come from three countries, the peasants who had helped him, and the water carrier Beronike.[53] All of them together, we are told, he made come to him in Baräso.

Maruya, the Mother, said to Deus: "That man whom I made my husband on earth and who died of longing and love for me while I was in the position of *biruzen*, please let him partake of salvation too." And he was immediately saved. Deus made them a couple and accorded them a rank. This rank was called *on-mi-ni-zejusu*.[54]

It is said that in addition he gave to Beronike the water carrier the rank of *anesude*[55] and assured forever the efficacy of her prayers in favor of this world.[56]

Chapter Six

The "Galilean" Revolution in Seventeenth-Century Japanese Art

The Japan that the Dutch encountered after 1640 was considerably changed. From 1603 on, the Tokugawas succeeded one another as shoguns almost without a ripple; the fall of the Osaka castle in 1615 and the extermination of the descendants of Hideyoshi had long since put an end to the bloody civil wars of the preceding period. The foreign missionaries had been chased out, and most of Japanese Christendom were forced to abjure the faith or were massacred. The remaining secret Christians, subsisting on the islands and in the mountains of Kyushu, no longer represented a danger. The *bakufu*, or military government, owned one-fourth of the country's land and all its mines, had a monopoly on the minting of money, and controlled all the large cities. The *daimyo*, or high lords, had a certain amount of autonomy in their own realms but were at the mercy of the shogun: he could confiscate their land at will, or displace, enlarge, or reduce their fiefs. All the *daimyo* had to reside half the year, or one year in two, with the shogun at Edo to pay him tribute. The merchants from the Dutch East India Company, confined to the tiny island of Deshima in Nagasaki harbor, also had to go to Edo once a year to pay their respects to the shogun.

From the mid-seventeenth to the late eighteenth century, the warrior class (*bushi*) grew progressively more impoverished. This was, however, the best-educated class, and it was to the skills of the *bushi* that the *daimyo* and the shogun had recourse when in need. A large number of these fiefless warriors (whether they had been dispossessed of their land or had rid themselves of it intentionally) came to be *ronin*, "warriors without a master." They became, depending on bent or circumstances, teachers, artists, wandering monks, or brigands. The merchant and artisan classes, on the other hand, were rapidly gaining in wealth during this time. This wealth engendered a strong demand for cultural goods, which the great writers did everything to satisfy; among them were the novelist Ihara Saikaku (1642–93), the playwright Chikamatsu Monzaemon (1653–1724), and the poet Matsuo Basho (1644–94). The richest and most active cities at the time were Osaka, a large commercial center through which passed all the rice in the country, as well as oil, wood, fertilizer, and metals; and Edo, where artisans' workshops and commercial establishments proliferated to meet the needs of the *daimyo* who spent half their time there.

Tokugawa Yoshimune, who came to power in 1716, was the first shogun to open Japan to the exterior. He made significant economic, fiscal, and administrative reforms and, to spur the renewal of his country, surrounded himself with men of science concerned more with utility than with speculative research. He also decided to cautiously address the West. In 1720 he lifted the prohibition on books written by Chinese Jesuits, provided they did not contain religious propaganda; most of the authorized works treated astronomy and geography. It was also around this time that the "ambassadors" the Dutch East India Company sent from Nagasaki to Edo each year began to be taken seriously. Until then, these visits had mainly benefited the Western scientists who sometimes joined the delegation, such as Willem ten Rhijne, then Engelbert Kaempfer, beginning in the latter half of the seventeenth century. The interpreters from Nagasaki, for their part, had long profited from all the small innovations and practical formulas they could glean from their daily tasks on Deshima.

Not content to have books brought from China, Yoshimune took a personal interest in what his guests brought with them. He questioned them and ordered books, medicines, plants, exotic animals, scientific instruments such as telescopes, and clocks to measure time. The artisans of Nagasaki began to construct imitations of these objects. Noro Genjo (1693–1761) and Aoki Konyo (1698–1769), two of the shogun's scientists who had already taken an interest in what the Dutch had to offer, were given the respective tasks of examining the works of Western natural history now in the shogun's library and of studying the Dutch language, its vocabulary and syntax. The year was 1740: the Dutch had been on Deshima for one hundred years.

The Dutch in Nagasaki

The Dutch presence in Nagasaki was quite unlike that of the Christian mission of the late sixteenth and early seventeenth centuries: the Dutch were not in Japan to win souls or gain knowledge; they were there to do business, and it was on this express condition that they were allowed to remain. Moreover, for them Deshima was only one more link in an immense net spread from the Baltic to the Levant, from the Americas to the Cape of Good Hope and Batavia.

The founders of the Dutch East India Company were staunch Calvinists, but they were more concerned with their struggle to best the Spanish powers on land and sea than with disputing the empire of souls with the Jesuits and the Franciscans. After the fall of Anvers in 1585, Calvinists and dissenters of all sorts who deserted the southern Netherlands either rejoined like-minded comrades in Holland and Zeeland or dispersed across northern Europe. For the most part rich, they reinforced by local support the oligarchy that monopolized power in the western Netherlands, or lent it the network of family and associates they had already established throughout the world. The East India Company (VOC) was founded in 1602. It was managed by a council of seventeen directors who could, at will, make treaties, construct fortifications, mount defensive wars, and recruit civilian and military personnel. They swore allegiance to the company and to the States General at the same time. By the middle of the seventeenth century, the Dutch had become the greatest trading nation in the world.

By the third quarter of the seventeenth century, however, decline had set in. The enterprise in effect fell victim to its own success. Those who had launched it, all too pleased to collect the profits, soon lost the spirit that had been its driving force. In 1677 a witness compared the soldiers and sailors the VOC maintained on its more than two hundred ships to "wild boars." Drunkards, debauchers, and thieves, they were treated as beasts by their own officers. Many, moreover, were not Dutch. They were adventurers mainly from Scandinavian and Germanic countries; there were even good Catholics among them. But all had a single desire: to get rich quickly, by any means.

One reads in the 1774 edition of Abbot Raynal's *Philosophical History of the Two Indies*, regarding the Deshima trading syndicate:

> Since 1641, [the Dutch] have been relegated to the artificial island of Deshima, built in the harbor of Nagasaki and linked to the city by a bridge. Their ships are disarmed as soon as they arrive, and the powder, guns, swords, artillery, even the rudder, are brought to land. In this sort of prison, they are treated with unimaginable disdain, and are permitted no communication except with the administrators in charge of regulating the price and quantity of their merchandise. The patience with which they have suffered this treatment for over a century cannot have failed to debase them in the eyes of the nation witnessing it, and the love of profit that has induced in them such numbness to these outrages must surely have corrupted their character.[1]

It must be said in their defense that these merchants, soldiers, and sailors endured atrocious living conditions on board their ships. In the late seventeenth century, out of every three hundred men who left Holland for Asia, eighty to one hundred died en route or deserted. It is understandable that in the eighteenth century very few citizens of the United Provinces, even among the laboring classes, would be tempted by overseas adventure. Little by little, those who had capital to invest stopped risking it on VOC trade. It was asserted in 1758 that Dutch creditors held a third of the total debt owed by England, which had taken over as the top commercial power in the world; they no longer invested in naval armaments for their own country, too risky a bet, or in local industry, which yielded too little profit. The war that broke out in 1780 between Holland and England would be the company's ruin.

The "Holland" that had charmed so many of the Japanese in the eighteenth century was thus a myth, having very little to do with what they saw at Deshima or at Edo during the envoys' annual visit to the shogun. When the Swedish naturalist Carl Peter Thunberg, then serving as a physician with the VOC, lived in Deshima in 1775–76, he found on the island, mingled with the Dutch sailors, Swedes, Danes, Germans, and even Portuguese and Spaniards, to say nothing of thirty-four slaves of various origins. But those who chanced to be intelligent, educated, and curious like himself, ten Rhijne and Kaempfer in their time and later Titsingh and Siebold, stood out in such contrast to the enclave's general population that the Japanese gave them an extraordinarily warm welcome: their admiration for them was as extreme as their disdain for the others. Thunberg, indeed, shared this disdain. He especially reproached the Dutch for their failure, in one hundred thirty years, to produce even a rudimentary dictionary. The one he used was a Portuguese-Japanese dictionary printed by the Jesuits in the late sixteenth century and handed down in a family of interpreters from father to son.[2]

In their isolation on Deshima, the native-born or naturalized Dutch suffered less from moral and intellectual privation, of which they most likely had little consciousness, than from sexual privation. Only prostitutes were allowed to enter the enclave. They were, of course, under guard, as were the interpreters, and both contributed to the Japanese authorities' surveillance of the tiny island. The women who frequented the Dutch were not those who frequented the Chinese, and neither of these groups of women frequented the Japanese. The Dutch, for their part, used the women to send into town all sorts of contraband merchandise, sold at exorbitant prices. There were few if any Dutch women in Deshima before the early nineteenth century.[3]

Henri Mechoulan has shown quite ably the major role played by the lust for profit and the mercantile mind in transforming seventeenth-century Holland into one of the most brilliant centers of intellectual freedom the modern world has known.[4] Voltaire had already remarked of England in the tenth of his *Letters on England:* "The trade that enriched England's citizens contributed to making them free, and this freedom in turn spread the trade; this has shaped its greatness as a State." The same was true of Holland.

The freedom in question had little to do with the spirit of tolerance, of course. As Diderot would note in his *Voyage de Hollande*, "The [Dutch] nation is superstitious and inimical to philosophy and free religious thought."[5] The strict Calvinism espoused by the dominant oligarchy was no less obscurantist in practice than the theological philosophy taught at the University of Coimbra in the sixteenth century. This became obvious when the 1618–19 synod of Dordrecht expelled all members who did not believe, as Calvin did, in predestination. It was even more striking when Holland's Chief Advocate, Johan van Oldenbarnevelt (1547–1619), was executed by order of Maurice of Nassau because the statesman—along with dissident reformers but also Catholics and Lutherans—opposed the takeover of the church and state by a single faction, even a majority one.

But in a country where the commodity reigned supreme, everything was up for barter, even freedom of conscience. Thus, despite Dordrecht and the example made of van Oldenbarnevelt, the Remonstrant and Counter-Remonstrant reformists and the Lutherans—as well as Jews, Mennonites, and Unitarians—grew accustomed to cohabitation. This was in the interest of their own communities, of course, and in that of the society as a whole; Calvinism continued to be dominant but never became the state religion.

Artistically, seventeenth-century Holland reached a brilliant luster in the cities where the merchant middle class held sway. This lasted until the Glorious Revolution of 1688, up to the moment William and Mary took the throne of England. It was a supreme century for painting. Holland had neither princes nor cardinals nor great lords to commission monumental projects of sculpture or architecture; on the other hand, it was overflowing with fine houses where paintings of beauty and excellence were collected and hung on the walls. Landscape, portrait, and genre paintings charmed the good burghers of Holland. In these works they could admire themselves at leisure: here was the idealized image of what they wanted to be, the frame they wished to give their existence forevermore. The taste for simplicity imposed by their religious moralism was readily satisfied by the apparently commonplace subjects depicted, provided their concern for quality was not violated by mediocre workmanship. The more down-to-earth the subject matter, the finer the execution had to be.

But the great masters of seventeenth-century Dutch painting—Frans Hals, who died in 1666; Rembrandt, dead in 1669; Vermeer, dead in 1675—were to have no successors. After the Peace of Ryswick (1697) and again after the treaties of Utrecht, which put an end to the Spanish War of Succession (1713–15), the influence of French culture began to increase in Holland. The influx of French refugees after the revocation of the Edict of Nantes (1685) gave greater impetus to this trend.

Eighteenth-century Holland also had numerous artists, but for them the quest for refinement outweighed the concern for authenticity. The same forms were reproduced in surfeit, to the detriment of the originality that had characterized the "Old" Masters. "Artists seem to have been contaminated by the spirit of the Dutch patricians of the time, who were for the most part independently wealthy and no longer entrepreneurs; they preferred to live on the dividends from their capital, which were substantial, rather than try new adventures."[6]

Flemish art underwent a similar downturn after the taking of Anvers by Alessandro Farnese, and especially after the Treaty of Münster (1648), under which the Flemish were made subject to the crown of Spain, then that of Austria. "Originality in composition ceased to be an aspiration. Painters drew their themes from other works or imitated their own creations. All these productions were sold as original works on the art market. . . . The industrialization of art was indisputably the cause of its decline. This was already apparent in the second half of the seventeenth century."[7]

IMAGES OF THE FLOATING WORLD, FLOWERS AND BIRDS

What could the refined and subtle Japanese artists who created the art of etching, known as *ukiyo-e*, expect from the louts holed up on Deshima or, more broadly, from eighteenth-century Flemish and Dutch art, then in total decline?

In the early eighteenth century, the merchant class had become indispensable to the *bakufu* and the samurais, but its members did not call the tune the way their Dutch counterparts had in Amsterdam in the middle of the previous century. The military mistrusted them and kept the class on a tight leash. Foreign to the court culture that perpetuated the great classical tradition, the merchant class threw itself into the quest for pleasure, creating a demand for a multiplicity of light, unpretentious artworks. Towns, gardens, houses of pleasure, and theaters became settings for endless amusements. The artists themselves enjoyed deploying the thousand and one actors in the social comedy: courtesans, kabuki actors, romantic lovers at play, women poets and shamisen players, women in the bath or on a stroll, at the temple, daydreaming by their windows, or making a fool of some graybeard.

The art of the xylograph had been invented in China under the Han dynasty, at the beginning of the common era. It spread to Japan along with Buddhism, beginning in the eighth century, and for a long time remained confined to the didactic function to which Buddhism had relegated it, the dissemination of pious images.

The first artist to draw and print on individual sheets etchings suitable for the highly secular tastes of the merchants of Edo was Hishikawa Moronobu (1631–94). Early in the last quarter of the seventeenth century he established a trade that would prosper until the early twentieth. Later, in the eighteenth century, came Okumura Masanobu (1686–1764). A book trader, publisher, and engraver, he published his own works and presented them as series in album form. He was the first to attempt to imitate Dutch engravings in perspective *(uki-e)*. In the same period Nishimura Shigenaga (1697–1756) successfully used *uki-e* and painted flowers and birds *(kacho-ga)*, also inspired by Western painting via China.

In 1745 Suzuki Harunobu (1725–70) began using the process of printing colors in several passes, which he had not invented but to which he lent a decisive boost. These "brocade images" *(nishiki-e)* with rich, deep colors on high-quality paper became extremely popular. His disciple Shiba Kokan (1747–1818) continued in the same vein. In about 1782 Kokan conceived a passion for Dutch engravings, which arrived in Edo as contraband, and began to study the European art books that enthusiasts were beginning to collect. In this way he rediscovered the techniques of oil painting and copperplate engraving, forgotten since the time of Giovanni Niccolò.[8]

The end of the century was dominated by Kitagawa Utamaro (1753–1806). His first albums, especially *The Book of Insects* (1788) and *The Book of Birds* (1789), earned him a solid reputation at once. His

Johann Elias Ridinger and Martin Elias Ridinger,
Falconer with Hooded Hawk Sighting a Heron.
© *Bibliothèque nationale de France, Paris*

Wakasugi Isohachi,
The Equestrian Falconer,
oil on canvas (126.9 × 50 cm).
© *Academy of Fine Arts, Tokyo*

Utagawa Toyoharu, *View of the Grand Canal, Venice*, hand-colored woodcut, late eighteenth century. © *National Museum of Tokyo*

Antonio Visentini, *View of the Grand Canal of Venice* (after Canaletto)

Hans Vredemans de Vries, *Perspective*.
© *Bibliothèque nationale de France, Paris*

Okumura Masanobu, *The Nakamura Theater: Edo*,
ca. 1740, hand-colored woodcut. © *Municipal Museum of Kobe*

Ambrosius Bosschaert the Elder,
Bouquet in Arched Window, ca. 1620
(64 × 46 cm). *Photo: C. Mauritshuis,
The Hague, Inv. n° 679*

Tani Buncho, *Flowers and Birds*,
copy on paper of a copy of
a lost painting by W. F. van Royen
(232.8 × 106 cm).
© *Municipal Museum of Kobe*

Shiba Kokan, *The Serpentine River, Hyde Park, London*,
hand-colored copperplate engraving, late eighteenth century. © *Municipal Museum of Kobe*

図之藍伽ノカスシラフ花蘭門

Utagawa Toyoharu (?), *The Roman Forum*, hand-colored copperplate engraving, early nineteenth century. © *Museum für Ostasiatische Kunst, Cologne. Inv. no. R 10.6. Photo: Rheinisches Bildarchiv, Cologne* talents of observation were equally acute, whether trained on the courtesans of the Yoshiwara district or on flora and fauna.

The very end of the eighteenth century saw the birth of the Utagawa school, which in the nineteenth century would dominate the market for *ukiyo-e* etchings. Its founder, Utagawa Toyoharu (1735–1814), had trained at the Kano school. At Edo, he was fascinated by the works of *uki-e* masters such as Masanobu and began to specialize in that genre. He produced mainly landscapes inspired by Dutch engravings. His contemporaries saw with new eyes familiar landscapes whose depth and breadth had never been hinted at before. Through him they also discovered exotic sites entirely unknown to them. The Japanese, who for one hundred fifty years had not been permitted to leave their country, could now, thanks to Toyoharu, dream of an elsewhere all the more seductive in that it was, for the artist himself, almost entirely imaginary.[9]

Nagasaki and Edo were the principal poles of Japanese painting in the seventeenth and eighteenth centuries. But Nagasaki owed this status to the Chinese rather than the Dutch. The Chinese, in fact, had been authorized to establish a trading syndicate in Nagasaki as of 1688, and from the start they enjoyed a much greater freedom than the Dutch. The merchandise arriving in Japan through these merchants was also inspected by administrators, some of them specifically delegated to oversee artworks coming from China and the West. The special inspectors' office was hereditary, like that of the interpreters, and among the four families who from generation to generation fulfilled this function true artists occasionally appeared; their competence was acknowledged by an official title. None of them, however, seems to have taken an interest in Western art as such: Chinese works of art were much more numerous in Nagasaki, and what became known as the Nagasaki school was largely oriented toward China.

But the Chinese in Nagasaki were not ghettoized as were the Dutch on Deshima. They received visits from their compatriots from the continent, and Chinese painters would come to Japan to engage in their art. The most illustrious of them was Shen Nan-p'in (in Japanese, Chin Nampin), who lived in Nagasaki in 1731–32. Chin Nampin (ca. 1682–1780) was never well known in his own country, but in Japan he achieved renown within a few months and his fame endured long after his departure. It is interesting that he owed his success not so much to the subjects he painted (flowers and birds, a genre that had been cultivated for a very long time in China) as to the way he painted them. Like many artists of his generation, he had been influenced by the Western Jesuits established in China. They were under the protection of the emperor Kang Hsi (1655–1723), and in the eighteenth century the Society of Jesus could boast of having an official painter at the Peking court, Father Giuseppe Castiglione, alias Lang Shih-ning (1688–1766). The Jesuits in China were not unaware of perspective and chiaroscuro, and they knew how to incorporate them into traditional Chinese art without jarring the sensibilities of the people who were calling on their talents. This can be seen in a vertical panel by Father Castiglione preserved in the Musée Guimet, showing Emperor Chien Lung sitting before his palace amid the dignitaries of his court. The drawing is very stylized, the background treated in the Chinese manner, but the perspective is quite marked and the finely modeled faces seem to resemble their subjects. Indeed, it was for this that Castiglione's art was most appreciated at the Peking court.

This novelty was also pleasing in Nagasaki. Chin Nampin immediately acquired numerous pupils, and after his departure he maintained the movement he had inspired by sending many more of his paintings from China to his friends, clients, and admirers. His influence extended through Japan well beyond Kyushu, and scarcely an eighteenth-century artist of note was not touched by it in some way.

Chin Nampin's influence was relayed to Edo by So Shiseki (1712–86). He had traveled to Nagasaki in 1740 and studied painting there with a pupil of the Chinese master. In the work of Shiseki and other representatives of the Nagasaki school, such as Kakutei (1722–85), or even individualists such as Wakasugi Isohachi (1759–1805), Western technique merged so well with Chinese style that those who appreciated the "flowers and birds" genre in this period often did not see the difference. One must not underestimate the role of these often humble, even improbable, cultural intermediaries in the transmission of ideas and forms from one end of the world to the other. The surprising thing is to find among them, behind the emblematic figure of Chin Nampin, one of the Bateren Japan believed it had banished forever.[10] It is true that the Jesuits in China were no longer quite what they had been a century earlier in Japan: their artists were not bound in their work to a "program" as restrictive and ideologically charged as the one set out by Valignano in *De missione legatorum*. They had first to meet the expectations of the Chinese commissioning the art and secondarily to work for the glory of their order.[11]

IN PEDDLERS' BASKETS

Given that neither the Dutch nor the Japanese had any particular goal in organizing their cultural exchanges, for a long time the interchange was directed solely by chance. This explains the disparate character of the objects the merchants brought and the uneven quality of works that entered Japanese libraries through them. The works come from various places, and their dates range from the sixteenth century, at the earliest, to the time of their acquisition. When a noticeable trend finally emerges in these exchanges, it is due to increasingly precise demands by the Japanese, not to the merchants' offerings, which remain entirely haphazard. Moreover, the known titles of Western works that reached Japan between 1640 and the end of the eighteenth century form an inventory that is far from complete: no records were kept, many books have no doubt been lost, and given the customary secretiveness of collectors, in Japan as elsewhere, some may yet slumber in their hiding places.

Aside from books about medicine and surgery, which merit special treatment, the first illustrated Western book to enter a Japanese library was one written by Jan Jonston (1603–75), *Naeukeurige Beschrijving van de Natuur der Viervoetige Dieren, Vissen en Bloedlooze Water-Dieren, Vogelen, Kronkel-Dieren, Slangen en Draken* (Natural History of Animals), published in 1660 in Amsterdam. The head of the Deshima outpost made a present of it to the shogun Tokugawa Ietsuna in 1663. Its abundant illustrations were everything in the eyes of Ietsuna. Yoshimune, who found the book in his predecessor's library in 1717, was astounded at the plasticity of the forms represented and the artful way in which light and shadow produced the illusion of volume. Later, in 1768, another copy of Jonston's book was acquired at great cost by a *ronin* of extraordinary curiosity and talent, Hiraga Gennai

(1728–79). It was only then, more than one hundred years after arriving in Japan, that Jonston became a source of inspiration to scientists and artists.

Even in 1663 the book was not new: the first edition, in Latin, had been in print in Frankfurt from 1649 to 1653. The author, born in Posnania into an old Scottish family, had studied medicine and natural history in several universities in Germany, Holland, and Scotland. After becoming a doctor of medicine at the University of Leiden (1632), he spent the rest of his life in Silesia. There he wrote his *Natural History of Animals.*[12]

In spite of the craze for the book in Japan in the latter half of the eighteenth century, it was of scant scientific value: many of the plates are copies of previous works (for example, by Aldrovandi, a sixteenth-century Italian naturalist), and several of the animals shown are creatures of pure fantasy. The hippopotamus has a bulldog's head and taloned feet and occupies the plate with a classical gryphon: bird in front, lion in back. A triton and a siren are depicted amid the fish. The world of reptiles is even more surprising: one finds two types of seven-headed hydra; a crowned basilisk with a rooster's beak, feet like those of a frog or toad, and a snake's tail, said to live "in the African solitudes"; and a wingless, two-footed dragon captured, it seems, in the countryside around Bologna.

The text accompanying these plates is sparse, consisting of a few prefatory pages indicating the beneficial uses of the animals described and the name of the animal on each plate, given in German and Latin. Nothing in this hodgepodge, typical of pre-Linnaean natural history, would be worthy of attention were it not for a certain number of plates, some done from life, bearing the signature of Matthäus Merian the Younger (1621–87). Merian belonged to a family that had already been made famous by his father, who was especially noted for his topographical engravings. Born in Basel, the younger artist had studied his art in Amsterdam, then in London, with van Dyck. He had also worked in Paris in the style of Champaigne, Vouet, Le Sueur, and Poussin, and like many artists from the northern countries he had made the pilgrimage to Italy, in 1643–47.[13] Thus it was Merian, the artist, not Jonston, the scientist, who elicited the admiration of Yoshimune, Gennai, and others. They showed rather good taste, considering that via Merian's engravings they were sometimes unknowingly coming into contact with the work of great masters such as Dürer or Rubens. Indeed, Jonston's rhinoceros is a reproduction of another famous plate bearing that title, engraved by Dürer in 1515 at the peak of his talent. As for the lion, it appears to have come originally from Rubens's *Daniel in the Lions' Den*, cropping up again in Jan Brueghel's *Paradise* as well as in sketches and engravings by other seventeenth-century Flemish and Dutch artists.[14] By happy accident or keen instinct, this lion and this rhinoceros, animals previously unknown in Japan, became the most highly valued of all the animals Jonston described.

In 1729 a real Dutch painting was given to Yoshimune. The artist was a painter of modest renown, Willem Frederik van Royen (1654–1723), but the piece seemed to embody the quintessence of Western art as assimilated by Chinese bird and flower painting, represented at the time in Japan by pupils of Chin Nampin. It showed a large bouquet of flowers of all seasons, very colorful, bursting and cascading from a large vase standing on a pedestal in an arched niche. At the foot of the vase, birds were shown pecking at fruit scattered on the ground. Yoshimune found the painting so beautiful that he placed it in a temple in Edo, where several generations of the Japanese admired it. Late in the century, a witness wrote: "No painting in the world can compare to the work of the Dutch in the representation of nature, and it is said that there is no more beautiful painting, even in Holland, than the painting of birds and flowers in the Rakan-ji temple at Honjo, Edo. The paint is softened by oil; it is applied not onto paper but onto silk fabric, which is why it is called in foreign countries *oil painting on silk.*" The original has been lost, but one can imagine it rather well by viewing the numerous still lifes of the same sort displayed in European museums. One example is the magnificent bouquet by Roelant Savery (1576–1639), painted in 1612 and now in the collection of the Principality of Liechtenstein at Vaduz: against a very dark background, a large blue iris dominates a bouquet of irises, tulips, roses, and peonies of all colors; insects gather nectar from it; at the foot of the vase are a fat bumblebee, a green lizard, a cricket, and a mouse, looking quite astonished to have encountered one another there. Or the painting by Ambrosius Bosschaert the Elder (1573–1621) titled *Bouquet in a Vaulted Window*, painted in about 1620 and now at the Mauritshuis in The

Hague. It, too, is a bouquet of flowers of all seasons, with a preponderance of tuliplike blooms, their nectar also at harvest by insects. Arranged on the windowsill, on either side of the vase, are seashells, cut flowers, and a large insect.[15]

The first book to be adapted from the Dutch by Noro Genjo on orders from the shogun, around 1750, was another work of natural history, one that seems utterly antiquated considering the date. Its author was Rembert Dodoens, alias Dodonaeus. He was born in Friesland in 1517 and died at Leiden in 1585. He thus lived a century earlier than Jonston. In the Dutch version studied by Genjo, the work was titled *Cruydt-Boek*, or *Book of Plants*. It was published in Anvers by Moretus in 1644, but the first edition of the book actually dated back to 1544. It was an odd compilation centering on more than seven hundred plates initially gathered by the botanist Leonard Fuchs. The printer Jan van der Loe, who owned the collection, had rounded them out with perhaps one hundred more and had asked Dodoens, who was not a botanist but a doctor, to write an accompanying text. Dodoens's chief contribution was to reorganize them according to the "natural" families of the plants, rather than in alphabetical order. This classification was not yet Linnaean order but the manifestation, at least, of a trend in that direction.

After working for van der Loe, Dodoens went on to Plantin and added to his *Cruydt-Boek* a new series of plates, closer to life. From a complex collaboration on the part of Dodoens, his French translator Charles de l'Écluse—alias Clusius, a pupil of Guillaume Rondelet—and Matthias de Lobel, from Lille, there emerged in 1568 a *General History of Plants* (Pemptades) in six parts, thirty books, and 840 chapters, describing 1,340 plants, classified generally according to their medical use at the time. The best plates of the assembled lot are in all likelihood the handiwork of Pierre van der Borcht. They are distinguished from Fuchs's initial plates by their technique. "In these works," says the historian of Flemish engraving A. J. J. Delen, "[the artist] has taken particular care to show the plant as completely as possible, in all its detail, one might say scientifically, but without losing sight for a moment of the aesthetic nature of the image. Meticulously observed, the figures possess a decorative aspect that is pleasing to the eye."[16]

Noro Genjo's adaptation, preserved in the National Archives of Tokyo, contains only one section of the *Cruydt-Boek* and none of the illustrations. It thus holds no interest for art historians except insofar as it might have stimulated those who had the means to buy the book and study the plates for themselves.[17]

As mentioned, Jonston's book had been bought in 1768 by Hiraga Gennai. Gennai was a brilliant jack-of-all-trades, part encyclopedist, part Rameau's nephew, who would take a keen interest in things Western from the moment there was the slightest loosening of the iron ring around the islet of Deshima. He built his first compass in 1755, after a model probably acquired in Nagasaki; bought Dutch, Chinese, and Cochinchinese ceramics to learn how domestic production might be improved; spent several years in a center for Confucian studies at Edo; studied medicinal herbs and plants with a naturalist; organized exhibits of Japan's natural resources; systematically researched the Dutch and Chinese curiosities available in Nagasaki to determine whether Japan held the same things; devoted himself to several mining expeditions; organized the extraction and refinement of sodium sulfate on the Izu Peninsula; studied the properties of asbestos and tried to make a fire-resistant fabric from it; became a sheepherder to make use of the wool; and took it into his head one day to build a balloon.

In 1773 Gennai traveled to Akita at the invitation of the lord of the realm, Satake Yoshiatsu (1748–86). Although a good two weeks' march northward from Edo and even more distant from Nagasaki, Akita had become, thanks to Yoshiatsu, an active artistic and cultural center. Yoshiatsu, who also had himself addressed by the name Shozan, was interested in painting, especially the genre cultivated at Nagasaki after Chin Nampin's historic stay in that city. Gennai, it seems, did not paint but had seen and read a great deal, and at Akita he taught the fundamentals of Western drawing.[18] He had begun this activity on his journey there by teaching Odano Naotake (1749–80), who was traveling with him. He also taught Satake Shozan and Satake Yoshimi (1749–1800). Thus was founded what would come to be known as the Akita school. As with the Nagasaki school, the goal was to be true to nature and to marry traditional Japanese techniques regarding paper and pigments with Western procedures for creating the illusion of perspective and volume. Retained from the "birds and flowers" genre was a taste for strong foregrounds, with a tree, plant, flower, or animal standing out boldly against a low horizon and a distant background. But thanks to

Gennai and to the "Dutch" models he had contemplated, something more was added, a concern with direct observation: the finished works of the Akita school are usually the end products of a long and patient preparation that was, as shown in several sketchbooks of studies, almost scientific.[19] Shozan and his friends were thus unknowingly rediscovering the great tradition of the European Renaissance, which their seventeenth-century Christian predecessors had bypassed all but unawares because their teachers, at the time, had not themselves discerned its enduringly innovative character.

Shozan left three essays on painting, written around 1778, one of which, *Gaho Koryo* (Elements of the Art of Painting), is said to be the first treatise on Western-style painting written in Japan. In it one reads: "A painting has value when it exactly represents the object depicted. Paintings of celestial or terrestrial objects, humans, flowers, or birds have value when all their details are faithfully reproduced. If a painting of a tiger looks more like a rock than an animal, people will laugh at it. . . . There is a theory that the spirit of a painting is more important than realistic representation; this conceit, however, loses sight of the true object of painting. In the end, how may one distinguish objects such as plants, trees, birds, animals, fish, seashells, insects, gold, precious stones, and earth, if their true shapes are not exactly represented?" Shozan's sketchbooks of studies, some of them from before his encounter with Gennai, for the most part contain drawings and engravings of flowers, plants, birds, insects, and reptiles, observed in nature.

In another 1778 essay, *Gato Rikai* (Understanding Painting and Composition), Shozan reproduces studies of perspective borrowed from a book by Gérard de Lairesse, *Het Groot Schilderboek* (The Big Book for Painters), published in Amsterdam in 1707.[20] Lairesse (1641–1711) was an engraver and painter from Liège who spent most of his life in Amsterdam. He wrote the book when he was past fifty. In it we find the quintessence of Dutch academicism as it existed in the last quarter of the seventeenth century, after the generation that had produced Rembrandt had faded away. It was a return to antiquity in the spirit of the French masters of the time, such as Poussin and Lebrun, decidedly more rational than the Fiamminghi of a century earlier. Translated into several languages and often reissued, Lairesse's book exerted a great influence on all of eighteenth-century Europe: it was still being reprinted in Paris in 1787. One sentence from it sums up his thinking: "Geometry is . . . the first step that leads us to drawing, and one can never really get there without it."[21] There is a blatant contradiction between Shozan's concern for a return to nature and his infatuation with Lairesse's treatise. The same contradiction is evidenced by eighteenth-century European theoreticians and art critics, who did not have the excuse, as did Shozan, of being limited to a single book.

For a long time the Akita school remained virtually unknown. As its representatives were of noble origin and had no need to sell their output to live, their work did not circulate on the art market. Even today, most of the pieces signed by Shozan or Yoshimi are in public or private collections in Akita. Naotake is the most famous of the group's members, because he lived for some time at Edo and because Hiraga Gennai and Satake Shozan liked to make presents of his works to their friends.[22]

Paradoxically, the genre that made the greatest and most lasting contibution to changing the way the Japanese looked at creatures and things was the least theoretical of all, the most free of prejudice, the most eager to please, and only to please. It is not known where or how Okumura Masanobu discovered the Dutch engravings that gave him the idea of introducing perspective into his "images of the floating world." Nor do we know which ones, precisely, were his models. It is agreed that his concept of perspective is close to that of Hans Vredeman de Vries (1527–1604/23), a painter and designer of architecture and ornaments, who was himself strongly influenced by Italian decorative painting and whose theories about perspective and architecture were disseminated throughout northern Europe. He first studied painting on glass, soon discovered the work of Vitruvius, and traveled all over central and northern Europe, as far as Danzig, Leipzig, and Prague. He never made the pilgrimage to Italy, but he was well acquainted with the various Italianate series preserved or published by Cock, his publisher in Anvers. Beginning in 1560 he published several series of scenographies, in 1577 a treatise on architecture in the style of Vitruvius, and in 1604–5, in The Hague and Leiden, a manual titled *Perspective*.[23] It contained studies of palaces, squares, and gardens in the Italian Renaissance style. Certain of the perspectives he proffered were absolutely dizzying and were often copied from him by artists with a taste for imaginary architecture.[24]

The wooden architecture of eighteenth-century Edo's pleasure houses and popular theaters confronted the eye with a multitude of vertical and horizontal lines that could be tiring. Masanobu saw the advantage of imitating Dutch engravings of de Vries's style, transforming an interplay of lines that usually cross perpendicularly on the image plane into an interplay of verticals, horizontals, and obliques that make the eye forget that the image is flat, leading it from one imaginary plane to the next and finally to an ideal point beyond which nothing more can be discerned. He put this way of seeing to use in a 1740 hand-colored woodcut depicting the Nakamura Theater in Edo. The orchestra and loge are full of spectators of both sexes who chat with each other, eat, drink, and stroll beneath bulging paper lanterns hanging from the ceiling. In the vast hall, lit by daylight from above, the show is everywhere, including on stage where a Kabuki actor holds forth, sitting on a sort of dais in the middle ground. At stage left, a servant waves a fan. At stage right, musicians and chorists crouch. Still farther off, glimpsed through an open screen, is the setting of the play, Mount Fuji, its size diminished by distance.

Masanobu, who was not a theoretician and had never read anything on perspective, did not understand its rules. Thus there are several perspectives in his print. The summit of Mount Fuji is indeed at the crossing point of the image's bisectors, but the diagonals do not all converge toward it. Yet what for the theoretician is an error, the artist has used to unquestionable practical advantage. Before a rigorously three-dimensional print, the eye would not "forget" only that it is flat; it would be tempted to forget as well the "compartments" in which the multiform spectacle in the hall is taking place, to return always to the center, even though it is less important than the periphery. In *The Nakamura Theater*, on the contrary, there is every inducement for the eye to wander at its own leisure and rhythm among all the dimensions of the image.[25]

The *optique*, which probably arrived from Europe via China in the early eighteenth century, soon brought great popularity to the *uki-e* genre. The *optique* was a very simple machine that came in two versions. One was a magnifying glass mounted on a stand, through which one observed, via a mirror inclined at a forty-five-degree angle, an image placed on the ground with its upper edge tilted toward the viewer. The other was a camera obscura–style box having a hole fitted with a lens through which one viewed an image slipped vertically into the back of the box.

These devices were all the rage in Europe from the middle of the eighteenth century up to about 1830. A popular art sprang up, the production of *vues d'optique* for use with the machine. The scenes shown were often topographies of famous sites, real or imaginary. The surprising and appealing aspect of the device was that it vastly augmented the depth illusion already produced by drawing in perspective: looking through the viewing lens, the spectator experienced the delicious sensation of being somehow inside the scene, on the very site being observed.[26]

The first Japanese artisan to have plumbed the resources of the *optique* was Maruyama Okyo (1733–95). He had first worked painting dolls for a toy maker, and it was there, no doubt, that he discovered the device. He saw at once the possibilities for making engravings in perspective and accentuating the effect by using this machine. He also decided it would be stimulating to place the vanishing point off center, to surprise viewers who might tire of repeated images constructed on the same model. He kept to traditional subjects, however: Chinese and Japanese landscapes and architecture.[27]

Shiba Kokan, born in Edo in 1747, first studied painting in the tradition of the Kano school, then devoted himself to the "birds and flowers" genre in the style of Chin Nampin. He discovered Western engraving in Jonston's book, which was shown to him by Hira Gennai and from which he copied some plates. Then he tried in various ways to rediscover the secret of copperplate engraving, which had been lost after the departure of Giovanni Niccolò for Macao. The task was enormous in scope: he had not only to reestablish the technique, but also to reinvent the press and reconstitute the paper for printing. Kokan succeeded, at the cost of unflagging effort, helped along by the Dutch translation (Leiden, 1778) of Noël Chomel's *Dictionnaire œconomique*, an illustrated text that had first been published in Lyon in 1709. Kokan did not know Dutch, but his friend Otsuki Gentaku, who had learned it to carry out his anatomical studies, translated the relevant passages for him.

Kokan's first copperplate engraving came off the press in 1783. It was a hand-colored view of the Sumida River in Edo, seen from the Mimeguri sanctuary. The perspective is masterful, the vanishing point slightly off center. The open space appears immense, and the impression of depth is analogous to that given by a *vue d'optique*. The detail work includes elements resulting from immediate observation (water, boats, and human figures) and others treated in the Western style (sky and trees).[28]

The following year Kokan constructed one of these mirror devices, and the landscapes he drew and engraved for several years were intended to be seen through it. To the blend of perspective and optics he added the flavor of exoticism. One copperplate engraving bearing his signature from this period shows the Serpentine River in London's Hyde Park. It imitates, necessarily, a Western model, but whatever this unknown model may have looked like, several aspects of Kokan's composition seem to be highly personal: the large tree overlooking the scene, which appears to be ready to burst from the frame, the extremely sinuous shapes of the swans swimming in the river, a certain diagrammatic tendency, the accentuation of the shadows.[29]

Kokan's philosophy is revealed in these excerpts from a letter he wrote at the end of his life to one of his freinds: "I describe everything in detail, down to the last cup of tea or sake I drink." Or again: "A painting that does not represent reality faithfully is not well done. . . . Oriental paintings do not have preciseness of detail, and without this preciseness, a painting is not really a painting. To paint reality is to paint all objects . . . exactly as they appear to us, in their singularity. No technique except the one that comes to us from the West can fully render this sensation of reality."[30]

Kokan was not the only one in his time to offer his compatriots, to whom all foreign travel was prohibited, the chance to escape through exoticism. I have already mentioned Utagawa Toyoharu, one of the masters of the *ukiyo-e* print at the turn of the nineteenth century. His *Grand Canal, Venice*, is a wood engraving in color. The engraving that inspired him is known: it was done by Antonio Visentini (1688–1782) after a painting by Canaletto (1697–1768).[31] The Grand Canal is seen from what is now the Piazzale Roma, looking toward San Simeone Pàccolo and, a little to the left, the campanile of San Geremia. Today, the only things missing are Santa Croce, at the far right, and the convent of Corpus Domini, on the left.

Visentini had been an architect before becoming a painter and an engraver, and his *Grand Canal* clearly brings out the topographic art of his times: it is a work created for touristic purposes, intended for very wide distribution. To the Japanese of that era, the name Venice no longer meant anything. It would have been different two centuries earlier, at least for those who had heard about the journey of the four young men Valignano had sent to Portugal and Italy. In the caption calligraphed on the border of the print, Toyoharu wrote *Oranda*, "Holland," which in the minds of his contemporaries and himself signified "Europe." The artist was evidently charmed by the sight of the gondolas crisscrossing the canal in all directions, the flared chimneys, so typical of the city of the Doges, the severe architecture of the churches. But he was unable to render the depth of the original. He has brought the background buildings close to the viewer and attenuated the contrast of light and shadows so greatly that the perspective, although well-defined in a linear sense, feels flattened.[32]

The source of another engraving, identified as "View of the Roman Forum," is unknown but could be a *vue d'optique*, itself derived from one of the fantastical reconstitutions of which the Italians and the Fiamminghi were so fond. That the Temple of Saturn is on the left and the Coliseum on the right, with the Arch of Titus at the center, suggests that it may be a converse image: this sort of inversion is common in the copies. Other details, such as the Trajan column at the right and the statue of Marcus Aurelius in the center of the square, establish that Toyoharu's model was itself an imaginary composition, called in Italy a *capriccio* or *veduta ideata*. In any case, the Japanese artist did not know what he was copying: the caption calligraphed at the top of the engraving speaks of a "Franciscan church, in Holland." What interested him more than anything was the highly decorative nature of the scene, the equilibrium of mass on either side of the arch and the statue, the figures and animals wandering about on the square, the play of light and shadow, the frontal perspective. There is a single Japanese touch: the odd shape of the clouds, which recalls the stereotyped skies of Kano school screens.[33]

Wakasugi Isohachi, who is linked to the Nagasaki school although not a pupil of Chin Nampin, is another of the artists who responded in one way or another to the taste for Occidentalism held by some of the Japanese at the end of the century. He was an independent artist whose life remains obscure and whose tastes seem to have been eclectic. One of his works that has been preserved is a painting on fabric of a falconer on horseback. Standing up in his stirrups, his head raised to the sky, the horseman is in Western dress. He holds in his right hand the reins of a galloping horse and on his left fist lifts a hooded falcon. The horse dashes through an undulating countryside beneath a vast pink and blue sky. On the horizon, very low in the frame, are houses, a tower, and a few trees, hazy with distance. Behind the horseman, in the background at left, the towers and walls of an immense fortified castle look out over a tall cliff, pink against the blue part of the sky.

The model for this painting is known: it is an engraving by Johann Elias Ridinger (1698–1767). Ridinger was a German painter and engraver who specialized in pictures of horses and hunting scenes. He left a voluminous body of work, engraved sometimes as etchings, sometimes as mezzotints. He published several collections that were appreciated throughout Europe and sometimes as far as Nagasaki, among them *Grosser Herren Lust in allerhand Jagen* (Gentlemen's Pleasures at All Types of Hunt, 1722), *Jäger und Falconier und ihren Verrichtungen* (Hunters and Falconers in Action, 1729), *Türkischer Pferdsaufbutz samt einem die nöthigen Anmerkungen hierzu enthaltenden Brief* (Turkish Horse-drawn Carriages, with a Letter Containing All the Remarks Necessary for Their Explication, 1752).[34] It should be noted that several of Ridinger's engravings were reproduced as authoritative in volume 3 of the *Collection of Plates* in Diderot and d'Alembert's *Encyclopédie* published in 1767, under the rubric "The Hunt, Venery."

Ridinger's *Falconer* is entirely typical of his style. The horse and its rider are powerfully sculpted by a ray of light that seems to come from a point very low on the horizon, outside and to the right of the image area. The rays of the sun that traverse the sky diagonally, as when it is about to rain, also emanate from this invisible point. Great black clouds, with only their edges lit by the rising sun, loom threateningly over the rider, his mount, the shrubbery on his left, and the village huddled around its bell tower in the distance. High above in the sky is the frightened heron on whom the man will soon loose the raptor.

The Japanese artist did not feel, or chose to ignore, the drama in Ridinger's scene, and by omitting the heron has even destroyed its original meaning. The blue and pink sky and the horseman's blue jacket make it instead a pleasant scene of riding through fields at the start of a lovely spring morning. As in the secular paintings of Niccolò's time, the fantasy castle, dwarfing with its mass the surrounding countryside, connotes both the European city and the glory of those who wield power within it.[35]

———

Exoticism played a modest role in eighteenth-century Japanese painting and engraving, and the works inspired by this new taste are for the most part minor ones. The Akita school's part in the diffusion and illustration of Western theories of art was also limited, due to the social origin of its members, their distance from Edo, and their indifference to the art market.

None of the great names in seventeenth- and eighteenth-century European art was known in Japan before the nineteenth century; not a single Rembrandt or Rubens, none of the great Dutch or Flemish works from the early seventeenth century reached its shores. The admiration inspired by a van Royen bouquet is a measure of the profound ignorance imposed on the Japanese, despite their curiosity, by their political isolation. Had they even the means to discern that among the engravers Merian, Pierre van der Borcht, or Ridinger were infinitely better than the others offered them by a far too restricted and haphazard market? To discriminate and to select in art requires an abundant and sufficiently varied stock. The Dutch had little to offer and generally did not themselves know the true value of what they were selling or bartering.

As for theory, the role of books arriving in Japan in the second half of the century should not be overestimated. Before Otsuki Gentaku, it was extremely rare to find any Japanese who knew enough Dutch to read even a minimally challenging text. There remained the image, on which the artist could always dwell without necessarily understanding its logic or its meaning.

Does this mean that the "Dutch" period was comparable to the "Portuguese" period? A flash of Occidentalism that, after briefly illuminating Nagasaki, Akita, or Edo, left behind only a few ashes? If this was not the case, it is because artistic life in Edo was so vital, and possessed of such great inner resources, that it could make creative capital out of even the mediocre. It is also because the Chinese influence, which remained constant throughout the period, had served as a carrier of the Western "values" discovered in Peking through Italian artists at the Jesuit mission. Last and most important, the artists who did the most to change their contemporaries' gaze were neither scientists nor theoreticians but artisans, printers, and decorators quite capable of observing and discerning intuitively the expectations of their clients. The expectations, that is, of a broad middle-class public little interested in metaphysical or spiritual questions, for whom, to paraphrase Shiba Kokan, a cup of tea was a cup of tea and a cup of sake a cup of sake. Members of this public had to be amused but not disconcerted: they wished to be surprised, to have their curiosity piqued, but not, in the process, forget the way to the theater or the house of pleasure, or lose their taste for sake. The genius of the artists who cultivated the *uki-e* and *vue d'optique* genre was to open their contemporaries' eyes to perspective and the perception of volume without straying from the subject matter typical of Floating World painting and without disrupting the framework within which the customary social drama was played out. It was the same world, still floating, but no longer on the "puddle" Rimbaud speaks of at the end of *The Drunken Boat*—from then on it was afloat on an open sea.

Thanks to these visionaries, Japan reproduced in the eighteenth century the experiments in perspective done by fifteenth-century Italian inventors, the very ones who had inspired Vredeman de Vries and Gérard de Lairesse. As Georges Gusdorf very ably demonstrates in *The Galilean Revolution*, "nature as mechanism" had been foreseen and brought into play by artists before being analyzed and reconstructed by scientists; the "mathematization of shapes" allowed them to master the appearance of things well before their material reality was conquered by science and technique.[36] It took more than a century in the West to make the final step from the artist's vision of space to its scientific construction; it took less than forty years in Japan, the interval between *The Nakamura Theater* and Satake Shozan's close reading of Gérard de Lairesse. Thus a few "Dutch" engravings, not all of them of high quality, succeeded in doing what all the volumes of Thomas Aquinas stacked on top of those of Aristotle and Sacrobosco could never have achieved, even had the missionaries been able to implant them in Japan in some lasting way: they drew Japan gently into modernity, more than one hundred years before it opened up to the rest of the world politically.

Chapter Seven

The Two Faces of "Dutch Science"

While the Galilean revolution swept Europe and spread through nearly every realm of knowledge, for a long time the Japanese could glimpse only the shadow face of what they called the "Dutch science"—a hodgepodge of books translated into Dutch, most often illustrated, of very diverse age and origin, and not always the best, as in the case of the natural history works that nonetheless charmed the Akita school. Usually unable to comprehend the language in which these books were published, Japanese viewers were forced to make great leaps of the imagination to reconstitute their meaning however they might: image by itself does not necessarily deliver the key to its interpretation, especially an image constructed with rules (perspective, chiaroscuro) and symbolism previously unknown in the tradition of the importing country.

Looking at the example of medicine and surgery, one would have to admit that the knowledge transmitted by Almeida and Ferreira to their Japanese pupils must have been quite minor, skills rather than "secrets," and a few practical recipes, all of them surely but marginal additions to the immense treasure of the Chinese pharmacopoeia. The situation changed somewhat after 1641. The Dutch on Deshima would have a doctor or surgeon of their own, and it did not escape the notice of the interpreters assigned to the little colony that these men did not treat the sick and wounded the way doctors educated in the Chinese tradition did. They were at times better, at others not as good, and the interpreters retained from their conversations with the practitioners of these arts whatever seemed most useful. The doctors of the Dutch East India Company likewise profited from the exchange. Thus as early as 1683 Willem ten Rhijne made known in Europe certain applications of Japanese medicine,[1] as did Engelbert Kaempfer in 1712 and 1727–28.[2] But neither of them understood Japanese or Chinese, and neither one bothered to elucidate the principles on which these applications were founded; it was enough for them that in precise cases recognizable by known symptoms—colic crises, for example, or gout—they were shown to be effective.

The first modern Japanese medical "school" was that of Caspar Schambergen, an obscure German surgeon-barber who spent some time in Nagasaki and Edo in the mid-seventeenth century. He taught several interpreters the art of treating open wounds, and his pupils spread the knowledge they had gained, invoking the name of Kasuparu as though he were a recognized authority.[3] It appears that we owe to one of Schambergen's pupils the first Japanese-language adaptation of Ambroise Paré's writings on surgery, which had been translated into Dutch and published in Amsterdam in 1649 under the title *De Chirurgie, ende Opera van alle de Wercken van Mr. Ambrosius Paré*. The adaptation consisted only of excerpts and circulated for a long time in manuscript form. It was finally published by a Kyoto book printer in 1769.[4]

In 1688 another interpreter from Nagasaki, Narabayashi Chinzan, alias Shingobei (1643–1711), also managed to obtain a 1649 or 1655 edition of *De Chirurgie*. He had acquired a vague notion of Western medicine from a practitioner who resided at Deshima from 1671 to 1675, Willem Hoffmann, and after he left his post as interpreter, Chinzan applied and taught what he remembered of his lessons. His adaptation of Paré circulated, like the first, in manuscript form, beginning in 1706. It included twenty-two pages of drawings in color, imitating the plates in the Dutch edition, and some of his drawings found their way into the 1769 Kyoto edition.[5] A few years later Chinzan was imitated in turn by Nishi Gentetsu. Gentetsu reused Chinzan's drawings and interspersed into his text his own observations and reflections on the treatment of wounds. His work was not printed and like the others circulated as a manuscript throughout the eighteenth century.[6] It is significant that all these adaptations concerned only the treatment of wounds, the domain in which traditional Chinese medicine, lacking knowledge of anatomy, was virtually useless. This was especially true for wounds from the firearms the Portuguese had introduced in the previous century, much more damaging than wounds from the bladed weapons warriors had employed until then.

Paré was incontestably a great surgeon and a bold innovator, but by 1688 or 1735, let alone 1769, his work was beginning to be quite dated in Europe. He had become a master barber-surgeon in 1536, and his *Méthode de traiter les plaies faites par haquebutes et autres bâtons à feu* (Method of Treating Wounds Made by the Harquebus and Other Firearms) had first been published in Paris in 1545. The observations it contained had been made during the campaign in Italy, in which he had participated in his official capacity from 1536 to 1542.

It is hard to overemphasize the strictly utilitarian nature of this early research, performed by men who had no previous medical training and whose methods, it seems, involved no pro-Western bias. It is true, however, that their efforts were of the greatest interest to the *bakufu*, as was everything concerning the art of warfare. In 1650 the shogun ordered the Dutch to bring him a book of anatomy when they sent their delegation to his court in Edo, and in 1654 he appointed a doctor named Mukai Gensho (1609–77) to compile all the information he could gather in Nagasaki on "Dutch" medicine. Gensho entered the school of a Deshima surgeon named Hans Jonson and wrote down everything he learned from him in a book titled *Komo ryu geka komo* (The Secrets of the Surgery School of the Red-Hairs).

Daniel Busch, a surgeon on Deshima from 1662 to 1666, was the first foreign practitioner authorized to treat patients in the city of Nagasaki itself. He was also authorized to teach, and the first medical certificate granted to a Japanese was bestowed by him in 1665. This first "certified" Japanese physician, Arashiyama Hoan (1633–93), went on to practice his art in Hirado. In 1683 he published a sort of manual of Western medicine that for a long time served as a guide for those who wished to study the "Dutch science" at Deshima.[7]

It would be nice to think that ten Rhijne and Kaempfer, who were in Japan in 1674–76 and 1690–92, respectively, and returned with so much new and useful knowledge, especially in the field of medicine, had also influenced a few good minds while they were there. To inform themselves, the two necessarily worked with interpreters and doctors, but the exchange was apparently all one way: there was no ten Rhijne school or Kaempfer school as there had been a Sawano Chuan school and a Caspar school. Yet it is thought that Narabayashi Chinzan may have met ten Rhijne, Cleyer, and Kaempfer.[8]

In the late seventeenth century, Deshima ceased to be an essential point in the Dutch East India Company's trading strategy, and none of the successors to ten Rhijne or Kaempfer was of their caliber. It was not until the late eighteenth and early nineteenth century that Deshima once again became an active intellectual pole, with Thunberg, Titsingh, and Siebold.[9]

THE "SENDOSIVISTES"

By the barbaric name *sendosivistes*, a mangled version of the word *siudosja* (pl. *siudosju*), used by Kaempfer in his *Natural History . . . of the Empire of Japan*, Diderot designated in his *Encyclopédie* the Confucianist Japanese philosophers, in whom he saw the Far Eastern equivalent of the French philosophers of his own generation.[10] The comparison was risky, perhaps, but not entirely foolish. There was indeed in Japan, in the eighteenth century, a strain of thought that was Confucian in origin and in a sense called into question the usual manner of thinking. It tended, as well, to direct the mind away from pure metaphysical speculation toward more positive forms of knowledge. The "sendosivistes" in Japan never reached as wide an audience as the philosophers finally enjoyed in France and a large part of Europe, but they came to exercise a certain influence on the power of the shogun and thus have their place in the comparative history of ideas.

Neo-Confucian philosophers[11] had already exerted some influence in Japan in the early seventeenth century, an influence that played no small part in discrediting the Christian missionaries' teachings in the eyes of the country's political authorities. Hayashi Razan (1583–1659), who would have a decisive role in closing Japan to the Portuguese and Spanish, had already distinguished himself in 1605 in an adamant debate with Fabian Fukan. He was not yet twenty-three years old when he recorded this debate in a sort of pamphlet whose title, *Hai yaso*, could be read with equal accuracy "Against Jesus" or "Against the Jesuits."[12] However, given that Razan's arguments rely on common sense and have no actual scientific basis (he even uses common sense to oppose Fukan's well-founded arguments for the roundness of the earth), they cannot be said to manifest a real advance in thought over the scholastic tradition of his Christian adversary.

Thinkers such as Ogyu Sorai and especially Arai Hakuseki (1657–1725), who was for a time the financial adviser to the shogun Tokugawa Ienobu, were another matter. Sorai, who died in 1728 but whose influence was felt chiefly in the second quarter of the eighteenth century, had an encyclopedic curiosity, taking an equal interest in the military arts, law, history, and music as well as the analysis of Confucian classics. The movement known as *kokugaku*, promulgating the defense and illustration of the national wisdom, proceeds more or less directly from him. Motoori Norinaga (1720–1801), a good representative of this movement, was highly critical of everything that came from China but also rejected the old Shintoist beliefs and even the parts of Confucianism that were pure speculation, such as the notions of Yin and Yang, of elements, or of karma. He recommended a stance of humility before the facts and called for an attitude of mind receptive to an objective knowledge of nature.[13]

The era in which Hakuseki was most active (1688–1704) corresponded to what has been called the "culture of *genroku*." It was characterized, especially in the large cities, by a profound and long-lasting secularization of minds. It took as its ideal mode of expression the neo-Confucianism of Chu Hsi, developed in China in the twelfth century but free of all the cosmological presuppositions that typically encumber ancient Confucianism. This philosophy was well suited to a society dominated by merchants, more avid for profit and pleasures than concerned with humanity's origins and final purpose.

Hakuseki was a *ronin*, a samurai without a master, the son and grandson of *ronin*. His family was poor, but like Hiraga Gennai in later times, he was a free spirit. Like many *ronin* Hakuseki was in large part self-taught, and he came to the attention of a lord related to the Tokugawas; in 1709 the lord, through adoption, was called to become shogun under the name Tokugawa Ienobu. Hakuseki had already become Ienobu's reader when he was adopted; he remained in that post when Ienobu became shogun and was tutor to his son when the latter succeeded his father. Hakuseki retained the enviable position of counselor to this prince until 1716. He was then expelled by his pupil's successor and lived in isolation. He nonetheless continued to write, and his work, characterized by rationalism and pragmatism, encompasses fields as varied as history, linguistics, geography, ethnology, cultural anthropology, politics, and economics.

One of Hakuseki's first works was based on his interviews in 1709 with Giovanni Battista Sidotti, an Italian Jesuit who had entered Japan clandestinely the previous year and was being held captive in Edo. From these interviews, and from a collection of memoirs he obtained in Nagasaki, he compiled in 1715 a three-volume work titled *Seiyo kibun* (Information on the West). The first volume recounted the "Sidotti affair"; the second consisted of world history and geography that encompassed Europe, Africa, Asia, and the two Americas; the third was an exposition and refutation of Christian beliefs. But this work was not published in Hakuseki's lifetime: the section on Christianity was compromising, if critical, and the philosopher's descendants kept the manuscript hidden. In 1713 he wrote the first Japanese book on world geography, *Sairan igen* (Selections from the Information Brought by the Foreigners), which he revised in 1725. The book contains information on physical and social geography and the products, customs, and political divisions of all the continents. Its contents came from his talks with Sidotti, from the memoirs gathered in Nagasaki, but also from Chinese atlases and geography books, and were based on modern maps given to the Tokugawa government by the Dutch merchants.[14]

Yet neither Hakuseki nor Sorai seemed to take a serious interest in "Dutch science," whether medicine, natural history, astronomy, or technology, and there is a wide gulf between their concerns and those of the interpreters at Deshima or Edo, who tried to cull the best of the foreign doctors' teachings and the books they used. Moreover, their influence was only limited (Hakuseki) or diffuse (Sorai), and they were unable to truly *predispose* the minds of their contemporaries to any sort of intellectual revolution. Rather, their work must be considered a symptom, an appeal, an attempt, opaque to the majority of their contemporaries, plainer to others, but in no way necessarily oriented toward the Western "Enlightenment." Today it is clear that the rationalism and pragmatism of Chu Hsi's Japanese disciples would have to have encountered those of the West sooner or later, but neither Sorai nor Hakuseki could have imagined such an encounter, for the reason that the Dutch they knew were no more "philosophers" than were the Portuguese in the times of the Jesuit mission. And they had not brought along in their trunks Locke or Leibniz, Bayle or Fontenelle. But we must credit Hakuseki with the perspicacity to have seen the distinction between the West's scientific and technical contributions and the Christian tradition, paving the way for political authorities like Yoshimune to welcome innovations from the West without breaking the prohibition on Christian propaganda that had been in effect since the early seventeenth century.[15]

Ando Shoeki, who was active during the period 1751–62, may have been more receptive to "Dutch science" than his predecessors if it is true that he practiced medicine. But he was principally concerned with political philosophy, denouncing the pillage to which the peasantry was subjected and the ideologies that justified it—even neo-Confucianism. He traveled to Nagasaki to meet the Dutch there, which served mainly to reinforce his belief that Dutch society was very close to his ideal: a society where one lived in peace and without inequality, since it was made up mostly of independent farmers.[16]

Tominaga Nakamoto (1715–46) was more of an iconoclast when it came to ideas. He was from an Osaka merchant family and had the turn of mind of his class: pragmatic, relativistic, mistrustful of all "metaphysical" speculation. A sort of Japanese Voltaire, says one of his biographers. But his reflections remained theoretical, and his audience in his own times was scarcely any broader than Shoeki's.[17] In a certain sense, minds like Nakamoto came too soon, and it is not by chance that he became well known and appreciated only after the Meiji Restoration.

Miura Baien (1723–89) is a perfect illustration of the contradiction in which Japanese followers of neo-Confucianism found themselves in the eighteenth century. He was the son of a physician, and he traveled to Nagasaki twice to question the Deshima interpreters on Dutch thought regarding the origin of the world. He was a rationalist who wished to keep himself free of any system or prejudice. He forbade himself all speculation on absolute reality and rejected belief in super-natural beings. He also rejected the principle of authority. "In truth," he wrote to a physician friend in 1777, "those who study under a master feel ashamed to be in disagreement with his opinions, and the masters, for their part, do not like to have their disciples disagree with them. The cause of this error is taking a person as a master. . . . I consider as my friends and fellow students even the little children I have taught to read. Thus I can never feel ill will toward them because their views diverge from mine, and this I never cease to tell them, so they will be clear on this point." Baien even mistrusted the authority of books; he found them useful but only if read with a critical eye and always measured against the great book of nature. He also thought that no one could claim to be the possessor of the truth: the truth would spring up inevitably from the friction of minds in contact with each other.

Thus everything should have inclined Baien to seek contact with this "Dutch science" that was all the rage among his less deep-thinking contemporaries, from untaught interpreters to madmen like Hiraga Gennai. Yet he did nothing of the sort, his two trips to Nagasaki notwithstanding. He allowed that the Westerners had good instruments and were good experimenters but reproached them with taking an interest only in the surface of things, even in medicine. And he was not entirely wrong, if we consider only the appearances offered by the majority of physicians or claimed physicians who resided on Deshima one after the other and the illustrations in the various books they furnished their Japanese clients and partners from time to time.

Moreover, Baien did not conceive of experimentation in the Western way. He was not an empiricist. For him, an experiment did not constitute proof. The best way to prove a theory, even in natural phenomena, he thought, was by speculative reasoning. He reproached Westerners, too, for their conception of the subject. Their error, he said, was "to envisage heaven and earth [i.e., nature] from the point of view of human beings, instead of seeing humans from the point of view of heaven and earth." Humans are, in effect, no more than a part of the great whole that constitutes nature, and have no other master than nature itself.[18]

One can always dream of the ways this "sendosiviste" would have profited from communicating with his European equals, Hume, Diderot, or Kant, for example. But as Rousseau said, "Individuals may go hither and thither; it seems that philosophy does not travel. The reason for this is obvious, at least for distant countries: there are but four sorts of men who make long journeys—sailors, merchants, soldiers, and missionaries."[19] At the time Japan was a country very distant from Europe, and none of Europe's great philosophers was moved to go there. There is no indication that Miura Baien wished to leave his country either, and had he so wished, it would have been forbidden him.

REVOLUTION IN JAPANESE MEDICAL SCIENCE

The revolution that occurred in Japanese medical science between 1754 and 1774 was not the work of the interpreters of Nagasaki or the neo-Confucian philosophers of the times. It took place first in the field of Chinese traditional medicine, at the instigation of practitioners who had reflected deeply on their art and dared to call into question *from within* the authority of the tradition in which they had been trained.

The first actual dissection of a corpse in Japan was carried out in 1754, on the initiative of a physician from Kyoto named Yamawaki Toyo (1705–62). Toyo, like all his contemporaries, went by plates of Chinese origin representing the five vital organs and six hollow viscera that together performed the major functions of the organism. Corresponding to these different functions were points on the surface of the body, aligned along conceptual "meridians" that could be acted on by needles planted in the epidermis or moxibustion applied to its exterior. These plates made no pretense of being anatomically accurate; they were, as one historian of science put it, merely "navigational charts." They served essentially to mark the relationships of points or series of points to the corresponding regions of the organism and were quite indispensable, since often there was quite some distance between the ailing part and the location on the epidermis where the needle or moxibustion should be placed. Toyo had observed a great deal and had perhaps had the opportunity to see Western anatomical plates.[20] He questioned the validity of the Chinese plates he had at his disposal and decided that the best assurance was direct verification, despite the taboo reigning at the time throughout the Asiatic world, especially for

Confucianists, against the mutilation and handling of cadavers. In so doing, he did not intend to refute the principles of traditional medicine; he wished on the contrary to restore them to the purity of their original state.

Toyo had the dissection performed by three of his students and published his observations in 1759 in a book titled *Zoshi* (Description of the Entrails), which stirred up heated debate. His colleagues reproached him in substance for turning the attention of physicians to organs that were dead and consequently nonfunctioning. For them, the shape of the organs was of no importance; all that mattered was the spirit that animated them when alive.[21]

Despite this opposition, one of Toyo's students performed two more dissections, in 1758 and in 1759. The second cadaver was that of a woman; its dissection allowed for the first description in Japan of the female reproductive organs.

Within the current of this purely endogenous curiosity about the anatomical makeup of the human body, renewed interest arose in the Nagasaki interpreters' attempts to translate or adapt Western models late in the previous century. The 1769 publication in Kyoto of Ambroise Paré, as adapted by a student of Caspar Schambergen, was one such attempt. Three years later came the publication of an adaptation completed in 1690 by Motoki Ryoi (1628–1702) of *Pinax microcosmographicus*, by Johannes Rümelin or Remmelin (1583–1632), which had been published in Germany in 1615 and in Holland in 1634.[22] Ryoi was an interpreter in Nagasaki, but his publisher in 1772 was a physician, Suzuki So-un. Remmelin's plates were unique in that they folded open to reveal the internal organs in the male and the female. They consisted of several drawings superimposed and glued at one end in such a way that when opened progressively deeper anatomical cross sections appeared, from the epidermis to the skeleton. They allowed one to perform a virtual dissection without leaving one's desk, and they were met with only mild interest as long as Japanese physicians had not themselves performed actual dissections.

The work of Yamawaki Toyo and his students made a great impression on a young man of twenty-six who already had an interest in "Dutch science," Sugita Gempaku (1733–1818). Gempaku was the son of a physician and had studied both traditional Chinese medicine (*kangaku*) and Western medicine, or what passed for it, as taught by a government physician descended from Nishi Kichibei, or Gempo, who had been named interpreter for Deshima in 1641. Gempo had studied medicine first with Sawano Chuan, then with the physicians of the East India Company, and he had finally become both interpreter and surgeon to the shogun at Edo. The Nishi family was highly renowned, and Nishi Gentetsu, with whom Gempaku studied for several years, was, like his grandfather, physician to the shogun.

Gempaku left memoirs, published after his death in 1815, recording a detailed history of the true epistemological revolution in which he was one of the actors. He has a tendency to overestimate his role, and his memory fails him at times, but historians of medicine today consider his account essentially credible.[23]

He begins the story, after a brief preamble on the role of the Deshima interpreters in the beginnings of *rangaku*, at the point of his encounter with a physician ten years his senior, Maeno Ryotaku (1723–1803). Ryotaku had been raised by an eccentric uncle who had had him study traditional medicine in Kyoto, but also music and the burlesque drama form called *kyogen*. For good measure, Ryotaku added to his official schooling an apprenticeship in the basics of the Dutch language, which he studied under Aoki Konyo. It was Konyo whom the shogun had ordered in 1740 to learn Dutch, while Noro Genjo was delegated to examine the Western natural history books he had in his library. "He was definitely the first physician who learned Dutch privately," wrote Gempaku.

Another doctor, Nakagawa Junan (1737–80), who belonged to the same clan as Gempaku and like him was from Obama, north of Kyoto, was also inspired to learn Dutch from a master who had been trained at Nagasaki. Junan was sixteen years younger than Ryotaku, and they were apparently not in contact. It is significant that across several years of distance they each thought to learn the language of the men with red hair, with no apparent goal. Neither Ryotaku's teacher nor Junan's could really teach his student much—the alphabet, a few isolated words. There was no question of being able to read a book, let alone a scientific work, with these rudiments. But their need to learn was very strong. They would probably not have been able to say what they were waiting for, but they were waiting.

One day in 1767 or 1768 ("I have forgotten the exact date, it was so long ago"), Ryotaku went to see Gempaku; it was in the spring, and as the Dutch were in Edo for their annual visit to the shogun, Ryotaku invited him along to visit them at their inn and question them. They went. The head interpreter accompanying the Dutch did everything possible to discourage the visitors. He explained to them that Dutch was an impossible language, that he himself was a long way from mastering it, despite many years of practice; it was impossible, in any case, to learn it in Edo. Gempaku left the inn completely discouraged.

The following year, nonetheless, he returned to the inn where the Dutch had come to stay as usual. Another interpreter showed him a book he had purchased. It was a rare book, he said. It dealt with surgery, and its author was called Hesuteru. A rare book, indeed: Lorenz Heister (1683–1758) was a German physician who had studied at Giessen, Amsterdam, then Leiden with the greatest masters. He was a doctor of medicine at the University of Harderwijk, and after having served in military hospitals in Flanders and in the Marlborough army, he had been called on to teach anatomy and surgery in Amsterdam in 1709, then in Basse-Sax, Altdorf, in 1710, and in Helmstedt, near Nuremberg, in 1718. His book also had an extraordinarily distinguished history: it had seen seven printings in German, three in Latin, and ten in English and had been translated into Spanish, French, Italian, and Dutch. The copy Gempaku saw was undoubtedly Dutch.[24]

Gempaku was unaware of this history, of course, but the book made an overwhelming impression on him: "When I opened it and looked inside, the illustrations I saw looked very different from those in Japanese and Chinese books, even though I could not decipher a word of the descriptions. But once I had contemplated these precise and finely executed images, I had the sense that my mind had opened wide. I borrowed the book for a time to copy the illustrations, if nothing more. I worked at it without respite, day and night, and before the [interpreter's] trip was over, I had copied them all. This work sometimes kept me up so late that I heard the cock crow."

The episode reveals that the part played by aesthetic sensibility was at least as great as the role of scientific intuition. At such times the history of science and the history of art tend to blend together, as often happened in Europe during the Renaissance.

At the time it was not permitted for private individuals to have Dutch books in their possession. These were to be kept only in the shogun's library and the libraries of the Nagasaki interpreters. But the desire to learn was so great that this prohibition was violated with increasing frequency. Nakagawa Junan and several other physicians began to acquire books from the interpreters who accompanied the Dutch to Edo each year. Thus it was that in early 1771 Junan showed his friend Gempaku two illustrated treatises on anatomy that he had just purchased. The first was *Ontleedkundige Tafelen, Benevens de daar toe behoorende Afbeeldingen en Aanmerkingen* (etc.); it was written by a physician from Danzig, Johann Adam Kulmus (1689–1745), and had been published in Amsterdam in 1734. The second was a treatise by Caspar Bartholin (1585–1629), *Anatomia nova*, probably the fourth edition, published in 1672 under the auspices of Bartholin's son Thomas (1616–80). To Sugita Gempaku it was a marvel, as Heister's book had been: "I was certain that they had been drawn and written from direct experience, and I would have given everything in the world to have those books. I wished them for my library all the more since for a long time my office was like that of a surgeon of the Dutch school."

Gempaku went to seek his lord's intendant and obtained from him the money to buy the Kulmus book. He did not yet know how he would gain from it intellectually, but he was certain it would be a useful purchase. He was also sure (he spoke of this often with Hiraga Gennai) that the expected reawakening in the study of medicine *would never come from the Nagasaki interpreters:* it was up to the physicians themselves, assuming they were willing to abandon speculation for fact. He knew that Yamawaki Toyo and his students were not alone in having practiced dissection. He knew at least two government physicians who had performed six or seven dissections themselves. They had certainly noticed that what they observed did not correspond to what was shown in the plates of traditional medical treatises. But rather than call into question the tradition, they preferred to argue that it was a matter of the diversity of the human species: Japanese anatomy was different from that of the Chinese, that was all.

Soon enough, Gempaku and his friends had the opportunity to verify the matter for themselves. The date was March 3, 1771. An execution was to take place the following day in Edo, and a government physician would preside over the dissection. Gempaku went to the site with a group of friends, including Junan and Ryotaku. He had brought Kulmus's book with him so as to compare the twenty-eight plates it contained with what they were about to see. Without prearrangement, Ryotaku also arrived at the meeting place with this book, which he had bought in Nagasaki. He held a slight advantage over Gempaku. He knew how to decipher a few words of Dutch: "Long" *(rongu)* for the lungs, "Hart" *(harutu)* for heart, "Maag" *(mâgu)* for stomach, "Milt" *(miruto)* for spleen.

As was customary, the dissection itself was carried out not by the physician but by a "demonstrator," in this case a ninety-year-old untouchable of the *eta* caste. In a country obsessed with the distinction between the pure and the impure, only untouchables could handle and cut into dead flesh; it was from this class that executioners were recruited. The old man had long practiced this work, but except for the bile duct, which was profitable for those of his profession because bile was highly prized in the pharmacopoeia of the time, he did not know the name of anything he touched. Moreover, he said in his defense, he had already performed this work before many physicians, and none of them had ever asked him what things were.

Gempaku and his companions compared the organs they saw to the illustrations in Kulmus and were astonished to see that everything seemed to coincide perfectly. They also rummaged in the bones scattered on the ground around the execution site and saw that their shape corresponded to the parts of the skeleton detailed by Kulmus.

Ryotaku, Junan, and Gempaku returned to the city together, deploring the fact that no physician had thought to perform this experiment before and determined to do without the mediation of the interpreters in the future. There was only one way out of the impasse. Ryotaku put it in these terms: "I have been to Nagasaki several times and I learned a few words of Dutch there. What do you say, shall we start from there and learn to read it together?"

The adventure commenced the next day. It was sheer madness: they had not only to decode the Dutch writing, reconstitute its syntax, and establish a concordance between the text and the pictures but also—above all—to invent from nothing a language of their own. "When we were first in the presence of the book *Taheru anatomia* [the

Japanese transliteration of *Tafel anatomia* (Anatomy Plates), probably taken from the Latin on the title page, *Tabulae anatomiae*] we were as the sailor who is left oarless and rudderless in the middle of the ocean, with no hope of aid for as far as the eye can see. We were completely overwhelmed."

The decryption took four years, at a rate of six or seven sessions per month. This work was interspersed with consultations with professional interpreters and new dissections. More physicians joined the efforts of the tiny group. Gempaku wrote up the minutes of each session the same night. He was also responsible for preparing the final manuscript, which was rewritten eleven times.

One of the most active members of the group was Katsuragawa Hoshu (1751–1809). He belonged to an old family of physicians familiar with Western medicine and was himself a government physician. He was highly gifted intellectually, quite a bit younger than the others, and swifter than they at surmounting the difficulties of translation.

The hardest task was to invent a modern medical language. The European physicians of the Renaissance had encountered the same problem. They had solved it by going back to Greek and Latin and grafting new words onto ancient roots. Sugita Gempaku's group did the same thing, using Chinese. But it was not easy to find an exact Chinese equivalent for every word in the *Tafelen*. Gempaku wrote on this subject: "I was often perplexed, for many of the expressions were not easily defined with a one-to-one correspondence. I reflected for a long time and decided that, since I was pioneering the work, I should define the expressions in such a way that they could be easily understood."

The great British historian of Chinese medicine, Joseph Needham, ran into exactly parallel difficulties when he had to translate into a modern Western language—English as it happened—the technical terms found in treatises on traditional Chinese medicine. There was no better solution, he said, than "to construct from the ground up, out of Greek and Latin roots, a lexicon of terms following as closely as possible the meaning of the various Chinese medical terms, and use them systematically." The only prior condition for using such a language would be to make "a thorough analysis of the meaning of the Chinese terms" and to justify semantically the "linguistic components from which the equivalents have been built."[25]

The work completed, it then had to be made known as widely as possible and obtain the imprimatur of the highest authorities in the country. To this end a sort of prospectus illustrated with a few plates was drawn up and distributed in 1773. This was another small revolution: never before had anyone thought of popularizing the advances of science. Katsuraga Hoshu's father was a vital resource for gaining access to the shogun. He had an honorable name at the court and was acquainted with the shogun's wife. The publication was authorized. Other high-ranking personalities were also solicited. All looked favorably on the enterprise.

The translation of Kulmus's book was published in 1774 under the title *Kaitai shinsho* (New Book on Anatomy). It was made up of five quarto volumes, one of them consisting of xylographed plates. Odano Naotake, who was then working with Hiraga Gennai at Edo, was given charge of the plates. There were forty of them, of which eight (four double plates) came not from Kulmus but from *Anatomia humani corporis*, published in Amsterdam in 1685 by Govert Bidloo (1649–1713). The plates illustrating Bidloo's book were signed by Gérard de Lairesse.[26] The ones reproduced in *Kaitai shinsho* show the tendons of the hand and foot. The difference between the number of plates (28) taken from Kulmus and the number of plates (32) attributed to Kulmus in *Kaitai shinsho* is due to the fact that the contents of one of Kulmus's plates is sometimes spread out over several plates in the Japanese translation.

The frontispiece of the first edition of *Kaitai shinsho* was not borrowed from either Kulmus or Bidloo. It was adapted from the frontispiece of a work published for the first time in 1556, in Rome, by the Spaniard Juan Valverde de Amusco, physician to the cardinal of Toledo, under the title *Historia de la composición del cuerpo humano* (History of the Composition of the Human Body). The book had been reprinted by Plantin at Anvers in 1566, 1572, and 1583, sometimes in Latin, sometimes in Dutch, and had included plates by Vesalius, from whom Valverde had borrowed freely. The *Kaitai shinsho* frontispiece comes from one of the Anvers editions, rather than an Italian one. The original had been drawn for Plantin by Lambert van Noort (ca. 1520–71) and engraved by Frans Huys (1522–62). It shows Adam and Eve, nude, on either side of a portal framing the title and decorated with the arms of Philip II of Spain. Odano Naotake, who was not familiar with copperplate engraving, could not imitate his model perfectly, since xylography was not capable of this. And we do not know why he replaced the royal heraldry of Philip, who had become king, with the coat of arms he had had while still the dauphin of Charles V.

A few years after the publication of *Kaitai shinsho*, Sugita Gempaku welcomed to Edo a twenty-two-year-old student who had been recommended to him by one of his friends. His name was Otsuki Gentaku (1756–1827), the son of a physician, and Gempaku soon came to value his character: he undertook nothing unless he was on the surest ground and wrote and spoke only what he understood perfectly. Maeno Ryotaku also took an interest in Gentaku's education, and in 1785 they sent him to Nagasaki with the financial support of the *daimyo* of Fukuchiyama, himself a distinguished scientist. Gentaku perfected his Dutch with a seasoned interpreter, then went back to Edo where in 1788 he published a collection titled *Rangaku kaitei* (Introduction to Dutch Science); the first part was a history of *rangaku* and the second part an introduction to Dutch grammar. He revisited Gempaku's unfinished work on Heister and had it published in 1790 under the title *Yoi shinsho* (New Book on Surgery). Last and most important, he revised *Kaitai shinsho* from top to bottom for a second edition that was completed (but not published) in 1798. Twelve years earlier, he had opened a school of medicine in Edo that had quickly earned widespread renown.

During this time, "Dutch" studies had flowered in all domains, and there were now countless publications on the subject. *Kaitai shinsho* had been a decisive breakthrough: the thrust it provided in 1774 would continue to be felt throughout the nineteenth century.[27]

The translation of Kulmus's book did not contribute much to the actual practice of medicine; it was, after all, only a common treatise on anatomy. Heister's book made a much greater contribution in the realm of surgery. In practice, Western medicine and Sino-Japanese medicine remained rivals in Japan for quite some time, with neither one able to demonstrate a decisive advantage over the other. The threefold importance of *Kaitai shinsho* lay elsewhere: its publication was the result of a conversion of the gaze and the mind, as Gempaku's memoirs bear witness; it opened the way to the creation of a rigorous, modern scientific language built on solid linguistic bases; and it made available to all who knew how to read the advances of a science theretofore considered secret.

One would think that the neo-Confucianists, who from Arai Hakuseki to Miura Baien seemed to be clamoring for an intellectual revolution, would welcome enthusiastically these efforts by scientists, especially physicians, that were effectively changing habitual ways of seeing and thinking in their field. One might also expect the Nagasaki interpreters to understand, at the least. But no: Sugita Gempaku and his group, and Otsuki Gentaku after them, made quite a few enemies on both sides.

The first to rally against them were the interpreters, whose families had been profiting from their exclusive traffic with the Deshima physicians for a century and more. Gempaku wrote philosophically in his memoirs: "It had to be thus: until then, they had been interpreters, nothing more; they had never read or translated a book. . . . No one would have imagined that any of them would understand anything about, for example, medical theories or the internal structure of the body." One interpreter, seeing the prospectus of *Kaitai shinsho*, is said to have exclaimed in astonishment: "There is nothing in the body called *geru* [Dutch *Geer*, blood clot]; there must be a confusion with *garu*, meaning bile [Dutch *Gal*]." And Gempaku concludes: "It seems, at any rate, that the realization of our new work, undertaken in the Kanto region, elicited a strong surge of jealousy from the interpreters in the Seihi (Nagasaki) region, where everything had really begun."

Hostility from most philosophers was no more moderate. Gempaku attempted in vain to explain that the new science could not have developed if Chinese science had not paved the way; the neo-Confucianists saw only that Chinese tradition was being devalued at that moment. Otsuki Gentaku was more straightforward than his teacher. He made so bold as to say in his *Introduction to Dutch Science* that other countries besides China could claim as much merit as the "Middle Empire."

In this battle of ideas, the side of the modernist physicians received unexpected backing from the partisans of the national science, or *kokugaku*, who looked to Japan's past, Shintoism in particular, for validation of their cause. Some of them went so far as to claim that the Japanese had had their own writing system before the importation of Chinese ideograms. Thus it was their hostility to China, rather than any particular rapport with the intellectual advances of Europe, that led them to welcome *rangaku*.

The most disturbing thing about the situation was that the Tokugawa government always tended to favor the neo-Confucianists. Hence the imperative need for Gempaku and his friends to have the support of the shogun himself when the first edition of *Kaitai shinsho* was launched. Luckily for Gentaku, not all the neo-Confucianists were sectarian. Gentaku mentions Shibano Ritsuzan (1734–1807), an orthodox neo-Confucianist who nevertheless found the Dutch science not without value. Its promulgators were barbarians, no doubt, since they did not know how to read Chinese, but this did not preclude their elaborating a field of knowledge valid for all, on the basis of their own observations.[28]

The Hidden Face of "Dutch Science"

The Japanese proponents of *rangaku* were first enchanted by the beauty of the illustrations found in Western books; only later did they verify the pictures' conformity with observable reality, and it was still later before they comprehended the details of the texts explaining both the images and the facts. They were entirely unaware, of course, of the complex intellectual background of the several works that fell into their hands in haphazard array, and until now historians of medicine have not concerned themselves with this.

Paré, Vesling, Remmelin, Heister, Kulmus, Bartholin, Bidloo, Valverde, Vesalius—a disparate series of names at a glance. The list includes one Frenchman, Paré; four Germans, Vesling, Remmelin, Heister, and Kulmus; a Dane, Bartholin; a Dutchman, Bidloo; a Spaniard, Valverde; and a Belgian who was active chiefly in Italy, Vesalius. Their lives spanned two and one-half centuries of medical and surgical history, from the earliest, Vesalius, born in 1514 or 1515, to the latest, Heister, who died in 1758. Some became well-known names (Paré, Vesalius), others (Kulmus, Remmelin) remained largely obscure.

The heterogeneity is even greater if one takes into account that some of these authors did not produce entirely original work. Valverde had studied at Padua with Colombo, the successor to Vesalius, and like his teacher he defended tradition against Vesalius, whose anatomical research often ran counter to Galen. But he was not an anatomist, and his work owed its success largely to the fact that many of his plates were drawn from *De humani corporis fabrica*, published by Vesalius in 1543. Valverde also had the advantage of illustrations using copperplate engravings, while *Fabrica* contained only wood engravings.[29] Nor was Kulmus's work wholly his own. A number of his plates are copied or adapted from a physician-surgeon from the Brabant, Philippe Verheyen (1648–1710), whose treatise on anatomy, *Corporis humani anatomia*, had been first published at Louvain in 1693.

Did these nine authors, ten if we count Verheyen, have no more in common than to have been published at one time or another in Holland? This could be pure coincidence: Dutch book traders seem to have handled anything and everything throughout the seventeenth and eighteenth centuries. But the laws of the marketplace rule out sheer chance. If the Dutch published and sold these books rather than others, it is because they fulfilled the same demand: they belonged in a certain sense to the same family. Indeed, their authors had the same teachers, the same models; they had often been educated in the same universities. They frequently copied one another's work, as well, as we have seen with Valverde and Vesalius, Kulmus and Verheyen.

Vesalius and Paré were more or less contemporaries. They had the same teacher during the same period at the Paris Faculty, Jacques Dubois, known as Sylvius, and Paré had no more compunction than had Valverde about incorporating into his work illustrations from *Fabrica* such as the "ploughman skeleton," one of the most famous. It is found, for example, facing page 63 in *Dix livres de la chirurgie* (Ten Books on Surgery), published in Paris in 1564, with the skeleton's arm supported on a scythe that has replaced the original spade.

Remmelin took the idea for plates that could be opened in layers from a technique perfected by Vesalius in Padua, and on publication they were made available to students and the curious in the Leiden amphitheater of anatomy.[30]

Johann Vesling, born in Minden, Westphalia, had completed his studies in Vienna. He taught at the Venice Medical College beginning in 1629 and occupied the anatomy chair at the University of Padua from 1632 to 1648. At the beginning of his *Syntagma anatomicum*, he acknowledges among his eminent predecessors Vesalius, Fallope, Fabricius ab Aquapendente, Casserius, and Spigelius.[31]

Caspar Bartholin studied everywhere: in Denmark, Germany, the Brabant, Holland, England, Spain, France, Switzerland, and Italy. He taught philosophy in Basel, anatomy in Naples, Greek in Montpellier, and rhetoric, medicine, and theology in Copenhagen. In the preface to his anatomical guidelines he claims the honor of following in the footsteps of Vesalius, whose portrait is the frontispiece of the book.[32]

Bidloo was a lecturer in anatomy and surgery at The Hague in 1688, then superintendent of all the civilian and military hospitals in Holland. In 1693 he was inspector of military hospitals in England, and he was named professor of medicine and surgery at Leiden in 1694.[33] The introduction to his *Anatomia* twice renders homage to Vesalius, once in the notes to the reader and again beneath his portrait. And as Bidloo taught for some time at Leiden, we may suppose that he viewed Remmelin's plates in the anatomy amphitheater, where they had been kept since the beginning of the century.

Kulmus, before settling in Danzig, studied medicine in Strasbourg and in Basel, where Remmelin had also spent time and where Vesalius had published *Fabrica*. His *Tafelen* is dedicated to three teachers, Frederik Ruysch (1638–1731), a Dutchman who had long taught anatomy, surgery, and botany in Amsterdam; Willem Roëll (1700–75), who was first Ruysch's assistant and became his successor in 1731; and Johann Salzman (1679–1738), professor of anatomy, surgery, and pathology at the University of Strasbourg.[34]

Heister was a student at Amsterdam at the same time Bidloo was, in 1706. Among the teachers who educated Heister were Kulmus's master, Ruysch, whom he said he venerated as a father, but also the famous Boerhaave, as well as Albinus, who was also Boerhaave's student and who taught at Leiden for nearly fifty years until his death in 1770. Albinus was the first to republish Vesalius in an edition with copperplate engravings instead of wood engravings, in 1725. Valverde, whose treatise on anatomy was illustrated with copperplate engravings, had not republished Vesalius but emulated him.[35]

From Danzig to Naples, Augsburg to London, one could spend a lifetime following the strands of the veritable spider's web formed by the network of relationships—scientific, editorial, sometimes personal—linking all the Western authors found in eighteenth-century Japanese medical libraries. This network is anchored at a few solid mooring points in universities: Leiden, Strasbourg, Basel, Padua. Sugita Gempaku, his companions, and his disciples knew nothing of this web, and it is not certain that all the Western scientists who passed through Deshima, except perhaps Kaempfer and Thunberg, had a clear awareness of it either. But an underlying kinship linked all of these authors.

Paré and Vesalius were good Catholics, in appearance and perhaps in reality, but it is well known that they had no excessive respect for authority in their own field. Paré, who had been certified a master barber-surgeon in 1536 after a lengthy hospital training course and who had long served in the army, was looked on with suspicion by the Faculty of Medicine because he dared to intrude at times on areas considered the preserve of physicians, as in treatises on the use of antimony, for example, or the treatment of tumors. In 1575 the dean of medicine did all he could to prevent the printing of Paré's *œuvres*, which had not received prior approval from the Faculty. This he could forgo, since he was head surgeon and valet to the king, but until the end of his life he never ceased to arouse the envy and acrimony of his adversaries. Paré was a deeply religious man in a time when Catholics and Protestants were locked in a merciless war. In 1572 came the Saint Bartholomew's Day Massacre: one had to take sides. Paré was sometimes suspected of being a Huguenot. Nothing proves that he was. But the professions of faith sprinkled throughout his work have at least a tinge of Erasmianism. Catherine de Medici asked him one day if he thought he would be saved in the other world. He replied: "Yes, certainly, Madame, because I do what I can to be a good man in this one, and God is merciful, understanding all languages, and content that one pray in French or in Latin." He was a tolerant man who gave of his services equally to the wounded of both sides.[36]

In medicine, Vesalius soon incurred the hatred of those who swore by Galen, and when it came to religion, his biographers did not neglect to note that he had fraternized with Michaël Servetus on the benches of the Faculty of Medicine in Paris. One of them wrote: "Although he refrained from mingling physiology and theology, a snare which Servetus did not avoid, it seems almost certain that he was at the least a liberal Catholic, to judge by his Paris friendships."[37]

It was not by chance that Vesalius, in publishing *Fabrica*, went to great expense to transport his wood engravings to Basel, there to entrust them to the book publisher Johann Herbst, also known as Oporinus (1507–68). The Republic of Venice was hardly a fiefdom of religious obscurantism in Italy, but Basel was an even freer city and Oporinus was a Protestant. A liberal Protestant, it is true, and no simpleton. He drew notice in 1543 by two striking acts: he dared to publish the Koran, with the support of Luther and against the counsel of the town senate, and he agreed to shelter the humanist Sebastian Castellion (1515–63) after Calvin expelled him from Geneva. Basel, says Cushing, "was a place of knowledge where liberal Protestants and Catholics could regroup in reasonable comfort despite all the religious controversies, and this would have been widely known in 1536 when Vesalius left Paris. Erasmus, who had just died there, had chosen to make it his permanent abode, as was plain to all from the fact that the majority of his works had been printed there."[38]

Remmelin was a tormented spirit, engrossed in cabalism and alchemy. But he was also an active heretic: he was imprisoned in Ulm and later exiled, toward the end of his life, for having had printed and distributed without authorization anti-Catholic pamphlets written by a Protestant.[39]

Caspar Bartholin was a Lutheran. He was another tortured soul; his many travels and the sheer number of disciplines that consumed him are proof of this. Late in life, however, he gave up medicine and anatomy for religious reasons. His son Thomas, who had taken the opposite course, going from theology to medicine, saw it as his duty to issue his unpublished works. It should be mentioned in passing that Caspar Bartholin had another son, also a physician. His given name was Erasmus.

Caspar Bartholin had published in his lifetime a work of astrology (*Astrologia seu de stellarum natura*) that seemed to situate him among the partisans of influence by the stars. Among the problems he discusses: Was the star that appeared to the Magi a natural phenomenon or a miracle? What is the explanation for the solar eclipse that occurred on Good Friday, according to the Gospels? But his natural theology kept Bartholin from straying into foolishness, and if he allowed that the stars can have an influence on natural bodies, he rejected the idea that they can influence minds, which amounts to denying the very possibility of astrology.[40]

Verheyen, like Thomas Bartholin, first studied theology and then abandoned it for medicine. He was a Catholic, since he was a professor at Louvain, but he, too, was probably an Erasmian.

Bidloo was a Protestant. He had to be, to hold the high offices he exercised in Holland and England just after the Glorious Revolution. But to hold a chair in medicine and surgery at Leiden, one did not have to be a sectarian Calvinist: the civil authorities had in fact removed the University of Leiden from ecclesiastical authority quite early, and thus it enjoyed relative freedom throughout the seventeenth century. It is significant that in 1582 its directors declared their opposition to the Geneva Inquisition, as they had done with the Spanish one. After the Synod of Dordrecht in 1519, the execution of van Oldenbarnevelt, and the imprisonment of Grotius, the university was purged, but its trustees resisted the domination of the Contra-Remonstrants and Leiden was soon once again a locale where thought was relatively free. "Thanks to the wisdom of the University trustees," writes one historian, "and the prudence of the States of Holland, Leiden enjoyed quite an appreciable liberty in the seventeenth century. But this liberty must of course be measured by the yardstick of the times, meaning that it could not be absolute."[41]

Kulmus was a Lutheran. And although Danzig, now Gdansk, was a center of Socinianism in the late sixteenth and early seventeenth centuries, there is no reason to think he was a crypto-Socinian. But like his teacher, Ruysch, Kulmus was a proponent of natural theology: he thought that the very perfection of the human machine proved the existence of a creator. In this line of thought the Bible is not the sole source of Revelation, and reason, in its way, is every bit as valid a pathway to God as faith, in its way.

In 1722 Kulmus published in Gotha his *Elementa philosophiae naturalis* (reissued in Göttingen in 1727 and in Danzig in 1737), in which he confirms this orientation. Physical science, he wrote, is a means for "everyone, and especially theologians, to demonstrate that the existence of God is very useful and very necessary." In his historical review of the developments of natural philosophy, the first figure he cites is Descartes, "intrepid denouncer of scholastic errors." Descartes, he says, "put an entirely new face on physical science, and inaugurated the first method that allowed for freedom of philosophy. Other philosophers . . . followed him, others took further his research on truth in the natural sciences thanks to more precise observations and experiments, backed by the efforts of rationality and judgment." In this class were Leibniz, Newton, Mariotte, and Wolff. Kulmus writes: "In natural philosophy, nothing must be the product of the imagination, nothing must be negated by simple conjecture. Everything must be proved by reason alone, sustained by certain and unquestionable examples."[42]

Two of his dissertations in Latin, printed in 1733 and preserved in the Gdansk city library attest to the fact that Kulmus did not hesitate to subject the Scriptures themselves to the scrutiny of reason. The first concerns the darkness that seemed to fall upon Palestine as Christ was dying; the second addresses the rainbow that appeared in the sky after the Flood. Regarding the former, assuming the dates are accurate, it is not possible that the darkening of the sky was the result of an eclipse of the sun,[43] but one may imagine, as Kepler did, that the sky was filled at that moment with ash from some volcanic eruption. The latter case was not a miracle in the true sense of the word. Whenever there is water in the atmosphere under certain conditions of light, a rainbow inevitably appears; Newton and Wolff had demonstrated this. Thus rainbows had been witnesed before the Flood. The miracle, a purely moral one, was that Noah and his sons saw in it a sign of divine benevolence toward them.

Lorenz Heister was another Protestant and believer in natural science, like Ruysch. Altdorf, where he had been granted a professorship in 1710, was the seat of the Protestant university of Nuremberg. Helmstedt, where he was called in 1720, was another Protestant university; it had been founded in 1576 by Duke Julius von Braunschweig and was for a long time the most populous one in Germany. The *Compendium medicinae practicae* (Abstract of Practical Medicine), which he published in Amsterdam a few years after his *Institutiones chirurgicae* (General System of Surgery), distinguishes nine types of medicine, from the empirical and rational to the mechanical and Stahlian. For him, the "workings of the human body" (the title of Vesalius's famous treatise) are entirely mechanical. They are the reciprocal interplay of an assemblage of fluids and solids for which the anatomist can accurately make an account and formulate laws on the basis of observations grounded in physics, chemistry, and mechanics. From these laws, the means of maintaining health and caring for the sick may be deduced rationally.

At the opening of the *Compendium* Heister cites the master Boerhaave as among those who, "rejecting the yoke of authority, admit nothing as certain or true, no matter who affirms it, unless they know it to be proven, either by the witness of their own senses or by unequivocal observations and experiments."[44] He refers to Albinus (1697–1770) as much as to Boerhaave and Ruysch, and this is no less significant. Albinus was in effect the first to consider anatomy a province of geometry. For him, it was not merely a matter of describing shapes; it was also necessary to measure and model the body in space with the greatest precision possible.[45] He was returning, unknowingly, to the concerns of Leonardo da Vinci, whose notebooks were not yet known.

Today, if one delves down to the archaeological foundation of the science that the Dutch East India Company merchants and physicians brought to Japan, it becomes clear that beyond the differences that may separate its authors, and beyond their superficial affinities, all without exception participate in the deep current running from Erasmus to the Enlightenment. Those who belong to this current, liberal Protestants or moderate Catholics, are not strictly speaking dissidents; some even had shining careers under the aegis of lay or ecclesiastical protectors. But if they were able to work, to produce, and finally to make their mark, it is because they lived in a time and place—the Republic of Venice, the Germanic countries, the Netherlands—in which the orthodoxy, *whatever it was*, was being rocked by dissidence. Protestantism or Erasmianism was threatening the Church of Rome in Italy, Spain, and France in the time of Vesalius, Paré, and Valverde. Anabaptist and Socinian thought contended vigorously with Lutheran and Calvinist orthodoxy in Poland, Germany, Switzerland, and Holland in Remmelin's and Bartholin's day. The effect of this multiform contentiousness was felt in Leiden, Amsterdam, Strasbourg, and Basel when Rusych, Bidloo, Kulmus, and Heister were active. It was strengthened with each new gain of Cartesianism, then Newtonianism, in the academies and universities.

This luminous picture may elicit the objection that the earliest Japanese users of these Western sources could not read the texts and knew nothing of their authors' other publications, let alone the surrounding philosophical or religious debates. To which it may be replied that the images themselves, as well as the oral commentaries on them by the Deshima physicians, necessarily bore a relationship to this context and could orient in the right direction open minds such as Sugita Gempaku's or Maeno Ryotaku's. Above all, one must recall that cultivated Japanese society had already experienced for itself, as early as the late sixteenth century, the banefulness of the tradition the European intelligentsia was battling at the time: scholastic Aristotelianism, the principle of authority, and dogmatism lay at the very foundation of the missionaries' preaching and catechism, as revealed by the refutations made in the seventeenth century by Hayashi Razan, Fabian Fukan, and Cristóvão Ferreira and in the eighteenth by Arai Hakuseki. Japan, in rejecting this, had *already* taken the radical stand that many European scientists and philosophers would not formulate until later, on other grounds, with other arguments, and sometimes after considerable vacillation.[46]

FREEZE FRAME

The Japanese artists who copied plates from Paré, Remmelin, and others did not always reproduce them as they were, because the meaning of an image is never unequivocal. They often had to interpret them, and their manner of doing so reveals much about the nature of their receptivity to the transmitted message, beyond any verbal communication.

The Japanese copies of Paré hold a second layer of interest in that most of the time Paré himself was appropriating illustrations from earlier works. One example concerns the method of treating a dislocated shoulder by suspending the patient on a ladder (*Dix livres de chirurgie* [Paris, 1564]). To illustrate this Paré had taken an engraving by the Italian Guido Guidi (*Chirurgia e graeco in latinum conversa* [Paris,

1544]),[47] itself inspired by a Byzantine manuscript from the tenth century, preserved in Florence, which in turn reproduced Greek figures from the first century B.C.E. In Guidi, the patient on the ladder is a muscular, naked, curly-haired Adonis reminiscent of the figures of Michelangelo. The assistants, one holding him by the neck and the other pulling on his arm, are dressed in ancient style, in short flowing tunics. The artist who illustrated Paré's treatise had little concern for the appearance of the patient, whose position alone was of interest, and he dressed the assistants in the style of the era of Charles IX. He also placed them on a sort of platform surrounded with plants of indeterminate species and added, to the left of the ladder, a pedestal with a vase and a length of cloth. The Japanese artists eliminated this ornamentation, whose function was probably not clear to them; they reproduced the assistants' garments as best they could and Japanized the facial features of the three figures.[48]

Vesalius and Remmelin, or rather the artists who illustrated their works, Jan Stefan van Kalkar[49] and Lucas Kilian, are highly typical, each in his way, of a genre the art historian André Chastel refers to admiringly as "moralized anatomy." Indeed, in Europe the anatomical image was not at first accepted as such by the general sensibility. It was seen only secondarily as having scientific or even aesthetic interest. Its function was primarily moral and spiritual. In this regard the Renaissance took a long time to free itself of the medieval conception of the relation between the living and the dead, as ordained by the predominant religious beliefs.[50]

The paradigmatic example is the "ploughman skeleton." At the end of the fifteenth century, and even before, the skeleton had become the "moral symbol" of death. In *L'Art de bien mourir* (The Art of Dying Well) by Savonarola (1497), the skeleton symbolizes the battle between heaven and hell. In one wood engraving it is seen seated with its scythe at the foot of a dying man's bed. Above the altar facing the bed is a large Christ on the cross. In the sky a halo-ringed Madonna appears flanked by two angels. A monk kneels by the deathbed praying. Behind him, through the open doorway, several horned devils are seen.

In a painting by Brueghel titled *The Triumph of Death*, now in the Prado, "the skeleton is used with intentional extravagance as a universal symbol, featureless and inaccurate in structure but animated in an infinite array of gestures and attitudes. The moral lesson is underlined by the fact that the composition touches on all the forms of vice and sin, and a giant toad—the image of evil—hops along behind Death. The skeleton is a stand-in for each of us: it is at once executioner and victim; wearing a mask, it announces the death of the worldly man. In short, the symbol puts on the mask of each of us to draw us into an awareness of our destiny."[51]

The skeletons in Vesalius's *Fabrica* typify moralized anatomy in several ways. They are in positions normally taken by the living and appear against a background landscape that has been identified as a place in the Paduan countryside called Abano Terme. The ploughman (actually a grave digger) leans on his spade at the edge of an open grave, lifting his vacant eye sockets to the sky, his jaws open as though in a scream. Another skeleton, its head resting on its left elbow, which leans on the entablature of a stela, seems to be meditating on a skull that it holds dreamily in its right hand. A third, seen from the rear, knees bent and head leaning on its two crossed hands, seems to be lamenting over the trunk of a small tree that has been cut down, while a lizard scurries by.[52]

Clearly this scene has a pedagogical function, and it addresses every viewer of these pictures: each one has a skeleton inside; each, sooner or later, will be reduced to this skeleton.[53] The allegory is even more telling in the versions of *Fabrica* where the stela on which the skull is resting bears the Latin inscription *Vivitur ingenio, caetera mortis erunt:* "Genius survives, all else is mortal." Art historians have also noted that the skeleton seen from the back is in a position similar to that of one of the disciples in Titian's *Entombment of Christ* in the Louvre.[54]

Those who copied the "ploughman" in Europe assimilated the message quite well. Paré, who was a believer, understood the moral value of such representations. The "ploughman" appears twice in the 1636 Dutch edition of his *De chirurgie*, the second time at the end of the book in a section on the plague, where it is accompanied by a rhyming text to the effect that Death is not looked on in the same way by the rich and the poor, the virtuous and the villainous; for all it is "the end of all misery and the beginning of eternal life."

Lairesse, illustrating Bidloo, did not copy Vesalius, but following on his model created variations faithful to the genre. The standing

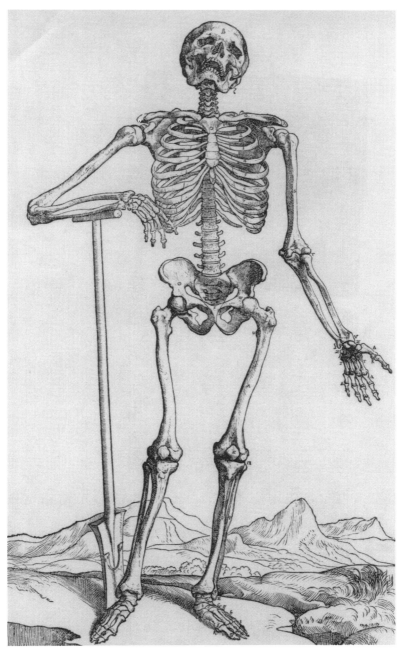

Andreas Vesalius, De fabrica humani corporis (1543), *"The Ploughman Skeleton."*

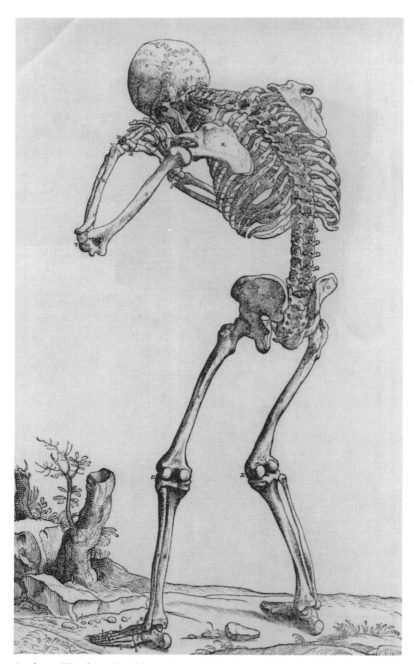

Andreas Vesalius, *De fabrica humani corporis* (1543).

skeleton in plate 87 of *Anatomia illustrata* is seen against a mountainous landscape, an open grave at its feet and in its hand an hourglass, the symbol of the inexorable flow of time. The skeleton seen from the rear in plate 88 is hardly Kalkar or Titian but does them one better in moralizing: holding a shroud in its hand it is about to descend into the grave, beneath a stone archway. In the middle distance is a truncated pyramid resting on sphinxes. The background is a landscape in the ancient style.

Among the plates with which Otsuki Gentaku enriched the second edition of *Kaitai shinsho*, there is also a "ploughman" leaning on his spade with his head raised toward the sky. The exact model the Japanese artist followed in 1798 is unknown, but it is certain that he did not apprehend the message embedded in the European imagery. The landscape and grave have disappeared, and the spade, in a shape that was unknown in Japan, functions only as a comfortable support for the subject's bent forearm. To further reduce the image to its scientific function, the artist has given it a totally original composition: the skeleton is slightly taller than the frame surrounding it, so that its feet seem to go past the bottom of the frame, as though it is walking toward the viewer. There is also a back view of a skeleton in this second edition of *Kaitai shinsho*, but the artist has omitted the allegorical tree, which evokes nothing for him. In the space where it had been, he has added a view of the shoulder blade. The pose is thus restored to the significance that, in the end, Vesalius and Kalkar had in mind: it demonstrates a stretched spinal column and gives an excellent view of the attachment of the ribs to the vertebrae, seen between widely parted shoulder blades.

Motoki Ryoi subjected Remmelin to an even more radical trimming in the last half of the seventeenth century, at or near the time when the Bavarian's plates were on display at the University of Leiden amphitheater. Perhaps because Augsburg and Ulm, where the author lived, was somewhat on the sidelines of the great currents of innovation streaming through the major Western universities, or perhaps due to Remmelin's particular sensibility, the plates in *Pinax microcosmographicus*, and even more so those in *Catoptrum microcosmicum*, are so overloaded with symbols and biblical quotations in Latin, Greek, and Hebrew that they finally obscure the images' properly anatomical function in favor of pious didacticism.

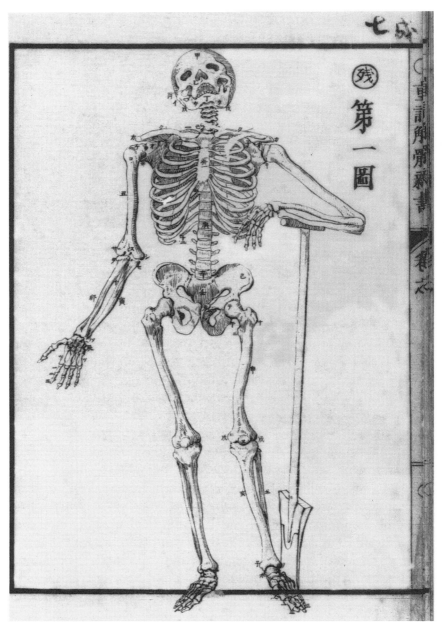

Preparatory drawing for the second edition of *Kaitai shinsho* (ca. 1798). Library of the University of Waseda, Tokyo.

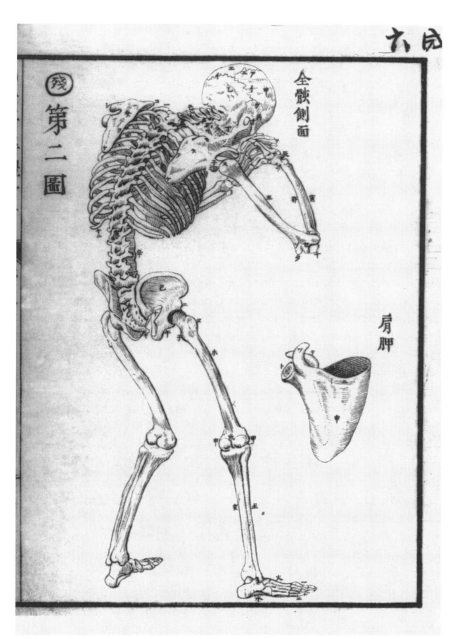

Preparatory drawing for the second edition of *Kaitai shinsho* (ca. 1798). Library of the University of Waseda, Tokyo.

There are only three plates in the original edition of *Catoptrum*—Remmelin had baptized them "visions"—and four in the original edition of *Pinax*, but it would be an endless endeavor to draw out in all their detail and specificity the messages that the text and the image, in interplay with each other, are meant to convey. In addition, the plates are meant to be read in reverse order, from the image of the woman (Eve), to whom the serpent is presenting the fatal apple at the bottom of the third plate, to the halo beaming from the mystical tetragram of Yahweh in the first. The entire story of salvation is condensed here, in a discourse in which symbolic images and Bible quotations reflect and oppose each other at the same time, and for those who know how to "read" it, all sorts of correspondences and antitheses emerge between macrocosm and microcosm, high and low, birth and death, humans and nature, mind and body, redemption and damnation. The plates of *Pinax*, less crowded than those of *Catoptrum*, are somewhat more legible, but the intent behind them was the same.[55] All this goes far beyond moralized anatomy and situates Remmelin's work, even though he was a Protestant, within the baroque madness of the Counter-Reformation rather than among the sober *vanitas* themes that Dutch artists were painting during the same period.

The extraordinary success of *Pinax microcosmographicus* in Europe was largely due to this demonstrative exuberance, but one may wonder why the University of Leiden would give it such eminent exposure. The anatomy amphitheater had been conceived from the start as a theatrical site, where the great drama of life and death would be staged. Petrus Pauw (1564–1617), who created it in the late sixteenth century, had studied for a time at Padua. He was well acquainted with Vesalius's *Fabrica* and placed real human and animal skeletons, as well as stuffed animals, everywhere throughout the amphitheater, so that students and visitors found themselves mingling in life with a ubiquitous cast of extras from the world of the dead. The subjects were frozen in dramatic poses, the human skeletons holding placards with mottoes such as *Memento mori* (Remember that one must die), *Pulvis et umbra sumus* (We are dust and shadow), and *Nosce te ipsum* (Know thyself). But the symbolism of the precariousness of human life set in this space took on its fullest significance in the summer, during the university vacation, when the amphitheater was open to visits from the public. Two

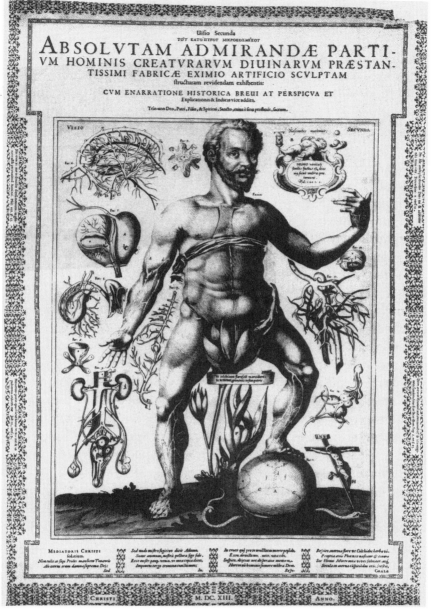

Johannes Remmelin and Cornelius Danckersz, *Pinax microcosmographicus*, Amsterdam 1634, pl. II.

skeletons would be placed on the dissection table in the center of the hall to represent Adam and Eve, on either side of the Tree of Knowledge, symbolizing "naturally" (with no need for an explanatory text) the Fall and Original Sin, which were responsible for the presence of evil in the world and the omnipresence of death. A 1610 etching drawn by J. C. Wondarius (ca. 1570–1615) and engraved by W. Swanenburg (1581/82–1612) gives a fairly good idea of the spectacle that greeted summer visitors to the amphitheater. The unexpected presence of a dog, stage right, makes it seem almost a scene from daily life. Stage left, a woman ponders a human skin displayed by a docent, her gaze as tranquil as though she were examining a swatch of fabric.[56]

It is certain that in Japan the rash of texts and symbols smothering the *Pinax* plates seemed completely exotic. Had a hundredth of their meaning been deciphered, the work would have been banned under the edicts prohibiting from the empire Christian propaganda in any form. This happy incomprehension saved Remmelin's work. Motoki Ryoi kept nothing but its strictly anatomical aspect, though this had been secondary in the mind of the original creator. He retained more than anything its pedagogical concept.

This concept was not entirely new in Europe. In Strasbourg in 1544, a work was printed by Jacob Fröhlich that contained colored wood engravings, made in 1539, with drawings that could be opened. One shows a pregnant woman, seated, knees apart. The part of the image from the neck to the pubis can be lifted to reveal the organs. These are represented again separately, above and on either side of the main figure, with explanations in German. Between the spleen and the intestines is the womb, containing a curled-up fetus.[57]

Vesalius used the same technique in a work that was not meant for anatomists and artists, as was *Fabrica*, but for practicing physicians, barber-surgeons, and students. This summary *(Epitome)* included several plates "presented so that the pictures of internal organs may be cut out and mounted on a larger figure, such that when they are lifted or moved aside the organs may be seen, in order, from the surface to the deepest level of the organism."[58]

Motoki Ryoi and those who later reprinted his adaptation of Remmelin quickly grasped the innovative nature of this new mode of presentation, and that is what they retained from *Pinax*, to the exclusion of everything else encumbering the plates. The result can seem comical. The Japanese copies show a man and a woman in very strange positions. Each one is lifting an arm and a leg for no apparent reason, and the raised leg is deformed as though atrophied, because the artist did not understand the use of perspective. A look at the original shows why. In *Pinax*, the woman's right foot is placed on an upside-down skull; slithering out of the skull is a snake that seems to be offering her with its raised head a branch with a hanging apple. The man's left foot rests on a skull shaped like a globe of the earth; again a snake emerges, this time with its head pierced by a crucifix.

A Bateren, in his time, would no doubt have drawn from it a somber sermon. Motoki Ryoi perceived instinctively, eighty years ahead of his time, that the future belonged to images that opened. He surely did not suspect that one day Japanese physicians would open with their own hands the great book of nature, by the light of reason alone. They were aided, it is true, by the books of Kulmus and Heister, at last fully unencumbered by the aura of "moralizing anatomy." But would anyone have understood *Kaitai shinsho* in 1774 if Ryoi's book had not circulated for several decades in specialized milieus and been released to the public in 1772?

Epilogue

On June 27, 1598, a company of Dutch merchants headed by Johann van der Veeke and Pieter van der Hagen sent a small fleet of five ships from Amsterdam to the East Indies. Being good Calvinists, and no doubt a tinge superstitious, they had given the ships names inspired by the Gospels: *Faith, Hope, Charity, Fidelity,* and *Gospel.* The commander of the expedition was Jacques Mahn. The pilot was an Englishman, William Adams.

Four years earlier Philip II, king of Spain and Portugal, had closed the port of Lisbon to Dutch commerce to punish his former subjects for rebelling against him. The flotilla sailed across the Atlantic toward the Strait of Magellan, traveled along the coast of Chile and Peru, then veered west across the Pacific in the direction of the Asian continent. This was the route Magellan had forged in 1519. It had been subsequently recognized by the English explorers Francis Drake in 1577–80 and Thomas Cavendish in 1586–88, and would be followed much later, in 1766–69, by Louis Antoine de Bougainville.

The expedition encountered all manner of difficulties, and only one vessel made it to shore on the north of the Japanese island of Kyushu, where it landed in the Bay of Beppu in mid-April 1600. It was the *Charity* (in Dutch, *De Liefde*), with William Adams aboard. Of the 110 men who had sailed, no more than 80 remained, and of these only

5 were able to walk. Their strength was completely exhausted, and several of them died of hunger the day after disembarking.

The Portuguese, sworn enemies of the Dutch, wanted the Japanese authorities to severely punish the intrusion of these strangers. They considered Kyushu a sort of private hunting ground; it was there that their missionaries had done their most effective evangelizing. And they themselves did not feel safe. Twenty-six Christians, including nine missionaries, had been crucified in Nagasaki the year before, and Spanish missionaries from the Philippines had already begun to compete with them here, right in Miyako, where the emperor's residence was located. But the Japanese, for their part, were curious to see "barbarians" different from the ones they were used to. These had red hair, did not attend Mass, and did not come from the south.

The "Dutch" were taken prisoner, and Adams was questioned by the shogun about the situation in Europe. He was freed after forty-one days and sent to Edo, where his talents were put to use, particularly for naval construction. But he was not permitted to return to Europe.

De Liefde, towed from its landing point to Funai, was quickly demolished and its debris dispersed. Nothing remained except a wooden statue that had been affixed to the stern, as was the custom at the time. It is possible that Adams was allowed to keep it and later gave it to some Japanese noble of distinction, who kept it at home. It was not seen again until after World War I, when it reappeared in the Ryukoji temple, in the Tochigi prefecture north of Tokyo.

For a long time the identity of the person represented by the statue was uncertain, until one day it was noticed that the statue had in its hand a scroll, on which one could still read the letters *E, R, M, U, S* and a date: 1598. Its resemblance to the statue of Erasmus found in the Rotterdam market square eliminated all doubt: it was indeed Erasmus. Moreover, the ship that carried William Adams, before being renamed *De Liefde*, had been called *Erasmus*.[1] In the hall of the National Museum of Tokyo, where it is preserved today amid other polychrome wood statues representing the sages and saints of Japan, Erasmus looks like the legendary Socrates conversing with his disciples before a dialogue with Plato. It looks as though the author of *Colloquies* has been there forever, *among his own kind*. The European passerby, eavesdropping on the silent dialogue, stops and falls silent too.

The Philosophical Canons of Coimbra

The detailed contents of the courses that made up *O Cânone filosófico conimbrense* and the names of their authors are presented in a book published in German in 1931 and translated into Portuguese in 1959. The author was Friedrich Stegmüller, and the Portuguese title was *Filosofia e teologia nas universidades de Coimbra e Évora no século XVI.*

If the name of Aristotle is mentioned in the very title of the *Curso*, it is because references to his work are everywhere. Several are found in the first part of volume 2 (Coimbra, 1592), signed by Manuel de Góis. The first four books concern "The Heavens." In it one learns that "Aristotle was not merely a philosopher who praised order and method in the transmission of knowledge but also a particularly attentive observer." The first book of "The Heavens" begins with the Aristotelian proof of the perfection of the universe. This is followed by "a few problems regarding the four elements that constitute the world." There Aristotle proves in three different ways that earth may be considered a "pure element." In the book "Meteors," Aristotle's *De generatione* is used as the basis for discussing "common doctrine" about the elements and "divisible substances" in general. Aristotle's name is found three more times in the book that treats various subjects in natural history: in the title, in the text regarding dreams, and in the text on youth and age.

The second part of volume 2 of the *Curso* (Coimbra, 1594) is also compiled by Manuel de Góis. It contains the *Nicomachean Ethics*, in ten books. Góis again signs volume 3 (Coimbra, 1597), titled *De generatione et corruptione*.

Volume 4, published in Coimbra in 1598, is edited by Cosme de Magalhães. It contains three treatises. The first is by Manuel de Góis and concerns the soul. The third part refers the reader directly to Aristotle, as does the treatise by Baltasar Alvares, *De anima separata*. Volume 5 (Coimbra, 1606) contains a course by Pedro de Fonseca, edited by Sebastião de Couto, and titled *In universam dialecticam Aristotelis*. The title is significant.

However, important parts of the course were not included in the *Commentarii* published at Coimbra. Omitted were the fours parts of Pedro de Fonseca's already dated *Metaphysics*, published respectively in Rome in 1577 and 1589, in Évora in 1604, and in Lyon in 1612. Also absent was *Logic*, released in 1604 without the authorization of the College of Coimbra and published simultaneously in Frankfurt, Hamburg, Cologne, and Venice; its two volumes were titled *Collegii conimbricensis S.J. commentarii doctissimi in universam logicam Aristotelis*. Its author was Gaspar Coelho, and the lessons had been given at Évora in 1584. Coelho himself was following a lecture course given at Coimbra in 1571 by Francisco Cardoso.

Although the first of the *Commentarii* was published in 1592, the material was already old. The decision to publish them had been made by the Provincial Congregation in 1579, and Góis's work had consisted largely of polishing, perfecting, and concretizing teachings that went back to Pedro de Fonseca in the years 1567–70 and even further, to the first days of the Coimbra College of the Arts and the University of Évora.

Chronology

1492   Granada is retaken from Muslims. Edict expels the Spanish Jews. Christopher Columbus departs from Palos (August 3).

1493   Papal bull divides the non-Christian world into two parts, one granted to Spain, the other to Portugal.

1494   Treaty of Tordesillas, fixing the meridian line dividing the Spanish and Portuguese zones of influence at 370 leagues west of Cape Verde.

1496–97 Forced conversion of Jews and Moors residing in Portugal.

1498   Vasco da Gama reaches India.

1500   Cabral takes possession of Brazil in the name of Portugal.

1502   Jacopo Sannazaro publishes *Arcadia* in Venice.

1506   Pogrom in Lisbon (April 19); thousands of *conversos* are killed.

1508   (approx.) Titian paints *The Pastoral Symphony* (long attributed to Giorgione).

1509   (approx.) Birth of Ambroise Paré.

1510   Afonso de Albuquerque establishes territorial base in Goa as a Portuguese administrative seat.

1511   Albuquerque wins Malacca from the Muslims. *The Praise of Folly*, by Erasmus, printed in Paris.

1513–1514 The Portuguese gain a foothold in China.

1516   The first translation of Erasmus into Castilian is published in Seville. Erasmus is adviser to Charles V and publishes the New Testament in Greek. Thomas More publishes *Utopia*. Selim I, ruler of the Turkish Empire, conquers Mesopotamia, Syria, and Egypt.

1517   Luther nails his theses on the doors of the Castle Church of Wittenberg. Erasmus begins to organize the trilingual College of Louvain. The Portuguese establish themselves in Canton.

1519	Death of Leonardo da Vinci. Erasmus refuses to join with Luther. Cortés conquers Mexico.
1520	Death of Raphaël. Suleiman the Magnificent ascends to the Ottoman throne. Belgrade is taken by the Turks. First Portuguese ambassador arrives at the court of the emperor of Ethiopia.
1521	John III ascends to the throne of Portugal. Dürer arrives in Anvers. Luther is excommunicated, begins his translation of the Bible into German. Magellan discovers the Philippines.
1522	First edition of the *Colloquies* of Erasmus to be claimed by its author. The Inquisition is established in the Netherlands.
1523	First executions in Anvers for religious reasons.
1524	Erasmus publishes *Diatribè sive Collatio de libero arbitrio*, his treatise on free will.
1525	Luther replies to Erasmus with "Bondage of the Will." John III marries Catherine, a sister of Charles V.
1526	Charles V marries Jean III's sister, Isabel. Turks invade Hungary.
1527	At theological congress of Valladolid, Portuguese representatives are hostile to Erasmianism. Imperial sack of Rome.
1528	Death of Dürer.
1529	First siege of Vienna by the Turks.
1530	François I creates the Collège Royal (the current Collège de France).
1531	Portuguese humanist André de Resende publishes his *Eulogy to Erasmus* in Basel. Michaël Servetus publishes *De Trinitatis erroribus*. John III solicits authorization from Rome to initiate the Portuguese Inquisition; it is denied.
1532	François I comissions in Brussels a wall hanging devoted to the "Story of Scipion."
1533	Pizarro has the Incan ruler Atahualpa condemned to death and takes over Cuzco.
1534	Goa becomes a bishopric with jurisdiction over Asia and East Africa.
1535	Capture of Tunis by Charles V. Massacre of Anabaptists in Münster.
1536	Death of Erasmus. Calvin publishes *Institutes of the Christian Religion*, in Latin, in Basel. Signing of the "Capitulations" between

France and Turkey, a consular agreement followed by a military alliance against the Hapsburgs. Pope Paul III agrees to the establishment of the Inquisition in Portugal, with certain restrictions.

1537   German humanist Jean Sturm is called to Strasbourg for the renewal of the Schools. The senate of Venice authorizes Vesalius to teach in Padua.

1539   Cardinal Enrique, brother of the king of Portugal, becomes Inquisitor General (he will also become regent of the kingdom from 1562 to 1568 and king from 1578 to 1580).

1540   First auto-da-fé in Lisbon (September 20). Pope Paul II approves the creation of the Society of Jesus.

1541   Calvin initiates the Reformation in Geneva.

1543   Vesalius publishes *De humani corporis fabrica* in Basel and dedicates the work to the crown prince of Spain, the future Philip II. Copernicus publishes *De revolutionibus orbium celestium* in Nuremberg. The Portuguese land on the island of Tanegashima in southwestern Japan.

1544   Vesalius becomes physician to the court of Charles V.

1545   Ambroise Paré publishes *La Méthode de traiter les plaies faites par les haquebutes et autres bâtons à feu* (Method of Treating Wounds Made by the Harquebus and Other Firearms). Council of Trent begins.

1546   Death of Luther.

1547   Pope Paul lifts the last restrictions on the Inquisition in Portugal.

1547–48 Foundation of the Royal College, also called the College of the Arts and Humanities, by John III of Portugal. André de Gouveia is called to the College of Guyenne to establish programs, then returns to France to recruit professors for it. War in India between the Portuguese and the Muslim state of Bijapur, where Goa is located.

1548   Yajiro becomes first Japanese to receive baptism in Goa from the hand of Francis Xavier.

1549   Francis Xavier begins to preach in Japan.

1550   Completion of the first version of the Constitutions of the Society of Jesus. Christophe Plantin becomes a citizen of Anvers and a member of the guild of Saint Luke. In Portugal, two professors at the College of the Arts are accused of Lutheranism.

1551	Procedural dispute between Father Cosmo de la Torres and the Buddhist monks of Yamaguchi. Francis Xavier leaves Japan.
1552	Death of Francis Xavier off the Chinese coast.
1553	Michaël Servetus is sentenced to be burned alive in Geneva (October 28). First Japanese envoy to Europe, Bernardo, from Kagoshima, arrives in Lisbon.
1554	Humanist Sebastian Castellion publishes *De haereticis an sint persequendi* (Must Heretics Be Persecuted?).
1555	Abdication of Charles V; his states are divided between Philip II of Spain and Ferdinand of Austria. Coimbra College of the Arts is given over to the Jesuits. Spain establishes a "pure blood" statute that is ratified by the pope. The Portuguese establish a trading post on Macao.
1556	First printing press in Goa. Juan Valverde de Amusco publishes his *Historia de la composición del cuerpo humano* (History of the Composition of the Human Body) in Rome.
1557	Death of John III. His grandson Sebastião takes the throne under the regency of his grandmother Catherine, then of his great-uncle Enrique.
1558	A Jesuit university opens at Évora. In the Indies, Cochin becomes an ecclesiastical province.
1560	Inquisition established in Goa. The superior general of the Society of Jesus imposes in Japan the Constitutions of the order, approved by the General Congregation in 1558.
1562	Brother Valentim da Luz, of the order of the Hermits of Saint Augustine, is accused of Lutheranism and burned at the stake in an auto-da-fé in Lisbon. In Japan. the *daimyo* Omura Sumitada opens the port of Yokoseura to the Portuguese.
1563	Council of Trent ends. Omura Sumitada baptized with the name Dom Bartolomeu. First auto-da-fé in Goa.
1564	Birth of Galileo. Paré publishes *Dix livres de la chirurgie* (Ten Books on Surgery). Council of Trent promulgates the Tridentine Index.
1566	*Catechismus romanus* completed by Cardinal Borromeo. Publication in Anvers of *Vivae imagines corporis humani* by Juan Valverde and Vesalius. First wave of iconoclasm in Flanders and the Brabant; religious unrest begins in Anvers. Death of Suleiman the Magnificent; Selim II succeeds him.

1567	Initiation of the Terror in the Netherlands under the direction of the Duke of Alba.
1568	*Biblia regia* project begun by Plantin in Anvers, under the direction of Arias Montanus, chaplain to Philip II. In Japan, Odu Nobunaga enters Miyako (Kyoto).
1569	New "Capitulations" between France and Turkey: French consuls are henceforth considered protectors of the Frankish—meaning European—community in the Turkish Empire.
1570	Publication in Anvers of the *Theatrum orbis terrarum* by Ortelius. Publication in Rome of treatise *De sphaera* by John Holywood, known as Joannes de Sacrobosco. Turks conquer Cyprus. In the Philippines, the Spanish begin to build Manila.
1571	A Christian fleet commanded by Don John of Austria defeats the Turkish fleet in the Battle of Lepanto (October 7). In gratitude, Pope Pius V institutes the Feast of Our Lady of Victory, which in 1573 becomes the Feast of the Rosary. In Emden, the Algemeene Synode der Reformierten founds the Dutch Reformed Church. In Japan, Nobunaga destroys Buddhist sanctuaries on Mount Hiei in Miyako. Nagasaki becomes the first Portuguese trading port in Japan. Sebastião of Portugal launches an expedition against the Moors of Morocco.
1572	Publication of the *Lusiades* by Camoens (1525–80), the product of Portuguese humanism in the first half of the century. Saint Bartholomew's Day Massacre in Paris. In Portugal, the humanist Damião de Góis is sentenced to life in prison.
1574	Death of Selim II; accession of his son, Murad III.
1575	Ceremonial opening of the University of Leiden (February 5). Macao becomes the seat of an ecclesiastical province. The Battle of Nagashino in Japan demonstrates superiority of firearms over cavalry.
1576	French and Turks favor accession to the Polish throne of Stefan Bathory, who as prince of Transylvania had been a vassal of the sultan since 1571. Spanish pillage Anvers. In Japan, Nobunaga has the Castle of Azuchi built on the shore of Lake Biwa.
1578	Second expedition of Portugal's Sebastião II to Morocco; he dies there along with the flower of Portuguese nobility.
1579	In Japan, baptism of Arima Harunobu, "king" of Arima, under the name Dom Protasio. Alessandro Valignano's first visit to Japan. In

the Netherlands, seven provinces unite to form the Union of Utrecht, establishing mutual assurances of freedom and status under the leadership of William of Orange.

1580   Dynastic union of Spain and Portugal under the crown of Philip II. "Pure blood" is law now enforced in Portugal. Two seminaries open in Japan, at Arima and Azuchi.

1582   Assassination of Nobunaga in Japan; Hideyoshi takes power. Valignano sends four young Japanese to Europe as "ambassadors."

1583   Valignano publishes *Sumario de las cosas de Japón*. Arrival of Giovanni Niccolò in Nagasaki. Hideyoshi has the Castle of Osaka built. Christophe Plantin established in Leiden as printer for the new university. Philip II names his nephew, Archduke Albert of Austria, as governor of Portugal in his name.

1584   Giordano Bruno publishes *Dell'infinito, universo e mondi* in London. Father Fróis begins to compile his *History of Japan*.

1585   Birth of Jansen. Brief from Gregory XII gives Jesuits the monopoly on the mission to Japan. Final surrender of Anvers to the Spanish; emigration of publishers involved with the Reformation, including the son-in-law of Plantin and Louis Elzevir. Christophe Plantin leaves Leiden for Cologne, then returns to Anvers after the city is taken. Valignano's Japanese envoys are formally received by the Republic of Venice (June 26).

1586   Albert of Austria, the governor of Portugal, becomes Grand Inquisitor. Valignano publishes his *Catechismus christianae fidei* in Lisbon. A brief from Sixtus V seems to annul that of Gregory XIII granting monopoly on the mission to Japan to the Society of Jesus; Franciscans are authorized to work anywhere in the Far East.

1587   Hideyoshi bans Christianity in Japan; missionaries have twenty days to leave the country, on pain of death; Portuguese merchants tolerated as their presence appears indispensable. These measures have no immediate effect.

1588   First printing with movable type in Macao. In Japan, Funai becomes the seat of an ecclesiastical province.

1590   Return of the delegation sent by Valignano to Europe (October). Publication in Macao of *De missione legatorum*. Advent of the Kano school of painting, in Miyako.

1591   First edition of the *Ratio studiorum* by the Society of Jesus. Toyotomi Hideyoshi formally receives the young Japanese "ambassadors" after their return from Europe (March 3). The four "ambassadors" take the robes of novices at Amakusa (July).

1592   Galileo gets his start in Padua as a mathematics professor. Start of publication of *Commentarii Collegii Conimbricensis S.J. in Aristotelem*. Publication in Nagasaki of *Dochirina kirishitan* in romanized Japanese. The Society of Jesus expels *conversos* from its ranks. Japanese attempt to invade Korea.

1592 or 1593   Publication in Amakusa of *Tales of Heike*, containing, among other things, a Japanese translation of seventy of Æsop's fables.

1593   Beginning of thirteen-year war between Turkey and the Hapsburgs. On May 28, a conference of theologians meeting in Manila authorizes the entry of Franciscans to Japan. On arrival they begin to construct two hospitals in Miyako.

1594   Faustus Socinus publishes *De Jesu Christo Servatore* in Poland.

1597   First synagogue in Amsterdam is opened. Publication in Rome of *Dottrina christiana breve*, by Cardinal Bellarmini. Second Japanese attempt to invade Korea. Twenty-six Christians are crucified in Nagasaki, including seventeen Japanese converts.

1598   Death of Philip II and of Hideyoshi. Archduke Albert and Archduchess Isabelle rule in name only the South Netherlands, actually governed by the military leader Ambroise de Spinola. Brief by Clement VIII revokes Jesuit monopoly in Japan. In France, Henri IV promulgates the Edict of Nantes, assuring relative religious peace in the country until 1685.

1599   Campanella is tortured and imprisoned for his philosophical and political opinions; remains in prison twenty-seven years. Superior General Aquaviva promulgates the Society of Jesus' *Ratio et institutio studiorum*.

1600   Giordano Bruno sentenced to the stake in Rome (February 17). In Japan, Tokugawa Ieyasu conquers his rivals at the Battle of Sekigahara. Founding in England of the British East India Company. On April 19, the Dutch ship *De Leifde*, formerly named *Erasmus*, under the English pilot William Adams, lands at the Bay of Beppu, north of Kyushu.

1602   Publication in Vicenza of Cardinal Bellarmini's *Dottrina christiana breve* in translation for the German-speaking population of the diocese of Padua. Founding of the Dutch East India Company.

1603	Tokugawa Ieyasu takes command as shogun. Military government installed in Edo (Tokyo). In Leiden, Arminius begins teaching as professor of theology.
1604	In China, Ricci publishes *The True Meaning of the Lord of Heaven*. In Japan, Fabian Fukan, a Japanese Jesuit, writes the apologia in dialogue form *Myôtei Mondô*, and Father João Rodrigues publishes *Arte da lingoa de Japam*.
1605	Publication of the (Socinian) catechism of Raków by Schmalz, Moscorzowski, and Völkel. In England, Francis Bacon publishes *Of the Proficience and Advancement of Learning*.
1606	In Japan, Ieyasu forbids all proselytizing by Christians and declares that Japanese converts must abandon all foreign religions. Debate between the neo-Confucianist philosopher Hayashi Razan and Fabian Fukan at the Jesuit college in Miyako (July 22). Publication of the first treatise on the harquebus in the Japanese language, written by a Buddhist monk.
1609	Kepler publishes his *Astronomia nova*, founding modern astronomy. Start of the expulsion of the Moriscos from Spain. In Japan, the port of Hirado opened to Dutch merchants. Jesuit missionaries estimate Christian population of Japan at 20,000. In Holland, Grotius publishes *Mare liberum*, defending freedom of the seas.
1610	In Holland, forty-six pastors sign the *Remonstrantia* and reject, as did Arminius, the Calvinist concept of predestination.
1611	Kepler publishes his *Dioptrice*.
1613	English trading begins at Hirado. In Germany, Johann Remmelin publishes under the name Michael Spacher a work titled *Catoptrum microcosmicum*, an anatomical atlas with plates that open in layers.
1614	Great persecution begins in Japan. Edict expels all priests.
1615	First Dutch translation of surgical treatises by Ambroise Paré.
1616	The Holy Office (Index) condemns Copernican theories and forbids Galileo to defend or teach them. In Japan, death of Tokugawa Ieyasu.
1618	Beginning of Thirty Years' War. In the Netherlands, national synod of Dordrecht condemns "Remonstrants"; 200 pastors are suspended, 80 forced into exile; University of Leiden purged of all professors and students who refuse to sign Canons of Dordrecht. Descartes leaves France for Holland.

1619	Execution on May 13 of Johan van Oldenbarnevelt, Grand Advocate of Holland, director of civil administration for Holland and the United Provinces; he is officially accused of desiring peace with Spain, which is also the position of the "Arminians." Grotius is sentenced to life imprisonment for the same reason. Dutch establish a trading post in Batavia.
1620	In Japan, Fabian Fukan writes a refutation of Christianity under the title *Ha Daiusu*. In England, Francis Bacon publishes *Novum organum* and founds an inductive logic that opposes classical Aristotelian logic.
1623	English abandon their trading post at Hirado. In Edo, fifty Christians are burned at the stake (the Great Martyrdom).
1625	In France, Grotius flees Holland and publishes *De jure belli et pacis*.
1628	Harvey demonstrates that the dual motion of auricles and ventricles obey the same rhythm *(Exercitatio anatomica de motu cordis et sanguinis in animalibus)*; his book is published in Frankfurt.
1629	Birth of Christiaan Huygens.
1630	Death of Kepler. Dutch "Remonstrants" win freedom to reside as well as to build churches and schools. In Japan, Tokugawa Iemitsu bans thirty-two scientific and religious works written in or translated into Chinese by Jesuits in China, especially Ricci. Japan is off-limits to all foreigners except the Dutch.
1632	Galileo publishes *Dialogo sui massimi sistemi del mondo* in Florence, laying the groundwork for the new physics and the new cosmology; sentenced to abjuration by the Holy Office.
1633	Father Cristóvão Ferreira abjures the faith in Japan. Start of publication of edicts that will close off Japan from the outside world.
1635	All Japanese forbidden to leave the country, on pain of death. The *daimyo* must reside half the time in Edo.
1636	Deportation to Macao of all Japanese married to Portuguese and of everyone of mixed blood. Construction of artificial islet of Deshima in port of Nagasaki. Ferreira, now Sawano Chuan, writes refutation of Christianity *(Kengiroku)*.
1637	Revolt of Japanese Christian peasants in Shimabara in the south of Japan. Birth of Swammerdam. Descartes publishes *Discourse on Method* in Leiden.

1638	In Poland, Raków seminary is closed; numerous intellectuals flee Poland for Holland. Last Portuguese expelled from Japan.
1640	Separation of Portugal and Japan; Duke of Bragança becomes king of Portugal under the name John IV. Posthumous publication of Jansen's *Augustinus* in Louvain. Inquisition office established by the Japanese in Nagasaki.
1641	Dutch restricted to islet of Deshima.
1642	Death of Galileo.
1643	Birth of Newton.
1644	Birth of Japanese poet Basho.
1645–46	Rome disapproves "Chinese rites" tolerated by Jesuits in Peking.
1648	End of Thirty Years' War. Under the Treaty of Westphalia, United Provinces of the Netherlands recognized as free and sovereign, ending eighty years of warfare.
1649	Execution of Charles I of England (February 9). Caspar Schambergen, surgeon-barber in the service of the Dutch East India Company, takes disciples in Edo (Kasuparu-ryu, Caspar school).
1656	Excommunication of Spinoza in Amsterdam (July 27). Publication in Amsterdam of the Socinian collection *Bibliotheca fratrum polonorum*.
1657	States General of Holland grant nationality to all Jewish residents. Pascal publishes his *Provincial Letters*.
1660	Founding of the Royal Society of London.
1661	City of Danzig (Gdansk) orders the departure of all "Arians" (or Socinians).
1663	Hendrick Indijck, *opperhoofd* on Deshima, makes a gift to the shogun of a Dutch edition of Jan Jonston's *Natural History of Animals*.
1664	Robert Hooke publishes in England his *Micrographia*, based on extensive observation through a microscope.
1665	*Philosophical Transactions* (London) and *Journal des Savants* (Paris) begin regular publication.
1668	Birth of Hermann Boerhaave. Nishi Gempo, an interpreter on Deshima, receives a diploma in medicine from Arnold Dirckz, a physician in the service of the Dutch East India Company.

1669	Swammerdam publishes his *Allgemeene Verhandeling van bloede-loose Diertjens* (General History of Insects) in Utrecht. Death of Rembrandt.
1670	Spinoza's *Tractatus theologico-politicus* published anonymously.
1671	Publication in Grenoble of *Secrets of Chinese Medicine Consisting of the Perfect Knowledge of the Pulses*, supposedly by Cleyer, actually by Boym.
1673	Huygens publishes *Horologium oscillatorium* in Paris.
1674	Arrival on Deshima of Dutch physician ten Rhijne.
1677	William of Orange marries Mary, niece of Charles I and daughter of James Edward Stuart, Catholic heiress to the throne of England.
1678	Richard Simon publishes his *Critical History of the Old Testament*, the first attempt at a rationalist exegesis of the Bible; the author, an Oratorian, is expelled from his order.
1682	Andreas Cleyer publishes *Specimen medicinae sinicae*, plagiarized from the Polish Jesuit Michael Boym.
1683	Turks lift the second siege of Vienna after the Polish victory at Kahlenberg. Locke arrives in Rotterdam, stays only until the Glorious Revolution of 1688, harbored by the Dutch "remonstrants." Ten Rhijne publishes *Dissertatio de arthritide*, with an appendix on Sino-Japanese acupuncture; first review in *Philosophical Transactions* (June 10).
1684	Review of ten Rhijne's book in *Journal des Savants* (March 27).
1685	Revocation of Edict of Nantes in France. Bidloo publishes *Anatomia humani corporis*, with plates by Gérard de Lairesse, in Amsterdam.
1686	The Hapsburg kings retake Buda from the Turks. Father Couplet publishes *Clavis medica ad Chinarum doctrinam de pulsibus*, returning credit to Boym for work that had been attributed to Cleyer.
1687	Newton presents to the Royal Society of London the manuscript of *Philosophiae naturalis principia mathematica*, expounding the law of universal gravitation.
1689	Locke publishes his *Letter on Tolerance* in Holland. William of Orange overthrows James VII of Scotland (and II of England), his

father-in-law, and becomes king of England. Declaration of the *Bill of Rights* by the House of Commons and the House of Lords.

1690   Kaempfer arrives in Nagasaki (September 26). John Locke publishes *An Essay Concerning Human Understanding*. In Japan, Motoki Ryoi begins adapting a book on anatomy by Johann Remmelin; it will not see publication until 1772.

1694   In Leiden, Kaempfer defends a medical dissertation titled *Disputatio medica inauguralis exhibens decadem observationum exoticarum*; two chapters are devoted to acupuncture and moxibustion.

1695   Death of Huygens.

1696   Louis Le Comte, S.J., publishes *Nouveaux mémoires sur l'état présent de la Chine* (New Notes on the Current State of China).

1697   Peace of Ryswick. Birth of Giovanni Antonio Canal, known as Canaletto.

1701   Publication of Ruysch's *Thesaurus anatomicus* in Amsterdam.

1704   Newton publishes *Treatise on the Reflexions, Refractions, Inflexions, and Colours of Light*.

1706   In Japan, Narabashi Chinzan writes *The Heritage of Dutch Surgery*, based in part on a Dutch translation of Paré from 1649 or 1655; the work is still in manuscript form.

1708   Landing at Yakushima of Giovanni Battista Sidotti, S.J., who is immediately taken prisoner. Boerhave's *Institutiones medicae* published in Leiden.

1709   Publication in Lyon of Noël Chomel's *Dictionnaire œconomique*.

1712   Kaempfer publishes *Amoenitatum exoticarum politico-physico-medicarum fasciculi V* in Lemgo, Germany.

1713   Publication of the anti-Jansenist bull *Unigenitus*. Austrian Netherlands come under the rule of Charles Hapsburg, now emperor under the name Charles VI. In Japan, Arai Hakuseki writes the first Japanese book on world geography, *Sairan igen*.

1714   Posthumous publication in Rome, at the instigation of Lancisi, of *Tabulae anatomicae* by Bartolomeo Eustachi (1500/10–1574).

1715   Arai Hakuseki completes *Seiyokibum* (Information on the West). Publication in Paris of *Histoire de l'établissement, des progrès et de la décadence du christianisme dans l'Empire du Japon*, by Pierre François-Xavier de Charlevoix, S.J.

1716	Tokugawa Yoshimune becomes shogun.
1720	Yoshimune lifts the ban on foreign books other than religious works.
1721	Albinus becomes professor of anatomy and surgery at Leiden.
1724	Yoshimune commissions from Blankaart a book on surgery, *Anatomia reformata*, published in Leiden in 1687.
1727	Publication by Hans Sloane, president of the Royal Society of London, of Kaempfer's *History of Japan*, an English version adapted from the German by Johann Caspar Scheuchzer. Death of Newton.
1731–32	Chinese painter Chin Nampin resides in Nagasaki.
1735	Jean-Baptiste du Halde, S.J., publishes *Description géographique, historique, chronologique, politique et physique de l'Empire de la Chine et de la Tartarie chinoise* in Paris.
1740	In Japan, Aoki Konyo and Noro Genjo begin to study Dutch at the behest of Yoshimune. *Theater of Nakamura*, print by Okumura Masanobu using perspective.
1742	Benedict XIV definitively condemns "Chinese rites."
1751	Beginning of publication of Diderot and d'Alembert's *Encyclopédie*. Portuguese government bans autos-da-fé.
1753	Volume 3 of the *Encyclopédie* contains an article on China by Diderot. Benjamin Franklin receives a medal from the Royal Society of London and a letter of congratulation from Louis XV for his body of work on electricity.
1754	Yamawaki Toyo directs a dissection performed by three physicians; it is the first dissection done in Japan.
1756	In Montpellier, Théophile de Bordeu defends a dissertation titled "Recherches sur les pouls par rapport aux crises" (Research on Pulses in Relation to Crises).
1757	Catholic church recognizes the theories of Copernicus and Galileo are true. Galileo's works withdrawn from Index Librorum Prohibitorum.
1759	Yamawaki Toyo publishes *Zoshi* (Description of the Viscera), based on the dissection of 1754. Founding of the British Museum in London; Kaempfer's collections deposited there. In Montpellier, Aimé Félix Bridault defends a baccalaureate dissertation on

Chinese medicine, "Medicinae sinensis conspectus." Jesuits expelled from Portugal.

1763   In Japan, the physician Maeno Ryotaku begins to learn Dutch with Aoki Konyo.

1765   The last volumes of the *Encyclopédie* to be published contain an article on Japan by Diderot. The entry *Pulse* by Ménuret de Chambaud and *Sensitivity* and *Vesicatory* by Fouquet give significant weight to Sino-Japanese medicine.

1771   In Edo, Sugita Gempaku and his companions have the first "Western-style" dissection performed in Japan.

1772   In Japan, Suzuki So-un, a physician, publishes the translation of Remmelin's anatomical atlas that had been prepared by Motoki Ryoi at the end of the preceding century.

1773   Pope Clement XIV eliminates the Society of Jesus. Hiraga Gennai visits Akita.

1774   Sugita Gempaku and his collaborators publish in Edo the first Japanese treatise on modern anatomy, *Kaitai shinsho*. In Paris, Dujardin publishes *Histoire de la chirurgie depuis ses origines jusqu'à nos jours* (History of Surgery from Its Origins to the Present Day), part of it devoted to "Surgery of China and Japan."

1775   Swedish naturalist Thunberg arrives on Deshima (August 17).

1776   Independence of the United States of America. Thunberg goes to Edo where he meets Katsuragawa Hoshu, who will become professor of surgery at the shogunal school of medicine in Edo in 1794.

1780   War between Holland and England.

1783   Otsuki Gentaku translates a Dutch grammar into Japanese. Shiba Kokan produces the first Western-style engraving.

1784   Thunberg, now professor of medicine and botany at Uppsala and president of the Academy of Sciences in Stockholm, publishes *Flora japonica*. Shizuki Tadao, an interpreter in Nagasaki, writes "Treatise on the (Newtonian) Theory of Attraction," adapted from *Introductiones ad veram physicam et veram astronomiam* by John Keill (1671–1721), which he had read in a Dutch translation dated 1741.

1786   Otsuki Gentako opens the first private school of Western medicine in Edo.

1787	In Montpellier, Jean Joseph Deidié defends a medical dissertation on acupuncture and moxibustion, "Dissertatio medico-chirurgica de cucurbitulis, moxa et acupunctura."
1788	Otsuki Gentaku publishes *Rangaku kaitei* (Introduction to Dutch Science).
1789	French Revolution begins. In Japan, Utamaro publishes *The Book of Birds*.
1790	Otsuki Gentaku publishes *Yoi shinsho* (New Book of Surgery), an adaptation of a treatise by Heister that had been prepared by Sugita Gempaku.
1798	Otsuki Gentaku completes work on the second edition of *Kaitai shinsho*; the work is not published until 1826.

Abbreviations

AA	*Artibus Asiae*
AG	*Analecta Gregoriana* (Rome)
AHP	Arquivo Histórico de Portugal (Lisbon)
AHSJ	*Archivum Historicum Societatis Jesu* (Rome)
BHM	*Bulletin of the History of Medicine*
BIA	*Boletim do Instituto Alemão* (Coimbra)
BMFJ	*Bulletin de la Maison Franco-Japonaise* (Paris-Tokyo)
CC	*La Civiltà Cattolica* (Rome)
DGNVO	*Deutsche Gesellschaft für Natur- und Völkerkunde Ostasiens* (Tokyo)
ETR	*Études Théologiques et Religieuses* (Montpellier)
HJAS	*Harvard Journal of Asiatic Studies* (Cambridge, Mass.)
JA	*Journal Asiatique* (Paris)
JAS	*Journal of Art Studies* (Tokyo)
JQ	*Japan Quarterly* (Tokyo)
KM	*Die Katholische Mission* (Bonn)
MHSJ	*Monumenta Historica Societatis Jesu* (Rome)
MN	*Monumenta Nipponica* (Tokyo)
NZM	*Neue Zeitschrift für Missionswissenschaft*
PEFEO	Publications de l'École Française d'Extrême-Orient (Paris)
REJ	*Revue des Études Juives* (Paris)
RET	*Revista Española de Teología* (Madrid)
RHM	*Revue d'Histoire des Missions* (Paris)
RZL/ CHLR	*Romanistische Zeitschrift für Literaturgeschichte/Cahiers d'Histoire des Littératures Romanes* (Heidelberg)
SAGM	Südhoffs Archiv für Geschichte der Medizin

SRLF	*Saggi e Ricerche di Letteratura Francese* (Florence)
SSM	*Studia Sino-Mongolica* (Wiesbaden)
TASJ	*Transactions of the Asiatic Society of Japan* (Tokyo)
TPJS	*Transactions and Proceedings of the Japan Society*
TSCPP	*Transactions and Studies of the College of Physicians of Philadelphia* (Philadelphia)
ZKG	*Zeitschrift für Kirchengeschichte*

Notes

PROLOGUE

1. Paul Claudel, *Oeuvre poétique* (Paris, 1957), pp. 100–101.

2. Pierre Landry, *Exposition universelle d'Osaka, 1970. "Progrès dans l'harmonie." Section française. Rencontres franco-japonaises* (Paris-Osaka, 1970), pp. 23–24.

3. Henri Bernard, Pierre Humbertclaude, and Maurice Prunier, "Infiltrations occidentales au Japon avant la réouverture du XIXᵉ siècle," *BMFJ* 11, nos. 1–4 (1939): 127–61.

4. Jacques Proust, "Raison, déraison, dans les articles philosophiques de l'*Encyclopédie*," *SRLF* 18 (1979): 425–48.

5. See the second part of my article "Pékin-Paris-Saint-Pétersbourg. Les avatars d'un classique confucéen au XVIIIᵉ siècle," *RZL/CHLR*, Heft 1–2 (1996): 99–112.

CHAPTER 1. AESOP'S SMILE, ARISTOTLE'S SUBSTANCE

1. Georg Schurhammer, "Die erste japanische Gesandtschaftsreise nach Europa, 1582–1590," *KM* 49 (1921): 217–24. Reprinted in *Gesammelte Studien* 2, no. 35: 731–41. See p. 732.

2. *Le Discours de la venue des princes japonais en Europe tiré d'un avis venu de Rome* (Paris, 1586), p. 25, probably after Guido Gualtieri, *Relationi della venuta degli ambasciatori giapponesi a Roma fino alla partita di Lisbona* (Rome, 1586), p. 158.

3. See Francisco Rodrigues, *A Companhia de Jesus em Portugal e nas missões*, 2d ed. (Porto, 1935), on the Society of Jesus in Portugal.

4. Henri Bernard, "Valignani ou Valignano, l'auteur véritable du récit de la première ambassade japonaise en Europe, 1582–1590," *MN* 1 (1938): 378–82.

5. Franz Josef Schütte, "Der lateinische 'Dialog De missione legatorum japonensium ad Romanam curiam' als Lehrbuch der japanischen Seminare. Europäische Kultur auf japanischen Schulen im XVI. Jahrhundert," *AG*, Studi sulla Chiesa Antica e sull'Umanesimo, 70 (1954): 260–68.

6. Friedrich Stegmüller, *Filosofia e teologia nas universidades de Coimbra e évora no século XVI* (Coimbra, 1959), pp. 85 ff.

7. Eduardus Sande, *De missione legatorum japonensium ad Romanam curiam, rebusque in Europa, ac toto itinere anidmadversis* (Macao, 1590), pp. 356–58.

8. Francisco Rodrigues, *História da Companhia de Jesus na Assistência de Portugal* (Porto, 1931) pt. 1, vol. 1, p. 484, n. 2.

9. Francisco Rodrigues, *A Formação intellectual do Jesuíta* (Porto, 1917), pp. 115–28.

10. Notably those of Marco Girolamo, or Hieronymous Vida, bishop of Alba (1485–1566), published in 1535. This was a narrative of the Redemption written in Virgilian hexameter.

11. Rodrigues, *Histórie da Companhia de Jesus*, pt. 2, vol. 2, pp. 22–61.

12. See Appendix.

13. José Sebastião da Silva Dias, "O Cânone filosófico conimbricense, 1592–1606," *Cultura, História e Filosofia* 4 (1985): 315–18.

14. Teófilo Braga, *História da Universidade de Coimbra nas suas relações com a instrução pública portugueza* (Lisbon, 1892–1902), vol. 2, pp. 661–64.

15. Father Barradas had studied philosophy and theology at Coimbra. He taught theology at the College of the Arts and was renowned for his preaching.

16. Braga, *História da Universidade de Coimbra*, vol. 2, pp. 376, 384, 401.

17. Dias, "O Cânone filosófico conimbricense, 1592–1606," 267–314.

18. Ibid., p. 42 and n. 5.

19. Jesuits used the term "scholastic" to refer to young people still performing their studies.

20. Franz Josef Schütte, "Drei Unterrichtsbücher für japanische Jesuitenprediger aus dem XVI. Jahrhundert," *AHSJ* 8 (1939): 224–48.

21. Rodrigues, *A Formação intelectual*, pp. 59–76.

22. Jesús López Gay, "La primera biblioteca de los Jesuitas en el Japón," *MN* 15 (1959–60): 368–69.

23. Ibid., p. 377.

24. Kiichi Matsuda, *The Relation between Portugal and Japan* (Lisbon, 1965), p. 84. See also Johannes Laures, *Kirishitan Bunko: A Manual of Books and Documents on the Early Christian Mission in Japan* (Tokyo, 1957).

25. E. A. Satow, *The Jesuit Mission Press in Japan, 1551–1610* (1888), pp. 20 ff.; Matsuda, *Relation*, p. 81.

26. Ibid., pp. 12–18; Pierre Humbertclaude, "La littérature chrétienne au Japon il y a trois cents ans," *BMFJ* 8, nos. 2–4 (1936): 210–11; Matsuda, *Relation*, pp. 81, 101; George Elison, *Deus Destroyed: The Image of Christianity in Early Modern Japan* (Cambridge, Mass., 1988), pp. 145–48 and n. 15, pp. 429–30.

27. Hans Haas, *Geschichte des Christentums in Japan*, a supplement to the *DGNVO* (Tokyo, 1902–4) vol. 1, pp. 243–68; Léon Bourdon, *La Compagnie de Jésus et le Japon, 1547–1570* (Paris, 1993), p. 174.

28. Léon Bourdon, *La Compagnie de Jésus et le Japon, 1547–1570* (Paris, 1993), p. 175.

29. Quoted in Jacques Gernet, "Sur les différentes versions du premier catéchisme en chinois de 1584," *SSM* (1979): 414.

30. Bourdon, *Compagnie de Jésus*, pp. 269–70.

31. Luís Fróis, *História de Japam* (Lisbon, 1976–84), vol. 1, p. 177.

32. Bourdon, *Compagnie de Jésus*, pp. 311–12, after the testimony of Father Torres; see also Fróis, *História de Japam*, vol. 4, pp. 541 ff.

33. Bourdon, *Compagnie de Jésus*, p. 612.

34. There were two types in the Society of Jesus, "spiritual coadjutors," who were priests, and "temporal coadjutors," who were not.

35. Minako Debergh, "Deux nouvelles études sur l'histoire du christianisme au Japon. I. Bases doctrinales et images du sacrement dans l'eucharistie à l'époque des premières missions catholiques chrétiennes au Japon (XVIᵉ–XVIIIᵉ siècle)," *JA* 268 (1980): 397–402.

36. Alessandro Valignano, *Les Jésuites au Japon. Relation missionnaire (1583)*. Translation, introduction, and notes by J. Bésineau (Paris, 1990), pp. 24–40.

37. Ibid., p. 26.

38. Ibid., pp. 3–25.

39. For the "Chinese" side of the question, see Jacques Gernet, *Chine et christianisme. Action et réaction* (Paris, 1982), pp. 278–329.

40. MS. 426, fols. 122–432. For the history and content of this manuscript, see Schütte, "Drei Unterrichtsbücher," pp. 223–56.

41. Bourdon, *Compagnie de Jésus*, pp. 157–58.

42. For a partly conjectural biography of Fabian Fukan, see Pierre Humbertclaude, "Myôtei Mondô. Une apologétique chrétienne japonaise de 1605," *MN* 1, no. 2 (1938): 516–19 (224–27); Pierre Humbertclaude, "Notes complémentaires sur la biographie de l'ex-Frère jésuite Fabien Fukan," *MN* 4 (1941): 617–21; Franz Josef Schütte, *Monumenta historica Japoniae. I. Textus catalogorum Japoniae aliaeque de personis domibusque S.J. in Japonia informationes et relationes 1549–1654* (Rome, 1975), pp. 208, 223, 252, 273, 290, 318, 449, 503 n. 48; Elison, *Deus Destroyed*, pp. 143–58, 164, 232–33, 430, 432, 460. On Fukan's *Myôtei Mondô*, see Humbertclaude, "Myôtei Mondô," pp. 526–48; and "Notes," pp. 237–67; see also Elison, *Deus Destroyed*, pp. 166–84.

43. Humbertclaude, "Myôtei Mondô," p. 266.

44. *Problèmes de linguistique générale* (Paris, 1966), 63–74 [*Problems in General Linquistics* (Coral Gables, Fla., 1971].

45. Gernet, *Chine et christianisme*, p. 324.

46. Ibid., p. 274.

47. Hans Müller, "Hai Yaso. Anti-Jesus. Hayashi Razan's anti-christlicher Bericht über eine konfuzianisch-christliche Disputation aus dem Jahre 1606," *MN* 2 (1939): 268–75; Elison, *Deus Destroyed*, pp. 149–53.

48. Elison, *Deus Destroyed*, pp. 259–91; Jacques Proust, "L'echec de la première mission chrétienne au Japon (XVIᵉ–XVIIᵉ siècle)," *ETR* 3 (1991): 359–81.

49. See chapter 5.

1. For a history of the Marranes, see Cecil Roth, *A History of the Marranes* (Philadelphia, 1941).

2. *Les Juifs d'Espagne, histoire d'une diaspora, 1492–1992* (Paris, 1992), pp. 75–88.

3. João Lúcio d'Azevedo, *História dos Cristãos novos portugueses* (Lisbon, 1921), pp. 36–150, 497–99.

4. Rodrigues, *História da Companhia de Jesus*, p. 497 n. 1.

5. Israël Salvador Révah, "Les origines juives de quelques jésuites hispano-portugais du XVIᵉ siècle," *Quatrième Congrès des hispanistes français*, Poitiers, 1967, pp. 87–96.

6. Josef Wicki, "Die 'cristãos-novos' in der indischen Provinz der Gesellschaft Jesu von Ignatius bis Acquaviva," *AHSJ* 46 (1977): 354–55.

7. Dorotheus Schilling, *Das Schulwesen der Jesuiten in Japan, 1551–1614* (Munich, 1931), p. 49.

8. Dorotheus Schilling, "Os Portugueses e a introdução da medicina no Japão," *BIA* (1937): 14.

9. Braga, *História da Universidade de Coimbra*, vol. 2, pp. 768–90.

10. Israël Salvador Révah, "Les Marranes," *REJ* (1959–60): 54–74.

11. Israël Salvador Révah, "L'hérésie marrane dans l'Europe catholique du XVᵉ au XVIIIᵉ siècle," *Hérésies et sociétés dans l'Europe préindustrielle*, Colloquium of Royaumont (Paris–The Hague, 1968), pp. 320–36.

12. For Almeida's career, see Schilling, *Das Schulwesen*, pp. 44–64; Pierre Delattre, "Un institut de médecine des missionnaires au Japon au XVIᵉ siècle," *RHM* 11 (1934): 17–28; C. R. Boxer, "Some Aspects of Portuguese Influence in Japan, 1542–1640," *TPJS* 23 (1935–36): 48–49; Schilling, *Os Portugueses*, pp. 12–18; Bourdon, *Compagnie de Jésus*, pp. 69–85, corrected by Miguel Campo, "Luís de Almeida, cirurgião e mercador e sua entrada na Companhia de Jesus, 1555–1556," *AHP* 2, no. 1 (1958): 90–94; John Z. Bowers, *Western Medical Pioneers in Feudal Japan* (Baltimore, 1970), pp. 11–14; Bourdon, *Compagnie de Jésus*, pp. 305–6, 335–41, 372–73.

13. Valignano, *Les Jésuites*, pp. 241–43.

14. A. Sicroff, *Les controverses des statuts de pureté du sang en Espagne aux XVI et XVII siècles* (Paris-Toulouse, 1960), pp. 278–82; Léon Poliakov, *De Mahomet aux Marranes* (Paris, 1961), pp. 221–27; Révah, "Les origines juives," pp. 90–91; Wicki, "Die 'cristãos-novos,'" pp. 344–45.

15. Marcel Bataillon, *Érasme et l'Espagne* (Paris, 1937), p. 167.

16. José V. da Pina Martins, *Humanismo e Erasmismo na cultura portuguesa do século XVI. Estudo e texto* (Paris, 1973), p. 36.

17. Marcel Bataillon, *Études sur le Portugal au temps de l'Humanisme* (Paris, 1974), pp. 7–30.

18. Israël Salvador Révah, *La censure inquisitoriale portugaise au XVI siècle*, vol. 1 (Lisbon, 1960), pp. 22–70.

19. Bataillon, *Érasme et l'Espagne*, p. 761.

20. *L'Humanisme portugais et l'Europe*, Proceedings of the 21st International Colloquium of Humanist Studies (Paris, 1984), p. 825.

21. Bataillon, *Études*, pp. 97–104.

22. Martins, *Humanismo e Erasmismo*, pp. 81–137; *Humanisme*, pp. 24–28.

23. Bataillon, *Études*, p. 61.

24. Ibid., pp. 121–49.

25. Ibid., pp. 171–81.

26. José Sebastião da Silva Dias, *O Erasmismo e a Inquisicão em Portugal. O processo de Fr. Valentim da Luz* (Coimbra, 1975), passim, and on pp. 266–71 the text of the final confession.

27. Rodrigues, *História da Companhia de Jesus*, pt. 2, vol. 1, pp. 193–204.

28. Schilling, *Das Schulwesen*, p. 70; Rodrigues, *História da Companhia de Jesus*, pt. 1, vol. 1, p. 518.

29. Franz Josef Schütte, *Monumenta historica Japoniae*, 581.

30. Schütte, *El "Archivo del Japón." Archivo documental español*, vol. 20 (Madrid, 1964), pp. 394–96, 412.

31. On the life of Ferreira, see Léon Pagès, *Histoire de la religion chrétienne au Japon depuis 1598 jusqu'à 1651* (Paris, 1869–1870), vols. 1 and 2, passim; Schütte, *"Archivo del Japón,"* passim; Hubert Cieslik, "The Case of Christóvão Ferreira," *MN* 29, no. 1 (1974): 1–54; Schütte, *Monumenta*; Elison, *Deus Destroyed*, pp. 185–91.

32. The complete text of *Deception Unmasked*, translated into English, is found in Elison, *Deus Destoryed*, pp. 292–318. Page numbers for quotations are from Elison. The following analysis appeared in Jacques Proust, "L'échec de la première mission chrétienne au Japon (XVIe–XVIIe siècle)," *ETR* 2 (1991): 196–205.

33. Érasme, *éloge de la folie, Adages, Colloques, Réflexions, Correspondance*, edited by C. Blum, A. Godin, J.-C. Margolin, and D. Ménager (Paris, 1992), p. 1005.

34. Ibid., p. 650.

35. Ibid., p. 845.

36. Ibid., p. 653.

37. Ibid., p. 659.

38. This kinship between Erasmian thought in the broad sense and the ideas expressed in *Deception Unmasked* refutes the hypothesis advanced in Masaharu Anesaki, "Japanese Criticisms and Refutations of Christianity in the Seventeenth and Eighteenth Centuries," *TASJ* 7 (December 1930): 12, according to which the work attributed to Ferreira is based in Confucianism.

39. Bowers, *Western Medical Pioneers*, p. 18.

40. Armando Martins Janeira, *O impacto português sobre a civilização Japonesa. Seguido de um epílogo sobre as relações entre Portugal e o Japão do século XVII aos nossos dias* (Lisbon, 1988), p. 166.

41. Cieslik, "The Case of Christóvão Ferreira," p. 35.

CHAPTER 3. CONSULTING DR. VÁZQUEZ

1. *Catholicisme. Hier, aujourd'hui, demain,* encyclopedia published under the auspices of the Centre interdisciplinaire des Facultés catholiques de Lille (Paris, 1953); see vol. 4, entry *Épikie.*

2. Cieslik, "The Case of Christóvão Ferreira," pp. 17–36.

3. L. Vereecke, *Conscience morale et loi humaine selon Gabriel Vázquez* (Paris, 1957), pp. 143–44.

4. Shusaku Endo, *Silence* (Tokyo, 1976), p. 15.

5. Gay, "La primera biblioteca," pp. 350–79.

6. Fróis, *História de Japam.* Part of *História de Japam* had already been published in Tokyo thanks to J. A. Abranches Pinto, Y. Okamoto, and H. Bernard under the title *Tratado dos embaixadores Japões que forão de Japão a Roma no anno de 1582.* A complete translation into Japanese was published in 1963–78 in Tokyo.

7. He published it in Tokyo, in the original Portuguese with a German translation, in 1955.

8. For development of the question up to this point, see Luís Fróis, *Traité sur les contradictions de mœurs entre Européens et Japonais,* translated by Xavier de Casfro and Robert Schrumpf with an introduction by José Manuel García (Paris, 1994), passim.

9. Fróis, *Traité,* p. 174.

10. Ibid., p. 82.

11. Valignano, *Les Jesuítes au Japon,* pp. 74, 122, 165, 75, respectively.

12. The *dojuko,* or *dogicos,* were not actually members of an order but servants who aided the fathers in their daily tasks.

13. Valignano, *Les Jésuítes au Japon,* p. 55.

14. Ibid., p. 185.

15. Ibid., pp. 55–56.

16. Ibid., p. 124. As of 1576 the seat of the bishopric with domain over Japan was in Macao. A bishop was finally named to Japan in 1588, but he was a Jesuit.

17. Ibid., pp. 59, 65, 75, 81, respectively.

18. Ibid., p. 59.

19. Ibid., pp. 193–94.

20. Ibid., pp. 121–22.

21. Ibid., pp. 128–29.

22. Ibid., p. 188. Thomas de Vio, known as Cajetan (1468–1533), was a cardinal and the master general of the Dominicans. He was a committed Thomist. Martin de Azpilcueta, known as Navarro ("The Navarran"), was mentioned earlier for his *Manual for Confessors,* which was prominently featured in the Jesuits' library in Japan.

23. Luciano Pereña Vicente, "Importantes documentos inéditos de Gabriel Vázquez," *RET* 16, no. 63 (April–June 1956): 193–213.

24. Jesús López Gay, "Un documento inédito del P. G. Vázquez (1549–1604), sobre los Problemas Morales del Japón," *MN* 16 (1960–61): 118–60. Unless otherwise

noted, all the data used in this section comes from Gay , "Un documento inédito"; and Vicente, "Importants documentos."

25. From the *Vázquez* entry in the *Dictionnaire de théologie catholique* (Paris, 1950).

26. Vereecke, *Consience morale*, p. 154.

27. Gay, "Un documento inédito," pp. 144–45 n. 36.

28. *Les Conciles œcuméniques* (Paris, 1994) 2x, p. 439.

29. Ibid., 2x, p. 993.

30. Érasme, *Éloge de la folie,* p. 48.

31. These Shinto festivals with carts, dancing, and various performances are still celebrated. They are called *matsuri* and take place in great number everywhere, in both cities and countryside.

32. This is the Buddhist feast of *bon,* which takes place in mid-July.

33. Thomas Aquinas, *Somme théologique* (Paris, 1984), pt. 3, pp. 294–96.

34. This was also Vázquez's position on the worship of images in the Christian context.

35. Etymologically, in Greek and Latin, "stumbling block," the object that causes one to fall (into evil).

36. 2 Kings 5:17–19. Naaman was the head of the army of the king of Aram, and Rimmon was a pagan deity. Cured of leprosy by the prophet Elijah and converted to the faith of the Hebrews, Naaman asked for God's forgiveness in advance, since he knew he would have to return with his master to the temple of Rimmon to prostrate himself before the image.

CHAPTER 4. THE THEATER OF FAITH, CIVILITY, AND GLORY

1. Adriana Boscaro, *Sixteenth-Century European Printed Works on the First Japanese Mission to Europe: A Descriptive Bibliography* (Leyden, 1973).

2. *Discours* 1586, p. 29; Schurhammer, "Die erste japanische," p. 726; Pasquale d'Elia, "I primi ambasciatori giapponesi venuti a Roma (1585)," *CC* 1 (1952): 56–57.

3. Rodrigues, *Formação intelectual*, pp. 79–81.

4. Bourdon, *Compagnie de Jésus*, pp. 355–60.

5. Schilling, *Das Schulwesen* pp. 79–80.

6. Bourdon, *Compagnie de Jésus*, pp. 362, 365–66.

7. *De missione*, pp. 358–61.

8. For more on the internal debates in Catholicism during this era, see Fra Paolo Sarpi, *Histoire du concile de Trente*, 2 vols. (Basel, 1738); and especially Hubert Jedin, "Das Tridentinum und die Bildenden Künste." Bemerkungen zu Paolo Prodi, *Ricerche sulla teoria delle arti figurativi nella Reforma cattolica* (1962), *ZKG* 74 (1963): 321–39.

9. Émile Mâle, *L'art religieux après le concile de Trente* (Paris, 1932), pp. 5–82.

10. Bourdon, *Compagnie de Jésus*, pp. 586–87.

11. Georg Schurhammer, "Die Jesuitenmissionare des 16. und 17. Jahrhunderts und ihr Einfluss auf die japanische Malerei," Jubiläumsband herausgegeben von der *DGNVO* anlässlich ihres 60 jährigen Bestehen, 1873–1933, pt. 1, (Tokyo, 1933), pp. 116–26.

12. Satow, *Jesuit Mission Press*, nos. 1 and 3. *Fides no dôxi* was Pedro Ramón's adaptation into Japanese of *Introducción al símbolo de la fé* by Luis de Granada.

13. Tokihide Nagayama, *Kirishitan shiryo shû. Collection of Historical Material Connected with the Roman Catholic Religion in Japan*, 2d ed. (Nagasaki, 1927), p. 74; Yoshimoto Okamoto, *The Namban Art of Japan* (New York and Tokyo, 1972), no. 31.

14. Okamoto, *Namban Art*, no. 29.

15. It reads as follows: *Domina nostra s. Maria (cui ab antiquitate cognomen) cuius imago in summa aede dum Ferdinandus tertius Hÿspasim expugnarat in pariete depicta, inventa, Nuestra Señora de l'Antigua* (Our Lady, Saint Mary, owes her appellation to her antiquity; her image was found painted on a wall in the principal edifice when Ferdinand III triumphed over Hÿspasis).

16. Nagayama, *Kirishitan shiryo shû*, p. 74; Okamoto, *Namban Art*, no. 30 and p. 150. La Virgen de la Antigua was particularly venerated throughout the Hispanic world, and her image was reproduced everywhere, especially in South America. For more on this subject, see José María Medianero Hernández, *Las pinturas de la antigua mezquita-catedral hispalense, analisis cultural e iconografico de unas obras desaparecidas* (Seville, 1983), offprint of *Archivo hispalense*, no. 201, pp. 173–86; and *La Gran Tecleciguata: Nota sobre la devoción de la Virgen de la Antigua en Hispanoamérica* (Seville, 1984), offprint of *II Jornadas de Andalucía y América*, vol. 2, pp. 365–80.

17. *Japan und Europa, 1543–1929,* an exhibition at the "43. Berliner Festwochen," Martin-Gropius Bau (Berlin, 1993), pp. 247–48.

18. The Library of the Escorial has a beautiful specimen, a painting signed by Luis de Morales (early sixteenth century–1586).

19. *Japan und Europa*, pp. 251–52, nos. 3/8 and 3/9.

20. Ibid., pp. 249–50, no. 3/5.

21. Ibid., pp. 268–71.

22. Luis de Morales, mentioned above, painted primarily the Virgin and Child, on wood and copper, as well as Christ Crowned with Thorns. His faces have drawnout shapes in the style of Parmigianus, and volumes are treated with a chiaroscuro technique imitating the *sfumato* of Leonardo da Vinci (V. Thieme and F. Becker, *Allgemeines Lexikon der bildenden Künste*, 37 vols. [Leipzig, 1907–50]).

23. *Japan und Europa*, p. 267, no. 3/34; see also pp. 266–67, no. 3/33.

24. *De missione*, p. 323.

25. Entry *Ortelius* by E. Bénézit, *Dictionnaire critique et documentaire des peintres, sculpteurs, dessinateurs et graveurs* (Paris, 1976); entry *Hogenbergh* by Bénézit and by Thieme and Becker.

26. Entry *Hoefnagel* by Bénézit and by Thieme and Becker.

27. *Japan und Europa*, pp. 51–53, 240, no. 2/5; 255–56, no. 3/15. For more on the general topic of Western-style painting in Japan, see Mitsuru Sakamoto, *Namban bijutsu to Yōfū-ga* (Namban Art and Western-style Painting) (Tokyo, 1984).

28. Alfons Kleiser, "P. Alexander Valignanis Gesandtschaftsreise nach Japan zum . . . Toyotomi Hideyoshi, 1588–1591," *MN* 1 (1938): 79–86.

29. *Japan und Europa*, pp. 64–65, 240–42, no. 2/7. *Paternus* is part of a series of twenty-seven engravings depicting the lives of saints. Saint Paterne, bishop of Avranches, is said to have lived with a companion in a hermitage in Normandy, where he braved great dangers to evangelize the inhabitants of the region, who were still pagans.

30. See the catalog *Fiamminghi a Roma, 1508–1608. Artistes des Pays-Bas et de la Principauté de Liège à Rome à la Renaissance* (Brussels and Rome, 1995). For more on the very important role of Plantin during this period, see *Anvers, ville de Plantin et de Rubens*, catalog of the exhibition held at the Galerie Mazarine, Paris, March–April 1954.

31. Michel W. Alpatow, *Die Dresdner Galerie. Alte Meister* (Dresden, 1966), pl. 73 and p. 60.

32. F. W. H. Hollstein, *Dutch and Flemish Etchings, Engravings and Woodcuts, ca. 1450–1700* (Amsterdam, 1949 and subsequent years), vol. 4, p. 206.

33. *Du* (art magazine published in Zurich), no. 371 (January 1972): pl. 10.

34. *Fiamminghi a Roma*, pp. 216–18.

35. A. J. J. Delen, *Histoire de la gravure dans les anciens Pays-Bas et dans les provinces belges des origines jusqu'à la fin du XVIe siècle*, 3 vols. (Paris, 1934–35; reprint 1969). See 1969 ed. pt. 2, p. 82 and pl. 24. Stradanus, about whom more will be said later, also produced numerous drawings of hunting scenes, some of which were later engraved by Hieronymus Cock. Cock, Galle, and Collaert published in Anvers many series devoted to the hunt.

36. *Japan und Europa*, pp. 122–23 and 243, no. 2/9. Japanese collections include representations of heroes or royalty done in the same style (Grace Alida Hermine Vlam, "Western-style Secular Painting in Momoyama Japan" [Ph.D. diss., University of Michigan, 1976], 76–94, 105–19; Grace Alida Hermine Vlam, "Kings and Heroes: Western-Style Painting in Momoyama Japan," *AA* 39, nos. 3–4 [1977]: 220–50).

37. *De missione*, pp. 136–37.

38. Vlam, "Western-style Secular Painting," pp. 120–26.

39. *Carthage. L'histoire, sa trace et son écho*, catalog of the exhibition presented at the Musée du Petit-Palais (Paris, 1995), pp. 164–69.

40. The idea of perching huge towers on the backs of Hannibal's elephants does not come from Greek and Latin sources but from the first Book of Maccabees, 6:37. In the Bible, the battle described is the one at Antiochus in which Judas Maccabeus confronts Antiochus V Eupator, invader of Judea. It ends with the death of Eleazar, on Judas's side. The "pattern" painted by Jules Romain also served to illustrate the death of Eleazar in, for example, *Images bibliques du Vieux et du Nouveau Testament*, published by Melchior Küsel in Vienna in 1679.

41. *De missione*, p. 32.

1. Guy Bédouelle, Bernard Roussel, et al., *Le temps des réformes et la Bible* (Paris, 1989), p. 342.

2. Ibid., pp. 327–66.

3. Ibid., pp. 33–36.

4. Hubert Cieslik, "Die Heilige Schrift in der alten Japanmission," *NZM* 11 (1955): 31.

5. Fróis, *História de Japam*, vol. 1, p. 25 and n. 14.

6. Cited by Cieslik, "Die Heilege Schrift," p. 32.

7. Ibid., pp. 34, 37.

8. Reg. Lat. 459.

9. Franz Josef Schütte, "Christliche japanische Literatur, Bilder und Druckblätter in einem unbekannten vatikanischen Codex aus dem Jahre 1591," *AHSJ* (January–June 1940): 229–43; Cieslik, "Die Heilege Schrift," pp. 37–40.

10. Schütte, "Christliche japanische," p. 251.

11. Humbertclaude, "Myôtei Mondô," *MN* 2 (1939): 254–58.

12. Ibid., pp. 254–55.

13. Bourdon, *Compagnie de Jésus*, p. 346.

14. Debergh, "Deux nouvelles études," pp. 397, 401–2.

15. E. A. Satow, "The Jesuit Mission Press in Japan," *TASJ* 27, pt. 2 (1900).

16. Schilling, *Das Schulwesen*, pp. 37–39.

17. Art. *Kakure Kirishitan* from *Kodansha Encyclopedia of Japan* (Tokyo, 1983). For the current situation in these communities, see Christal Whelan, "Religion Concealed: The Kakure Kirishitan on Narushima," *MN* 47 (1992): 369–87, and "Japan's Vanishing Minority: The *Kakure Kirishitan* of the Goto Islands," *JQ* (October–December 1994): 434–49.

18. Valignano, *Les Jésuites au Japon*, 1990, p. 178.

19. According to Bourdon, *Compagnie de Jésus*, pp. 654–59. See also Minako Debergh, "Deux nouvelles études sur l'histoire du christianisme au Japon. II. Les pratiques de purification et de pénitence au Japon vues par les missionnaires jésuites aux XVIᵉ et XVIIᵉ siècles," *JA* 272 (1984): 167–216.

20. Bourdon, *Compagnie de Jésus*, pp. 367–368.

21. Masaharu Anesaki, "Psychological Observations on the Persecution of Catholics in Japan in the Seventeenth Century," *HJAS* 1 (1936): 27.

22. For a more detailed presentation of the *Commencements*, as well as a complete translation of the story from German into French, see *Commencements du ciel et de la terre, conte japonais*, translated from the German of Alfred Bohner by Jacques and Marianne Proust, in *Arquivos do Centro Cultural Português*, Fundação Calouste Gulbenkian, vol. 35 (Lisbon-Paris, 1996).

23. Whelan, "Religion Concealed," pp. 382–84.

24. Paul's first letter to the Corinthians, 1:18: "For the word of the cross is folly to those who are perishing, but to us who are being saved it is the power of God." For

more on voluntary death in Japan, see Maurice Pinguet's beautiful book by that title (Paris, 1984).

25. One of these calendars is reproduced and described as no. 32, Okamoto, *Namban Art*.

26. Valignano, *Les Jesuítes au Japon*, p. 259.

27. Bourdon, *Compagnie de Jésus*, pp. 175–78.

28. Georg Schurhammer, *Das kirchliche Sprachproblem in der japanischen Jesuitenmission des 16. und 17. Jahrunderts*, a publication of *DGNVO* (Tokyo, 1928), p. 106, and Janeira, *O impacto português*, pp. 217–21, give two lists of words that have passed from Latin or Portuguese into Japanese. Many are still in use.

29. Eighteen deciliters.

30. From *domêgo* to *sabato*, Sunday to Saturday, the names of the days of the week are borrowed from the Portuguese.

31. From the Latin *dominicus*, "belonging to the Lord."

32. Compare with the story of the manna in Exodus 16.

33. One *koku* equals eighty liters.

34. The number eight connotes a quantity that is undetermined but very large.

35. The lion-dogs or dogs of Korea (*koma inu*) are usually found in pairs in Shinto sanctuaries, one on either side of the entrance.

36. These items are rather small, flat wooden spoons, used to serve rice. As rice was sacred, the spoons are used as lucky amulets.

37. Mythical island.

38. This rowing race, Chinese in origin, still takes place each year in Nagasaki on the Sunday closest to June 15. Kaempfer, in an appendix to *History of the Empire of Japan*, recounts a similar story about King Peiruun, who ruled the vanished island of Maurigasima in ancient times.

39. Rice, used as currency.

40. Measure of length that varies, depending on the region, from 1.75 to 1.9 meters.

41. Compare with Acts 10:11 (narrative of Peter's vision when he is invited by Cornelius).

42. From the Portuguese *jejum*, "a fast."

43. For more on the Shinto rites of purification, see Debergh, "Deux nouvelles études," II, pp. 167–216. See also Leviticus 12 and Luke 2:22 for the corresponding rites in Judaism.

44. Herodes, or Herod. Compare this whole story with Matthew 2:1–12.

45. Matthew 2:12 does say that "they departed for their country by another way," but the Heavenly Floating Bridge belongs to a Shinto legend; it is the bridge on which Izanagi and Izanami stand when they plunge the celestial spear into the primordial water to create the islands of the Japanese archipelago.

46. See Isaiah 53:7 and all mentions in the New Testament of the symbol of the Lamb.

47. John 19:31.

48. Vinegar and hyssop, according to John 19:29; wine and gall, according to Matthew 27:34.

49. From the Portuguese *calvário*. The transliteration would normally give *karuwariyo*. But *ryû*, which means "dragon," is found in the composition of many names of mountains and temples.

50. This episode comes from the legend of Nichiren, the founder of one of the great Buddhist sects in the eighth century. Condemned to death, he could not be executed because the executioner was blinded by a storm.

51. John 19:34.

52. Jacques de Voragine's *La Légende dorée* (Garnier-Flammarion, 1967, vol. 1, pp. 234–35) recounts that the centurion who pierced Christ's side with his lance was named Longin. His vision had gone dark as a result of illness or age, and when he rubbed his eyes with the blood dripping from his lance, he miraculously recovered his sight. From that moment on he renounced military life and lived twenty-eight more years in a monastery in Cappadocia. He was finally decapitated because he refused to sacrifice to the idols, but his martyrdom converted the governor who had sentenced him to death. This man, who was blind, at once recovered his sight.

53. Veronica. In chapter 9, during the walk to Calvary, she wiped the face of Christ with a cloth and gave him water to drink.

54. From the Latin *in nomine Jesu*.

55. From the Latin *Agnus Dei*.

56. The presentation of Christianity made by Arai Hakuseki in book 3 of "Information on the West," written after his interviews with Father Sidotti in 1708–9, has much in common with the legend of the *Commencements*. For more on the subject, see Hisayasu Nakagawa, "Présentation et réfutation du christianisme par Hakuseki Arai," in *Problème de la traduisibilité des cultures* (Kyoto, 1994), pp. 5–10.

CHAPTER 6. THE "GALILEAN" REVOLUTION
IN SEVENTEENTH-CENTURY JAPANESE ART

1. Guillaume Thomas Raynal, *Histoire philosophique et politique des établissements et du commerce des Européens dans les deux Indes* (Geneva, 1774), vol. 2, p. 143.

2. For more on this subject, see C. R. Boxer, *The Dutch Seaborne Empire, 1600–1800* (New York, 1965), pp. 1–110; and Charles Pierre Thunberg, *Le Japon du XVIII siècle vu par un botaniste suédois* (Paris, 1966), pp. 164–65.

3. Frits Vos, "Forgotten Foibles. Love and the Dutch at Desjima, 1641–1854," in *Asien, Tradition und Fortschritt. Festschrift für Horst Hammitzsch zu seinem 60. Geburtstag* (Wiesbaden, 1971), pp. 614–33.

4. Henri Mechoulan, *Amsterdam au temps du Spinoza* (Paris, 1990).

5. Denis Diderot, *œuvres complètes*, ed. Assézat et Tourneux (Paris, 1875–77), vol. 17, p. 428.

6. Jakob Rosenberg, Slive Seymour, and E. H. Ter Kuile, *Dutch Art and Architecture, 1600–1800* (Harmondsworth, 1966), p. 207.

7. J. de Maere and M. Wabbes, *Illustrated Dictionary of 17th-Century Flemish Painters* (Brussels, 1994), vol. 1, pp. 13–14.

8. For more on Shiba Kokan, see Calvin French, "The First and Last Passion (Shiba Kôkan, 1747–1818)," *Hemisphere* 21, no. 1 (1977): 8–13; no. 3 (1977): 8–15.

9. For a broad discussion of this question, see René Neuer, Herbert Libertson, and Susugu Yoshida, *Ukiyo-e, 250 ans d'estampes japonaises* (Paris, 1985), pp. 20–40.

10. Chin Nampin was not influenced directly by Castiglione, who came after him, but by one of his more obscure predecessors. Henri Bernard, "Traductions chinoises d'ouvrages européens au Japon durant la période de fermeture, 1614–1853," *MN* 3, no. 1 (1940): 59, names several of these. The book also names their principal Chinese pupils.

11. For more on the Nagasaki school, see Calvin French, *Through Closed Doors: Western Influence on Japanese Art, 1639–1853* (Rochester, N.Y., 1978), pp. 61–68.

12. *Biographie Michaud*, entry *Jonston*.

13. Entry *Merian* in Bénézit and in Thieme and Becker.

14. Mitsuru Sakamoto, "Rubens and Western-Style Painting in the Edo Period," *JAS* 295 (September 1974): 26–34.

15. For more on the van Royen painting and its earlier history, see French, *Through Closed Doors*, pp. 164–65.

16. Entry *Dodonée* in the Biographie Michaud and especially Delen, *Histoire*, vol. 2, pp. 80, 83.

17. For more on Genjo's translation, see *Japan und Europa*, p. 326.

18. Hubert Maës, *Hiraga Gennai et son temps, PEFEO* 72 (1970).

19. French, *Through Closed Doors*, pp. 123–28.

20. Ibid., pp. 125–26; *Japan und Europa*, pp. 113, 129, 290.

21. Gérard de Lairesse, *Le Grand Livre des peintres ou l'art de la peinture considéré dans toutes ses parties et démontré par ses principes* (Paris, 1787), vol. 1, p. 7. For more on Lairesse, see entries under his name in Bénézit, Thieme and Becker, and Maere and Wabbes, *Illustrated Dictionary*.

22. French, *Through Closed Doors*, p. 125.

23. Entry *Vries* in Bénézit and in Thieme and Becker; see also Delen, *Histoire*, vol. 2, pp. 50, 143, 158; and vol. 3, pp. 65, 68, 86, 98, 139–42.

24. Rosenberg, Seymour and Ter Kuile, *Dutch Art and Architecture*, p. 188.

25. French, *Through Closed Doors*, pp. 99–100; *Japan und Europa*, p. 131.

26. For more on the introduction of the *optique* to Japan, see *Japan und Europa*, pp. 131–33; and French, *Through Closed Doors*, pp. 103–4.

27. French, *Through Closed Doors*, p. 96.

28. Ibid., pp. 130, 150. For a notably different version of the event, also dated 1783, see Donald Keene, *The Japanese Discovery of Europe, 1720–1830* (Stanford, Calif.,

1969). The Western book cited by Keene (p. 67) is a Dutch dictionary of the arts and sciences by Egbert Buys dated 1769, and the Japanese artist to whom the rediscovery is imputed is Honda Toshiaki. In the case of Honda Toshiaki, as in that of Shiba Kokan, the translator was said to be Otsuki Gentaku.

29. French, *Through Closed Doors*, pp. xxi, 152.

30. Cited in French, *Through Closed Doors*, p. 3; see also *Japan und Europa*, pp. 128–29.

31. For more on Visentini, see the catalog of the exhibition at the Museo Correr in Venice, September–November 1990, titled *I Rami di Visentini per le vedute de Venezia del Canaletto*. The painting *Veduta da S. Croce verso gli Scalzi* is no. 18. See also the complete reproduction of Visentini's works in J. G. Links, *Views of Venice by Canaletto, Engraved by Antonio Visentini* (Toronto, 1971), in which *Prospectus ab Aede S. Crucis* is no. 2 in part 2.

32. French, *Through Closed Doors*, pp. 111–12.

33. Ibid., pp. 114–15; *Japan und Europa*, pp. 133, 304 (the authors of the Berlin catalog, however, do not attribute *Roman Forum* definitely to Toyoharu, and they date it as early nineteenth century). As regards the "Japanese gaze" on Western works, see Hosono Masanobu, *Nagasaki Prints and Early Copperplates* (Tokyo and New York, 1978).

34. Entry *Ridinger* in Bénézit and in Thieme and Becker.

35. For more on Wakasugi Isohachi and Ridinger, see French, *Through Closed Doors*, pp. 65–66; and *Japan und Europa*, pp. 108, 112, 294–95.

36. Georges Gusdorf, *Les sciences humaines et la pensée occidentale* (Paris: 1969), vol. 3, pt. 1, p. 270.

CHAPTER 7. THE TWO FACES OF "DUTCH SCIENCE"

1. Willem ten Rhijne, *Dissertatio de arthritide: Mantissa schematica de acupunctura* (London, 1683). Accounts recorded in *Philosophical Transactions of the Royal Society*, no. 148 (June 1683): 222–35; and *Journal des savants* (March 27, 1684): 63–66.

2. Engelbert Kaempfer, *Amoenitatum exoticarum politico-physico-medicarum fasciculi V* (Lemgo, 1712), and *The History of Japan*, English translation by Scheuchzer (London, 1727–28; French translation, The Hague 1729).

3. Bowers, *Western Medical Pioneers*, 1970, p. 30; Pierre Huard, Zensetsu Ohya, and Ming Wong, *La médecine japonaise des origines à nos jours* (Paris, 1974), p. 54 and n. 25; see also Grant K. Goodman, *The Dutch Impact in Japan, 1640–1853* (Leiden, 1967), p. 44.

4. Janet Doe, *Ambroise Paré: A Bibliography, 1545–1940* (Amsterdam, 1976), pp. 98–99, 204.

5. Bowers, *Western Medical Pioneers*, p. 29; Huard, Ohya, and Wong, *La médecine japonais*, pp. 54–56; Doe, *Ambroise Paré*, pp. 204–5.

6. Doe, *Ambroise Paré*, p. 206.

7. Bowers, *Western Medical Pioneers*, pp. 30–31; Huard, Ohya, and Wong, *La Médecine japonais*, p. 54 n. 25.

8. Goodman, *Dutch Impact*, p. 45.

9. Bowers, *Western Medical Pioneers*, pp. 31–60.

10. Hisayasu Nakagawa, *Des Lumières et du comparatisme. Un regard japonais sur le XVIIIᵉ siècle* (Paris, 1992), p. 257.

11. Neo-Confucianism refers to a current of the reform of ancient Confucianism whose source is Chu Hsi (Tchou-Hi or Zhu Xi), a twelfth-century Chinese sage. Introduced into Japan by Zen Buddhism, neo-Confucianism achieved its full independence with Fujiwara Seika in the late sixteenth century (Carsun Chang, *The Development of Neo-Confucian Thought* [New York, 1957]; Masao Maruyama, *Studies in the Intellectual History of Tokugawa Japan* [Tokyo, 1979]; Theodore de Bary, *Neo-Confucianism Orthodoxy and the Learning of the Mind-and-Heart* [New York, 1981]).

12. "The Anti-Jesuit," says Elison, *Deus Destroyed*, pp. 149–53, in his English translation of the pamphlet; "L'Anti-Jésus" according to Gernet, *Chine et christianisme*, after Hans Müller, "Hai Yaso. Anti-Jesus. Hayashi Razan's anti-christlicher Bericht über eine konfuzianisch-christliche Disputation aus dem Jahre 1606," *MN* 2 (1939): 268–75 (introduction to the German translation of *Hai Yaso*).

13. Maruyama, *Studies*, pp. 101, 136–80.

14. Rev. W. B. Wright, "The Capture and Captivity of Père Giovan Batista Sidotti in Japan from 1709 to 1715," *TASJ* (1881): 156–72; Nakagawa, *Des Lumièras et du Comparatisme*, pp. 243–46, 269–291; Nakagawa, "Présentation et réfutation," pp. 1–18.

15. Goodman, *Dutch Impact*, pp. 61–62.

16. Maruyama, *Studies*, pp. 250–62.

17. Shûichi Katô, "Tominaga Nakamoto, 1715–1746: A Tokugawa Iconoclast," *MN* 22, nos. 1–2 (1967): 178–87.

18. Gino K. Piovesana, "Miura Baien, 1723–1789, and His Dialectic and Political Ideas," *MN* 20, nos. 3–4 (1965): 389–433 passim.

19. J.-J. Rousseau, *Discours sur l'origine de l'inégalité*, note 10.

20. Bowers, *Western Medical Pioneers*, p. 65, conjectures that this may have come from the German physician Johann Vesling (1598–1649), whose *Syntagma anatomicum* was published in 1641 at Padua, where Vesling occupied the chair of surgery. But the confused drawings in *Zoshi* are clearly done from life; they are not copies of Vesling's plates.

21. Goodman, *Dutch Impact*, p. 88; Bowers, *Western Medical Pioneers*, pp. 65–66; Huard, Ohya, and Wong, *La médecine japonais*, p. 70; Shigeru Nakayama, "Japanese Scientific Thought," *Dictionary of Scientific Biography*, edited by Charles Coulston Gillispie (New York, 1978), vol. 15, app. 1, p. 739.

22. They were engraved by Lucas Kilian (1579–1637), a Bavarian artist who had spent 1601–4 in Italy and had worked in Venice (entry *Kilian* in *Neue Deutsche Biographie*, Bayerische Akademie der Wissenschaften, vol. 11 [1977]).

23. The account that follows comes from Gempaku Sugita, *Rangaku kotohajime* (Die Anfänge der Holland-Kunde), translated by Koichi Mori, *MN* 5, no. 1 (January 1942): 144–46; and no. 2, pp. 215 (501)–236 (522), except where otherwise indicated.

24. Entry *Heister* in *Neue Deutsche Biographie*, Bayerische Akademie der Wissenschaften, vol. 8 (1969).

25. Joseph Needham, *Dialogue des civilisations. Chine-Occident. Pour une histoire œcuménique des sciences* (Paris, 1991), pp. 277–80 and n. 31.

26. Lairesse drew 106 plates for Bidloo. His elegant drawings are preserved at the old Faculty of Medicine in Paris, MS. 26. In the printed version, sadly, the engravings do no justice to the drawings.

27. Alain Briot, "Panorama de la médecine japonaise des origines à Meiji," in *Médecine et société au Japon* (Paris, 1994), pp. 21–25.

28. Keene, *Japanese Discovery*, pp. 25–29.

29. A. W. Meyer and K. Wirt Sheldon, "The Amuscan Illustrations," *BHM* 14 (1943): 668.

30. *Leiden University in the 17th Century: An Exchange of Learning*, edited by Th. H. Lungsingh Scheurleer and G. H. M. Posthumus Meyjes (Leiden, 1975), p. 228.

31. Entry *Vesling* in the *Enciclopedia italiana* and *Biographisches Lexikon der hervorragenden Aerzte aller Zeiten und Völker* (Munich-Berlin, 1962).

32. Entry *Bartholinus* in *Biographisches Lexikon*, in *Dictionnaire des sciences médicales. Biographie médicale* (Paris, 1820), and in the *Enciclopedia italiana*.

33. Entry *Bidloo* in *Biographisches Lexikon*.

34. Entries *Roëll*, *Ruysch*, and *Salzmann* in the *Biographisches Lexikon*.

35. Entry *Heister* in *Neue Deutsche Biographie* and the *Enciclopedia italiana*.

36. J.-F. Malgaigne in Ambroise Paré, *œuvres complètes* (Geneva, 1970), pp. ccxxiv–ccciv; see also Jean Céard, *La nature et les prodiges. L'insolite au XVIe siècle en France* (Geneva, 1977), chap. 12; and Paule Dumâtre, *Ambroise Paré, chirurgien de quatre rois de France* (Paris, 1986).

37. Harvey Cushing, *A Bio-bibliography of Andreas Vesalius* (New York, 1943), p. xxvii.

38. Ibid., p. 10. See also J. B. de C. M. Saunders and Charles Donald O'Malley, *The Illustrations from the Works of Andreas Vesalius of Brussels* (Cleveland, 1950), pp. 21–39; and Charles Donald O'Malley, *Andreas Vesalius of Brussels, 1514–1564* (Berkeley, Calif., 1964), p. 133. On the intellectual atmosphere in Basel in the sixteenth century, see Emmanuel Le Roy Ladurie, *Le siècle des platter, 1499–1628. I. Le mendiant et le professeur* (Paris, 1995), passim. On the Padua school, see John Herman Randall, Jr., *The School of Padua and the Emergence of Modern Science* (Padua, 1961).

39. On Remmelin, see Walther Pfeilsticker, "Johannes Rümelin," *SAGM* 22, no. 2 (1929): 174–88; 22, no. 4 (1929): 382–92; Karl Schadelbauer, "Zu Johannes Rümelin und Stephan Michelspacher," *SAGM* 24 (1931): 123–27; and W. B. McDaniel, "The Affair of the '1613' Printing of Johannes Rümelin's *Catoptron*," *TSCPP* 6 (June 1, 1938): 60–72.

40. Caspar Bartholin, *Astrologia seu de stellarum natura, affectionibus et effectionibus exercitatio*, 5th ed. (Copenhagen, 1612), passim.

41. *Leiden University*, p. 7.

42. Johann Adam Kulmus, *Elementa philosophiae naturalis, observationibus necessariis experimentis et sana ratione suffulta* (Danzig, 1737), pp. 2, 3, 4, 12.

43. According to Kulmus, astronomical calculations show that in the fourth year of the 202d olympiad there could not have been a solar eclipse in Palestine.

44. Laurentius Heister, *Compendium medicinae practicae, cui praemissa est de medicinae mechanicae praestantia dissertatio* (Amsterdam, 1743), p. 4.

45. Ludwig Choulant, *Geschichte und Bibliographie der Anatomischen Abbildung* (Leipzig, 1852), p. 113; John L. Thornton, *Medical Books: Libraries and Collectors* (London, 1949), p. 73.

46. For an overall comparison of the scientific tradition of China and Japan versus the Western scientific tradition, see Shigeru Nakayama, *Academic and Scientific Tradition in China, Japan, and the West* (Tokyo, 1984).

47. Guidi, who died in Pisa in 1559, had been physician to François I and a professor at the Collège Royal in Paris before becoming a professor at Pisa.

48. Huard, Ohya, and Wong, *La Médecine japonaise*, p. 51; Paule Dumaître, *Histoire de la médecine et du livre médical* (Paris, 1978), pp. 93, 168.

49. It is thought that the "ploughman skeleton" and the other skeletons illustrating Vésale's *Fabrica* were drawn and engraved by Jan Stefan van Kalkar, who worked in Venice in Titian's atelier (Saunders and O'Malley, *Illustrations*, pp. 26–27). But the extent of Kalkar's contribution to the preparation of *Fabrica* is still controversial, and the possible role of Titian himself is a subject of conjecture.

50. André Chastel, "Le baroque et la mort," in *Retorica e Barocco* (Rome, 1955), and "L'anatomie artistique et le sentiment de la mort," *Médecine de France* 175 (1966): 17–32; Gisèle Matthieu-Castellani, *Emblèmes de la mort. Le dialogue de l'image et du texte* (Paris, 1988).

51. Chastel, "Le baroque," p. 19. Also see Mathieu-Castellani, *Emblèmes*, p. 36, regarding *Simulacres et historiées faces de la mort* (The Dance of Death), drawn by Holbein after Dürer.

52. Saunders and O'Malley, *Illustrations*, p. 29 and plates 21, 22, 23.

53. The first artist to depict "anatomical" skeletons in dramatic postures was Jacopo Berengario da Carpi (ca. 1470–1550), a professor of surgery at Bologna, in a commentary published in 1521 on the work of the medieval anatomist Mundino (1270–1326). For more on the subject, see Dumaître, *Histoire de la médecine*, p. 123.

54. The man dressed in yellow to the viewer's right.

55. For the extremely complex story of the first editions of *Catoptrum* and *Pinax*, see McDaniel, "Affair of the '1613' Printing," pp. 60–72.

56. *Leiden University*, pp. 219, 222.

57. Mark David Altschule and Estrellita Karsh, "Pioniere in der medizinischen Abbildung," special issue of *Du* (Zurich) on art in medicine (October 1975): 25.

58. Saunders and O'Malley, *Illustrations*, p. 24. See also Pierre Huard and Marie-José Imbault-Huart, *André Vésale. Iconographie anatomique* (Paris, 1980), p. 207.

Epilogue

1. Oskar Nachod, *Die Beziehungen der Niederlaendischen Ostindischen Kompagnie zu Japan im siebzehnten Jahrhundert* (Leipzig, 1897), pp. 93–101; J. B. Snellen, "The Image of Erasmus in Japan," *TASJ* 11 (1934): 1–32.

Selected Bibliography

The bibliography has been limited intentionally and lists solely the books and articles cited in the notes and text, unless the complete reference is furnished in the notes or the text.

Alpatow, Michel W. *Die Dresdner Galerie. Alte Meister.* Dresden, 1966.

Altschule, Mark David, and Estrellita Karsh. "Pioniere in der medizinischen Abbildung." Special issue of *Du* (Zurich) on art in medicine (October 1975): 20–59.

Anesaki, Masaharu. "Japanese Criticisms and Refutations of Christianity in the Seventeenth and Eighteenth Centuries." *TASJ* 7 (December 1930): 1–15.

———. "Psychological Observations on the Persecution of Catholics in Japan in the Seventeenth Century." *HJAS* 1 (1936): 13–27.

Anvers, ville de Plantin et de Rubens. Catalog of the exhibition held at the Galerie Mazarine, March–April 1954, Paris, 1954.

d'Azevedo, João Lúcio. *História dos Cristãos novos portugueses.* Lisbon, 1921.

Bartholin, Caspar. *Astrologia seu de stellarum natura, affectionibus et effectionibus exercitatio.* 5th ed. Copenhagen, 1612.

Bary, Theodore de. *Neo-Confucianism Orthodoxy and the Learning of the Mind-and-Heart.* New York, 1981.

Bataillon, Marcel. *érasme et l'Espagne.* Paris, 1937.

———. *Études sur le Portugal au temps de l'Humanisme.* Paris, 1974. (First published Coimbra, 1952.)

Bédouelle, Guy, Bernard Roussel, et al. *Le temps des réformes et la Bible.* Paris, 1989.

Bénézit, E. *Dictionnaire critique et documentaire des peintres, sculpteurs, dessinateurs et graveurs.* Paris, 1976. (First edition 1911–23.)

Bernard, Henri. "Traductions chinoises d'ouvrages européens au Japon durant la période de fermeture, 1614–1853." *MN* 3, no. 1 (1940): 40–60.

———. "Valignani ou Valignano, l'auteur véritable du récit de la première ambassade japonaise en Europe, 1582–1590." *MN* 1 (1938): 378–85.

Bernard, Henri, Pierre Humbertclaude, and Maurice Prunier. "Infiltrations occidentales au Japon avant la réouverture du XIXᵉ siècle." *BMFJ* 11, nos. 1–4 (1939): 127–61.

Biographisches Lexikon der hervorragenden Aerzte aller Zeiten und Völker. Munich, 1962.

Boscaro, Adriana. *Sixteenth-Century European Printed Works on the First Japanese Mission to Europe: A Descriptive Bibliography.* Leyden, 1973.

Bourdon, Léon. *La Compagnie de Jésus et le Japon, 1547–1570.* Paris, 1993. (Dissertation delivered at the Sorbonne in 1949.)

Bowers, John Z. *Western Medical Pioneers in Feudal Japan.* Baltimore, 1970.

Boxer, C. R. *The Dutch Seaborne Empire, 1600–1800.* New York, 1965.

———. "Some Aspects of Portuguese Influence in Japan, 1542–1640." *TPJS* 23 (1935–36): 13–64.

Braga, Teófilo. *História da Universidade de Coimbra nas suas relações com a instrução pública portugueza.* 4 vols. Lisbon, 1892–1902.

Briot, Alain. "Panorama de la médecine japonaise des origines à Meiji." In *Médecine et société au Japon,* under the direction of G. Siary and H. Benhamou, pp. 11–25. Paris, 1994.

Campo, Miguel. "Luís de Almeida, cirurgião e mercador e sua entrada na Companhia de Jesus, 1555–1556." *AHP* 2, no. 1 (1958): 90–96.

Carthage. L'histoire, sa trace et son écho. Catalog of the exhibition presented at the Musée du Petit-Palais, March 9–July 2, 1995. Paris, 1995.

Catholicisme. Hier, aujourd'hui, demain. Encyclopedia published under the auspices of the Centre Interdisciplinaire des Facultés Catholiques de Lille, Paris. Vol. 4, 1953. Vol. 39, 1980.

Céard, Jean. *La nature et les prodiges. L'insolite au XVIᵉ siècle en France.* Geneva, 1977.

Chang, Carsun. *The Development of Neo-Confucian Thought.* New York, 1957.

Chastel, André. "L'anatomie artistique et le sentiment de la mort." *Médecine de France* 175 (1966): 17–32.

———. "Le baroque et la mort." In *Retorica e Barocco,* Atti del III Congresso Internazionale di Studi Umanistici, Venice, June 15–18, 1954, Rome, 1955.

Choulant, Ludwig. *Geschichte und Bibliographie der Anatomischen Abbildung.* Leipzig, 1852.

Cieslik, Hubert. "The Case of Christóvão Ferreira." *MN* 29, no. 1 (1974): 1–54.

———. "Die Heilige Schrift in der alten Japanmission." *NZM* 11 (1955): 30–41.

Claudel, Paul. *Oeuvre poétique.* Paris, 1957.

Les Conciles œcuméniques. 2x, pp. 439, 993–95. 2xx, pp. 1533–43. Paris, 1994.

Cushing, Harvey. *A Bio-bibliography of Andreas Vesalius.* New York, 1943.

Debergh, Minako. "Deux nouvelles études sur l'histoire du christianisme au Japon. I. Bases doctrinales et images du sacrement dans l'eucharistie à l'époque des premières missions catholiques chrétiennes au Japon (XVIᵉ–XVIIIᵉ siècle)." *JA* 268 (1980): 395–416; "II. Les pratiques de purification et de pénitence au Japon vues par les missionnaires jésuites aux XVIᵉ et XVIIᵉ siècle." *JA* 272 (1984): 167–216.

Delattre, Pierre. "Un institut de médecine des missionnaires au Japon au XVIᵉ siècle." *RHM* 11 (1934): 16–28.

Delen, A. J. J. *Histoire de la gravure dans les anciens Pays-Bas et dans les provinces belges des origines jusqu'à la fin du XVIᵉ siècle.* 3 vols. Paris, 1934–35. (Reprinted in one volume by F. de Nobele [Paris, 1969].)

Dias, José Sebastião da Silva. "O Cânone filosófico conimbricense, 1592–1606." *Cultura, História e Filosofia* 4 (1985): 257–370.

———. "Cultura e obstáculo epistemológico do renascimento ao iluminismo em Portugal." In *A Abertura do Mundo. Estudos de História dos descobrimentos europeus*, Hommage to Luís de Albuquerque. Vol. 1, pp. 41–52. Lisbon, 1986.

———. *O Erasmismo e a Inquisição em Portugal. O processo de Fr. Valentim da Luz.* Coimbra, 1975.

Dictionnaire des sciences médicales. Biographie médicale. Paris, 1820.

Dictionnaire de théologie catholique. Vol. 15, 2, pp. 2601–10, entry *Vázquez*. Paris, 1950.

Diderot, Denis. *Œuvres complètes*, ed. Asséžat and Tourneux. 20 vols. Paris, 1875–77.

Le Discours de la venue des princes japonais en Europe tiré d'un avis venu de Rome. Paris, 1586. (Probably by Father Jacques Gaultier.)

Doe, Janet. *Ambroise Paré: A Bibliography, 1545–1940.* Amsterdam, 1976. (Reprinted from the 1937 edition with additions and corrections in 1940.)

Dumaître, Paule. *Ambroise Paré, chirurgien de quatre rois de France.* Paris, 1986.

———. *Histoire de la médecine et du livre médical.* Paris, 1978.

d'Elia, Pasquale. "I primi ambasciatori giapponesi venuti a Roma (1585)." *CC* 1 (1952): 43–58.

Elison, George. *Deus Destroyed: The Image of Christianity in Early Modern Japan.* Cambridge, Mass., 1988. (First edition 1973.)

Endo, Shusaku. *Silence.* Tokyo, 1976 (English translation of the 1969 edition in Japanese.)

Érasme. *Éloge de la folie, Adages, Colloques, Réflexions, Correspondance*, ed. C. Blum, A. Godin, J.-C. Margolin, and D. Ménager. Paris, 1992.

Fiamminghi a Roma, 1508–1608. Artistes des Pays-Bas et de la Principauté de Liège à Rome à la Renaissance. Exhibition organized by the Société des Expositions du Palais des Beaux-Arts in Brussels and the Palazzo delle Esposizioni of the City of Rome. Brussels, February 24–May 21, 1995; Rome, June 7–September 4, 1995.

French, Calvin. "The First and Last Passion (Shiba Kôkan, 1747–1818)." *Hemisphere* 21, no. 1 (January 1977): 8–13; 21, no. 3 (March 1977): 8–15.

———. *Through Closed Doors: Western Influence on Japanese Art, 1639–1853.* Catalog of an exhibition of pieces from the collection of the Kobe Municipal Museum of Namban Art, organized by C. French, T. Sugase, and K. Usui and shown at the University of Michigan Museum of Art, October 9–November 13, 1977; the Denver Art Museum, February 12–March 19, 1978; and the Asian Art Museum of San Francisco, April 11–May 14, 1978. Rochester, 1978.

Fróis, Luís. *História de Japam.* 5 vols. Annotated edition by José Wicki. Lisbon, 1976–84.

———. *Traité sur les contradictions de mœurs entre Européens et Japonais.* Translated by Xavier de Castro and Robert Schrumpf with an introduction by José Manuel García. Paris, 1994.

Gay, Jesús López. "La primera bibliotéca de los Jesuítas en el Japón." *MN* 15 (1959–60): 142–72, 350–79.

———. "Un documento inédito del P. G. Vázquez (1549–1604), sobre los Problemas Morales del Japón." *MN* 16 (1960–61): 118–60.

Gernet, Jacques. *Chine et christianisme. Action et réaction*. Paris, 1982.

———. "Sur les différentes versions du premier catéchisme en chinois de 1584." *SSM* (1979): 407–16.

Goodman, Grant K. *The Dutch Impact in Japan, 1640–1853*. Leyden, 1967.

Gualtieri, Guido. *Relationi della venuta degli ambasciatori giapponesi a Roma fino alla partita di Lisbona*. Rome, 1586.

Gusdorf, Georges. *Les sciences humaines et la pensée occidentale*. Vol. 3, pts. 1 and 2. *La Révolution galiléenne*. Paris, 1969.

Haas, Hans. *Geschichte des Christentums in Japan*, a supplement to the *DGNVO*. 2 vols. Tokyo, 1902–4.

Heister, Laurentius. *Compendium medicinae practicae, cui praemissa est de medicinae mechanicae praestantia dissertatio*. Amsterdam, 1743.

Hollstein, F. W. H. *Dutch and Flemish Etchings, Engravings and Woodcuts, ca. 1450–1700*. Amsterdam, 1949 and subsequent years.

Huard, Pierre, Zensetsu Ohya, and Ming Wong. *La médecine japonaise des origines à nos jours*. Paris, 1974.

Huard, Pierre, and Marie-José Imbault-Huart. *André Vésale. Iconographie anatomique*. Paris, 1980.

L'Humanisme portugais et l'Europe. Proceedings of the XXIst International Colloquium of Humanist Studies. Tours, July 3–13, 1978, Paris, 1984.

Humbertclaude, Pierre. "La littérature chrétienne au Japon il y a trois cents ans." *BMFJ* 8, nos. 2–4 (1936): 158–220.

———. "Myôtei Mondô. Une apologétique chrétienne japonaise de 1605." *MN* 1, no. 2 (1938): 515–48 (223–56), and 2 (1939): 237–67.

———. "Notes complémentaires sur la biographie de l'ex-Frère jésuite Fabien Fucan." *MN* 4 (1941): 617–21.

Janeira, Armando Martins. *O impacto português sobre a civilização japonesa. Seguido de um epílogo sobre as relações entre Portugal e o Japão do século XVII aos nossos dias*. Lisbon, 1988. (First published 1970.)

Japan und Europa, 1543–1929. An exhibition at the "43. Berliner Festwochen," Martin-Gropius Bau, Berlin, 1993.

Jedin, Hubert. "Das Tridentinum und die Bildenden Künste." Bemerkungen zu Paolo Prodi, *Ricerche sulla teoria delle arti figurativi nella Reforma cattolica* (1962). *ZKG* 74 (1963): 321–39.

Katô, Shûichi. "Tominaga Nakamoto, 1715–1746: A Tokugawa Iconoclast." *MN* 22, nos. 1–2 (1967): 176–93.

Keene, Donald. *The Japanese Discovery of Europe, 1720–1830*. Stanford, Calif., 1969. (First published London, 1952.)

Kleiser, Alfons. "P. Alexander Valignanis Gesandtschaftsreise nach Japan zum . . . Toyotomi Hideyoshi, 1588–1591." *MN* 1 (1938): 70–98.

Kodansha Encyclopedia of Japan. 9 vols. Tokyo, 1983.

Kulmus, Johann Adam. *Elementa philosophiae naturalis, observationibus necessariis experimentis et sana ratione suffulta*. Danzig, 1737.

Lairesse, Gérard de. *Le Grand Livre des peintres ou l'art de la peinture considéré dans toutes ses parties et démontré par ses principes.* 2 vols. Paris, 1787.

Landry, Pierre. *Exposition universelle d'Osaka, 1970. "Progrès dans l'harmonie." Section française. Rencontres franco-japonaises.* Catalog of a collection of historical artifacts on relations between France and Japan from the seventeenth to the twentieth centuries. Paris and Osaka, 1970.

Laures, Johannes. *Kirishitan Bunko: A Manual of Books and Documents on the Early Christian Mission in Japan.* Tokyo, 1957. (First published 1940.)

Leiden University in the 17th Century: An Exchange of Learning. Ed. Th. H. Lungsingh Scheurleer and G. H. M. Posthumus Meyjes. Leiden, 1975.

Le Roy Ladurie, Emmanuel. *Le siècle des platter, 1499–1628. I. Le mendiant et le professeur.* Paris, 1995.

McDaniel, W. B. "The Affair of the '1613' Printing of Johannes Rümelin's *Catoptron.*" *TSCPP* 6 (June 1, 1938): 60–72.

Maere, J. de, and M. Wabbes. *Illustrated Dictionary of 17th-Century Flemish Painters.* 3 vols. Brussels, 1994.

Maës, Hubert. *Hiraga Gennai et son temps.* PEFEO 72 (1970).

Mâle, Émile. *L'art religieux du XIIIᵉ siècle en France.* Paris, 1990. (First edition Paris, 1898.)
———. *L'art religieux après le concile de Trente.* Paris, 1932.

Martins, José V. da Pina. *Humanismo e Erasmismo na cultura portuguesa do século XVI. Estudo e texto.* Paris, 1973.

Maruyama, Masao. *Studies in the Intellectual History of Tokugawa Japan.* Tokyo, 1979. (Translated from the Japanese edition of 1952.)

Masanobu, Hosono. *Nagasaki Prints and Early Copperplates.* Tokyo and New York, 1978. (Translated from the Japanese edition of 1969.)

Matsuda, Kiichi. *The Relation between Portugal and Japan.* Lisbon, 1965.

Matthieu-Castellani, Gisèle. *Emblèmes de la mort. Le dialogue de l'image et du texte.* Paris, 1988.

Méchoulan, Henri, et al. *Les Juifs d'Espagne, histoire d'une diaspora, 1492–1992.* Paris, 1992.

Meyer, A. W., and K. Wirt Sheldon. "The Amuscan Illustrations." *BHM* 14 (1943): 667–87.

Müller, Hans. "Hai Yaso. Anti-Jesus. Hayashi Razan's anti-christlicher Bericht über eine konfuzianisch-christliche Disputation aus dem Jahre 1606." *MN* 2 (1939): 268–75.

Nachod, Oskar. *Die Beziehungen der Niederlaendischen Ostindischen Kompagnie zu Japan im siebzehnten Jahrhundert.* Leipzig, 1897.

Nagayama, Tokihide. *Kirishitan shiryo shû: Collection of Historical Material Connected with the Roman Catholic Religion in Japan.* 2d ed. Nagasaki, 1927.

Nakagawa, Hisayasu. *Des Lumières et du comparatisme. Un regard japonais sur le XVIIIᵉ siècle.* Paris, 1992.
———. "Présentation et réfutation du christianisme par Hakuseki Arai." In *Problème de la traduisibilité des cultures.* Proceedings of the International Colloquium of Kyoto, September 9–11, 1991. Kyoto, 1994.

Nakayama, Shigeru. "Japanese Scientific Thought." *Dictionary of Scientific Biography.* Ed. Charles Coulston Gillispie. Vol. 15, app. 1, pp. 728–58. New York, 1978.

———. *Academic and Scientific Tradition in China, Japan, and the West.* Tokyo, 1984. (Translated from the Japanese edition of 1974.)

Needham, Joseph. *Dialogue des civilisations. Chine-Occident. Pour une histoire œcuménique des sciences.* Paris, 1991.

Neue Deutsche Biographie. Bayerische Akademie der Wissenschaften. Vol. 8 (1969), entry *Heister.* Vol. 11 (1977), entry *Kilian.*

Neuer, René, Herbert Libertson, and Susugu Yoshida. *Ukiyo-e, 250 ans d'estampes japonaises.* Paris, 1985.

Okamoto, Yoshimoto. *The Namban Art of Japan.* New York and Tokyo, 1972. (Translated from the Japanese edition of 1965.)

O'Malley, Charles Donald. *Andreas Vesalius of Brussels, 1514–1564.* Berkeley, Calif., 1964.

Pagès, Léon. *Histoire de la religion chrétienne au Japon depuis 1598 jusqu'à 1651.* 2 vols. Paris, 1869–70.

Paré, Ambroise. *(Œuvres complètes.* Ed. J.-F. Malgaigne. Geneva, 1970. (Reprinted from the original edition of 1840–41.)

Pfeilsticker, Walther. "Johannes Rümelin." *SAGM* 22, no. 2 (1929): 174–88; 22, no. 4 (1929): 382–92.

Piovesana, Gino K. "Miura Baien, 1723–1789, and His Dialectic and Political Ideas." *MN* 20, nos. 3–4 (1965): 389–421.

Poliakov, Léon. *De Mahomet aux Marranes.* Paris, 1961.

Proust, Jacques. "L'échec de la première mission chrétienne au Japon (XVIᵉ–XVIIᵉ siècle)." *ETR* 2 (1991): 183–206, 3 (1991): 359–381.

———. "Raison, déraison, dans les articles philosophiques de l'*Encyclopédie.*" *SRLF* 18 (1979): 425–48.

Randall, John Herman, Jr. *The School of Padua and the Emergence of Modern Science.* Padua, 1961.

Raynal, Guillaume Thomas. *Histoire philosophique et politique des établissements et du commerce des Européens dans les deux Indes.* 3 vols. Geneva, 1775.

Révah, Israël Salvador. *La censure inquisitoriale portugaise au XVI siècle.* Vol. 1. Lisbon, 1960.

———. "L'hérésie marrane dans l'Europe catholique du XVᵉ au XVIIIᵉ siècle." In *Hérésies et sociétés dans l'Europe préindustrielle,* pp. 327–42. Colloquium of Royaumont. Paris–The Hague, 1968.

———. "Les origines juives de quelques jésuites hispano-portugais du XVIᵉ siècle." *Quatrième Congrès des hispanistes français.* Poitiers, March 18–20, 1967, pp. 87–96.

———. "Les Marranes." *REJ* 1, no. 118 (1959–60): 29–77.

Rodrigues, Francisco. *A Companhia de Jesus em Portugal e nas missões.* 2d ed. Porto, 1935.

———. *História da Companhia de Jesus na Assistência de Portugal.* Pt. 1, vols. 1 and 2. Pt. 2, vol. 1. Porto, 1931.

————. *A Formação intellectual do Jesuíta*. Porto, 1917.

Rosenberg, Jakob, Slive Seymour, and E. H. Ter Kuile. *Dutch Art and Architecture, 1600–1800*. Harmondsworth, 1966.

Roth, Cecil. *A History of the Marranes*. Philadelphia, 1941.

Sakamoto, Mitsuru. *Namban bijutsu to Yôfû-ga* (Namban Art and Western-Style Painting). Tokyo, 1984.

————. "Rubens and Western-Style Painting in the Edo Period." *JAS* 295 (September 1974): 26–34.

Sande, Eduardus. *De missione legatorum japonensium ad Romanam curiam, rebusque in Europa, ac toto itinere anidmadversis*. Macao, 1590. (Facsimile edition produced in Tokyo in 1935, currently in the library of the Musée Guimet, Paris: 43566 204-V.)

Sarpi, Fra Paolo. *Histoire du concile de Trente*. 2 vols. Trans. Pierre François Le Courayer. Basel, 1738.

Satow, E. A. *The Jesuit Mission Press in Japan, 1551–1610*. 1888.

————. "The Jesuit Mission Press in Japan." *TASJ* 27, pt. 2 (1900).

Saunders, J. B. de C.M., and Charles Donald O'Malley. *The Illustrations from the Works of Andreas Vesalius of Brussels*. Cleveland, 1950.

Schadelbauer, Karl. "Zu Johannes Rümelin und Stephan Michelspacher." *SAGM* 24 (1931): 123–27.

Schilling, Dorotheus. *Das Schulwesen der Jesuiten in Japan, 1551–1614*. Munich, 1931.

————. "Os Portugueses e a introdução da medicina no Japão." *BIA* (1937): 5–46.

Schurhammer, Georg. "Die erste japanische Gesandtschaftsreise nach Europa, 1582–1590." *KM* 49 (1921): 217–24. (Reprinted in *Gesammelte Studien* 2, no. 35: 731–41.)

————. *Das kirchliche Sprachproblem in der japanischen Jesuitenmission des 16. und 17. Jahrhunderts*, a publication of *DGNVO*. Tokyo, 1928.

————. "Die Jesuitenmissionare des 16. und 17. Jahrhunderts und ihr Einfluss auf die japanische Malerei." Jubiläumsband herausgegeben von der *DGNVO* anlässlich ihres 60 jährigen Bestehen, 1873–1933, pt. 1, pp. 116–26. Tokyo, 1933. (Reprinted in *Gesammelte Studien* 2, no. 38, pp. 769–79.)

————. *Gesammelte Studien*. 4 parts in 5 vols. Rome-Lisbon, 1962–65. (*Bibliotheca Inst. Hist. S.I.*, vol. 20–23/2.)

Schütte, Franz Josef. "Christliche japanische Literatur, Bilder und Druckblätter in einem unbekannten vatikanischen Codex aus dem Jahre 1591." *AHSJ* (January–June 1940): 226–80.

————. "Der lateinische 'Dialog De missione legatorum japonensium ad Romanam curiam' als Lehrbuch der japanischen Seminare. Europäische Kultur auf japanischen Schulen im XVI. Jahrhundert." *AG*, Studi sulla Chiesa Antica e sull'-Umanesimo, 70 (1954): 247–90.

————. "Drei Unterrichtsbücher für japanische Jesuitenprediger aus dem XVI. Jahrhundert." *AHSJ* 8 (1939): 223–56.

————. *El "Archivo del Japón." Archivo documental español*. Vol. 20. Madrid, 1964.

————. *Monumenta historica Japoniae. I. Textus catalogorum Japoniae aliaeque de personis domibusque S.J. in Japonia informationes et relationes, 1549–1654*. Vol. 3 of *Monumenta historica S.J.* Rome, 1975.

Sicroff, A. *Les controverses des statuts de pureté du sang en Espagne aux XVI et XVII siècles*. Paris and Toulouse, 1960.

Snellen, J. B. "The Image of Erasmus in Japan." *TASJ* 11 (1934): 1–32.

Stegmüller, Friedrich. *Filosofia e teologia nas universidades de Coimbra e Évora no século XVI*. Coimbra, 1959. (Translated from a work originally published in German, Munich, 1931.)

Sugimoto, Tsutomu. *Zuroku Rangaku jiishi* (Beginnings of Dutch Studies via the Image). Tokyo, 1985.

Sugita, Gempaku. *Rangaku kotohajime* (Die Anfänge der Holland-Kunde). Translated by Koichi Mori, *MN* 5, no. 1 (January 1942): 144–46; and no. 2: 215 (501)–236 (522).

Thieme, V., and F. Becker. *Allgemeines Lexikon der bildenden Künste*. 37 vols. Leipzig, 1907–50.

Thomas Aquinas. *Somme théologique*. Pt. 2, question 78, and pt. 3, question 43. Paris, 1984.

Thornton, John L. *Medical Books: Libraries and Collectors*. London, 1949.

Thunberg, Charles Pierre. *Le Japon du XVIII siècle vu par un botaniste suédois*. Introd. Claude Gaudon. Paris, 1966.

Valignano, Alessandro. *Catechismus christianae fidei*. Lisbon, 1586.

————. *Les Jésuites au Japon. Relation missionnaire (1583)*. Trans., introd., notes J. Bésineau. Paris, 1990. (Cf. *Sumario de las cosas de Japón [1583].*) Annotated edition by José-Luis Alvarez-Taladriz, *MN*, monograph no. 9, Tokyo, 1954.)

Vereecke, L. *Conscience morale et loi humaine selon Gabriel Vázquez*. Paris, 1957.

Vicente, Luciano Pereña. "Importantes documentos inéditos de Gabriel Vázquez." *RET* 16, no. 63. (April–June 1956): 193–213.

Vlam, Grace Alida Hermine. "Kings and Heroes: Western-style Painting in Momoyama, Japan." *AA* 39, nos. 3–4 (1977): 220–50.

————. "Western-Style Secular Painting in Momoyama, Japan." Ph.D. dissertation, University of Michigan, 1976.

Vos, Frits. "Forgotten Foibles: Love and the Dutch at Desjima, 1641–1854." In *Asien, Tradition und Fortschritt. Festschrift für Horst Hammitzsch zu seinem 60. Geburtstag*. Wiesbaden, 1971.

Whelan, Christal. "Japan's Vanishing Minority: The *Kakure Kirishitan* of the Goto Islands." *JQ* (October–December 1994): 434–49.

————. "Religion Concealed: The Kakure Kirishitan on Narushima." *MN* 47 (1992): 369–87.

Wicki, Josef. "Die 'cristãos-novos' in der indischen Provinz der Gesellschaft Jesu von Ignatius bis Acquaviva." *AHSJ* 46 (1977): 342–61.

Wright, Rev. W. B. "The Capture and Captivity of Père Giovan Batista Sidotti in Japan from 1709 to 1715." *TASJ* (1881): 156–72.

Index

abortion, 61, 65
Abraham, 124
Acolastus (theater), 85
active scandal, 79–80
Adam, 117–18, 127, 130, 133, 210
Adams, William, 213–14
adultery, 62
Æsop, 5, 10–11
Alba, Duke of, 94
Albert VII, regent of Spanish
    Netherlands, 108
Albinius, 199
Alcalá, Pedro de, 119
Almeida, Estevam de, 39
Almeida, Luís de, 34–38
ambassadors. *See* Japanese envoys
Amida Buddha, 48, 132
Anatomia humani corporis (Bidloo), 189,
    194
Anatomìa nova (Bartholin), 186
Andrade, António de, 44
Anjiro, 61–62, 114, 135
anti-Semitism, 29–30
Antonio of Lebrija, 9–10
Anvers, Belgium, 103, 155
apostasy: Christians forced into, 91; of
    Ferreira, 46
Aquaviva, Claudio, 15, 38, 60
Arcadia (Sannazaro), 104
Aristotle: and categories, 25; common
    sense, 6; *De anima*, 68; *Ethics*, 9;
    Ferreira on, 52–53; and language
    pitfalls, 18; matter and form

distinction, 16; natural morality, 11;
Nicomachean Ethics, 59; and
Peripatetic tradition, 17; theology
based on, 10
Arius, 39
art: Akita school, 163–65; of
architecture, 165; brocade images,
156; cartography in, 94–96;
Chinese art, 157–59, 172; color
printing, 156; comparison of
Japanese and European artists, ix–x,
xvi–xvii; Counter-Reformation art,
xv, 87–93; Dutch influence, 155–56,
160–63, 165–66, 171–73; Eisei
collection, 100, 102, 105; European
pastoral genre, 100–107;
European Renaissance, 164;
exhibitions of, xiv–xv; fantasy
themes, 102–3, 106, 160; Flemish
art, 103–7, 155; Henry Walters
collection, 107; in Holland, 154–55;
hunting theme, 98, 106, 107,
170–71; of Japanese Counter-
Reformation, xv, 87–93; of Jesuit
school in Nagasaki, 90; Kano
school, 92, 96, 110, 157, 167;
landscapes, 168; media of, 90–92;
medical art copies, 200–211;
military battles, 110–12; moralized
anatomy, 201–2; Nagasaki school,
157–58, 163; *optique*, xvii–xviii,
166–67; as propaganda, 99;
religious art, 87–93, 104; royalty of

art *(cont.)*
    Europe, 107–8; story of Scipion,
    111–12; *ukiyo-e* etchings, 155–57,
    172; Utawaga school, 157; *vues
    d'optique*, 167, 168, 169, 172; as
    weapon in religious controversy,
    88; Western influence in Japan, 156,
    158, 163–64, 165–66, 168–71,
    171–73; xylograph art, 156
L'Art de bien mourir (Savonarola), 201
Augustine, Saint, 9
Azpilcueta, Martin de, 59

Baien, Miura, 180–82, 191
baptism, 121, 127–28, 134–35
Barradas, Sebastião, 7
Barreto, Belchior Nunes, 13
Barreto, Manoel, 115
Bartholin, Caspar, 186, 192, 194, 196,
    199
Bartholin, Thomas, 186, 196, 197
Basho, Matsuo, 150
Bataillon, Marcel, 38
Battle of Lepanto, 109–12
Battle of Lepanto (Cort), 111
Battle of Zama, 111
*Beginnings of Heaven and Earth: The
    Arrest of Zezusu* (excerpt), 146–47;
    on baptism, 127–28, 134–35;
    Buddhist influence on, 132–34; *The
    Choosing of Maruya* (excerpt),
    142–44; *The Creation of Human
    Beings* (excerpt), 140; and dogma,
    128–29; *The Flood* (excerpt), 141–42;
    foundation myth of, 135; *The Gift of
    Rice* (excerpt), 140–41; language in,
    135–36; *The Last Judgment*
    (excerpt), 148; as liturgical
    framework, 129–30; *The Magi*
    (excerpt), 145–46; on marriage, 128;
    Money Blinds (excerpt), 147–48;
    narrative line of, 126–27; *The
    Nativity* (excerpt), 144–45; oral

    tradition origin of, 121, 125–26;
    prayers in, 130; Shintoism influence
    on, 134–35; translation of, 125
being, 24–25
Bellarmin, Cardinal, 136
Bellini, Gentile, 84
Bemtalhado, Manuel, 32
Benveniste, Emile, 24–25
Bible: Fabian's version of, 116–19;
    Ferreira on, 53–54; Japanization of,
    130–32; Jesuit use of in Japan, 115;
    study of, 7; translation into
    Japanese, 114–15; translation into
    popular language, 113–15
Bidloo, Govert, 189, 192, 194, 197, 199,
    205
bile, value of, 187
blood purity statute, 30, 38, 44
Boerhaave, Hermann, 194, 199
Bohner, Alfred, 125
Bol, Hans, 105, 107
Bondage of the Will (Luther), 54
The Book of Birds (Utamaro), 156
The Book of Insects (Utamaro), 156
books: authors of Western medical
    books, 192–200; ban on possession
    of, 186; burning of, 40; "Dutch
    science," 174; Japanese difficulty
    with language of, 174; of natural
    history, 159–60, 162; prohibition
    lifted on, 150; publishing by Jesuits,
    9–11; role of in Japan, 171; treatise
    on Western-style painting, 164;
    Western books in Japan, 159;
    Yoshimune's interest in, 150–51
Borromeo, Carlo, 14, 120
Bosschaert, Ambrosius the Elder, 161
Bougainville, Louis Antoine de, 213
Bouquet in a Vaulted Window
    (Bosschaert), 161
Bourdon, Léon, x, 119–20
Boxer, C. R., x
Braudel, Fernand, xviii–xix

flight of from Portugal, 29; forcible baptism of, 29; and the Inquisition, 30–31; as medical practitioners, 33; prosperity of, 30–31; rationalism of, 34; usury practices of, 73

John, Gospel according to, 115

John II, King of Portugal, 29, 35

John III, King of Portugal, 2, 30–31, 41

John the Baptist, 87, 127–28, 134

Jonson, Hans, 176

Jonston, Jan, 159–60, 161, 163, 167

Judas, 127

judgment, 20

Julianus (Juliano Nakaura), 1–2, 4, 18–19, 27

Junan, Nakagawa, 184, 186, 187

Juvenal, 5

Kaempfer, Engelbert, 150, 153, 175, 176–77

Kakutei, 158

Kalkar, Jan Stefan van, 201, 205

Katai shinso, 189–92, 205, 211

Kengiroku. See Deception Unmasked (Ferreira)

Kichibei, Nishi, 184

Kilian, Lucas, 201

Kirishitan sho, Haiya sho (Arimichi), 125

Klau, Father. *See* Clavius

Kokan, Shiba, xvii–xviii, 156, 167–68, 172

kokugaku, 178, 191

Komo ryu geka komo, 176

Konyo, Aoki, 151, 184

Koya, Tagita, 125

Kukai, 133

Kulmus, Johann Adam: about, 194; *Elementa philosophiae naturalis*, 197–98; mentioned, 199, 211; nationality of, 192; *Ontleedkundige Tafelen*, 186–87, 189, 190, 194; religious orientation of, 197–98; sources of for book, 193

kyogen, 184

Kyushu, Japan, 213–14

Lacombe, Jean de, xii

La Fontaine, Jean de, 10

Laínez, Diego, 31, 37–38

Lairesse, Gérard de, 164–65, 172–73, 189, 202, 205

language: in *Beginnings of Heaven and Earth*, 135–36; categories, 25–26; clerical *vs.* vernacular, 136–37; impossibility of Dutch, 185; ingenuity in translation, 137–38; interpreters, 191; invention of modern medical language, 188, 190–91; Japanese difficulty with Western books, 174; Japanization of Christian texts, 130–32; loss of meaning in transliteration, 18; pitfalls, 18; study of biblical, 114; translation of Western medical books, 187–92; transliterations, 135–36

Lanzilotto (Italian Jesuit), 61–62

Last Judgment, 148

Latin: as educational language, 8; primer for, 9–10; study texts for, 19; Vulgate Latin Bible translation, 113

l'Ecluse, Charles de. *See* Clusius

Lent, 123

Leonardo da Vinci, 199

Letters on England (Voltaire), 153

Life of the Glorious Saint Sebastian, 116

Lighthouse at Alexandria (Heemskerck), 106

Lobel, Matthias de, 162

Lopes, Manuel, 32

Louis XIV, King of France, xii

Lourenço, Maria, 44

Lourenço (Japanese Jesuit), 12–13

Louvre, Paris, 111

Lucan, 5

Lucifer, 117

Luke, Saint, 18, 115
Lung, Chien, 158
Luther, Martin, 40, 41, 54–55
Lutheranism, 4, 41, 43–44
Luz, Valentim da, 42

Machado, João Baptista, 44
Madonna and Child, in art, 90–91, 93
Magalhaes, Cosmo de, 5
Magellan, Ferdinand, 213
Magi, story of, 131–32, 145–46
Mahavairocana, 135
Mahn, Jacques, 213
Mancius (Mancio Ito), 1–2, 4, 18–19, 27
Manual for Confessors and Penitents (Azpilcueta), 59
maps, 94–96
Marie of Hungary, 111–12
Mark, Gospel according to, 115
Marranism, 34
marriage, 70–72, 128
Martinus (Martinho Hara), 1–2, 4, 18–19, 27
Mary: artistic depictions of, 88, 90, 91–92; in *Beginnings of Heaven and Earth*, 128, 129–30, 134, 137–38, 139, 142–45, 148; Fabian's interpretation of, 118; Ferreira on, 53–54; grace of, 48; in Vatican manuscripts, 115
Mary Magdalene, 115
Masanobu, Okumura, 156, 157, 165–66
Mascarenhas, António, 44
materia prima, 23–24
Matsuda, Kiichi, 10
matter, form distinct from, 16–17
Matthew, Saint, 35, 88, 114, 115
Mauritshuis, the Hague, 161–62
Mazolini, Silvestre, 59
Mechoulan, Henri, 153
medicine: authors of Western books, 192–200; Chinese traditional medicine, 36, 175–76, 182–84; dissections practiced in Japan, 182–83, 186–87; illustrations, 200–211; invention of modern medical language, 188, 190–91; Japanese revolution in, 182–92; Jesuits and, 34, 37; Jews as practitioners of, 33; knowledge exchange between Dutch and Japanese, 174–77; medical literature, xviii; modern Japanese medical school, 175; rivalry between West and Japan, 190; surgeons distinct from physicians, 35; translation of Western books, 187–92; Western medical schooling in Japan, 36
Meid, Wolfgang, 136
Meiji Restoration, 125, 126
Melancthon, Philipp, 41
memorization *vs.* personal reflection, 7–8
men: in Europe, 98–99; in Japan, 62
Merian, Matthäus, the Younger, 160–61
Mesquita, Diogo de, 100
Méthode de traiter les plaies faites (Paré), 176
Michaël (Miguel Chijiwa), 1–2, 4, 18–19, 27
Michelangelo, 106, 201
Miguel (Japanese Jesuit), 36
Minerva, 95
missionaries: art displayed by, 89; canons of Council of Trent, 66; crucifixion of, 214; in debate, 21–22; discrediting teachings of, 177; dispensary in Funai, 35–37; Fróis in Japan, 59; and Islam, 108–9; Japanese envoys of, 1–6; principles' applicability to Japanese context, 66
Molina, Alonso de, 119
Molina, Luis de, 32, 54
Montaigne, Michel Eyquem de, 41
The Months (Collaert), 105
Monumenta nipponica (Bohner), xii, 125

Monzaemon, Chikamatsu, 150
Morales, Luis de, 93
moralized anatomy, 201–2, 211
Moronobu, Hishikawa, 156
mortifications, 122, 123
Municipal Museum, Kobe, 95
Musashi, Miyamoto, xvi
Museum of Namban Culture, Osaka, 107
Museum of the Prefecture, Nagasaki, 107
musical instruments, 105
Muslims, expulsion from Portugal, 29.
  See also Islam
Myôtei Mondô (Fabian), 23–25, 27, 116–19
Mystery of the Passion (Gréban and
  Gréban), 114

Naaman, 81
Nagasaki, Japan: Chinese artists in,
  157–58; Dutch presence in, 151–55;
  Japanese art in seventeenth and
  eighteenth centuries, 157
Nagataka Murayama collection, Kobe,
  110
Nagoya joshi shoka tandai kiyo, 125
Nakamoto, Tominaga, 180
The Nakamura Theater (Masanobu), 165,
  173
Nakaura, Juliano. *See* Julianus (Juliano
  Nakaura)
namban-ryu, 36
Nambanryu geka hidensho (Chuan), 56
Nampin, Chin, 157–58, 161, 163, 167,
  169–70
Nan-p'in, Shen. *See* Nampin, Chin
Naotake, Adano, 163, 165, 189–90
National Gallery, Spain, 93
National Museum, Tokyo, 214
Nativity, 144–45
Natural History of Animals (Jonston),
  159–60, 163, 167
Natural History . . . of the Empire of Japan
  (Kaempfer), 177
natural reasoning, 51

natural sciences, 7–8
Navarre, Marguerite de, 114
Needham, Joseph, 188
neo-Confucian philosophers, 177–82,
  191–92
"New Christians," 29–34, 44. *See also*
  Jews
Niccolò, Giovanni: about, 89–90; Battle
  of Lepanto screen, 110–11;
  departure for Macao, 167;
  mentioned, 156; students of, 104–5,
  107; surviving art of, 99; workshop
  of, 96
Nichiren, 133
Nicomachean Ethics (Aristotle), 59
Norinaga, Motoori, 178
Notationes in totam Scripturam sacram (de
  Sá), 7
Nuestra Señora ed l'Antigua, 90, 108

O Cânone filosófico conimbricense, 6
O Curso conimbricense, 6, 24
Oda Nobunaga, 48
Okyo, Maruyama, 167
Old Masters Museum, Dresden, 104
Ontleedkundige Tafelen (Kulmus),
  186–87, 189, 190, 194
Opera theologica (Vázquez), 67–68
Oporinus. *See* Herbst, Johann
optique, xvii–xviii, 166–67
Opuscula moralia (Vázquez), 58
oral tradition, 121–22, 125–26
Original Sin, 210
Ortelius, 94
Ortels, Abraham. *See* Ortelius
Osaka, Japan, 150
otherness of Japan, 62–66
Our Lady of Mercy of Bungo
  dispensary, Funai, 35–37
Ovid, 5

papal bulls, 39
Papinius, 5

Paradise (Brueghel), 161
Paré, Ambroise: circulation of works of, 33; *De Chirurgie*, 175–76, 202; *Dix livres de la chirurgie*, 193, 200–201; Japanese adaptation of works of, 175–76, 183; known in Japan, xviii; mentioned, 192, 199; *Méthode de traiter les plaies faites*, 176; and ploughman, 202; religious orientation of, 195; and Vesalius, 193
Pascal, Blaise, 81
Passion, 115, 123, 128
passive scandal, 79–80
Paternus (Vos), 103
Paul, Saint, 18, 129
Paul III, Pope, 30
Paul IV, Pope, 39
Paulo (Japanese Jesuit), 36
Pauw, Petrus, 208
Peace of Ryswick, 155
pedagogical theater, 85–87
penitential practices, 122–25
Penni, Giovanni Francesco, 111–12
Pentecost, 129
Peraldo, Guillermo, 59
Peripatetic tradition, 17
persecution, 45–46, 123
personal reflection *vs.* memorization, 7–8
Perspective (Masanobu), 165
Peter, Saint, 88, 90, 92, 116, 118–19
Philip II, King of Spain and Portugal, 30, 94, 107–8, 109, 189–90, 213
Philip III of Austria, 108
Philosophical History of the Two Indies (Raynal), 152
philosophy: in Japan, 177–82; of Remmelin, 196; study of, 6–7
Pinax microcosmographicus (Remmelin), 183, 205, 208, 210–11
Pius IV, Pope, 39
Pius V, Pope, 92

Plantin, 103
Plantin-Moretus Museum, Anvers, 107
Plato, 9
Plautus, 5
Pliny the Younger, 5
ploughman skeleton, 201–2, 205, 208
Polanco, Juan de, 38
politeness, 63
politics, of *Deception Unmasked*, 50
Polo, Marco, 92
Polybius, 110, 111
polygamy, 62, 65
Ponte, Niccolò da, 84
pope: Ferreira on, 50–51; and Holy Roman Emperor, 97
popular cults, 75
Portuguese period, xii–xiii
Prado Museum, Spain, 93
pragmatism, 179–80
The Praise of Folly (Erasmus), 75
preaching: in catechism, 11; Ferreira on, 52
predestinados, 47, 51, 54
Prieras. *See* Mazolini, Silvestre
principium efficiens, 16–17
principle, 21–22
problems of conscience: about, 67–69; homicide, 73–74; idolatry, 75–81; Japanese feudal lords, 74–75; marriage and divorce, 70–72; superstition, 77, 78–81; usury, 72–73
The Procession before Saint Marc (Bellini), 84
Propertius, 5
property, 24
prostitution, 153
Protestantism, sympathy with, 43
Provincial Congregation of Jesuits in Japan, 67
Provincial Letters (Pascal), 81
Punic Wars, 111
Pure Land sect, 123, 132

purification rites, 122–23, 134–35
Pyramus and Thisbe (Heemskerck), 103

quintessence, 12

Ramón, Pedro, 10
rangaku, 184, 190
Rangaku kaitei (Gentaku), 190
rationalism, 34, 179–80
Ratio studiorum, 4, 32, 45, 85
Raynal, Guillaume Thomas, 152
Razan, Hayashi, 26, 177–78, 200
Reiko's Smile (Ryusei), xvii
Reinoso, Rodrigo, 33
Relation de l'empire du Japon (Caron), xi–xii
religion (*see also specific religions*):
    Ethiopian Christianity, 41–42;
    Ferreira's refutation of
    Christianity, 46–56; of medical
    authors, 195–200; sympathy with
    Protestantism, 43
religious art, 87–93, 104
religious sphere, distinction from
    secular sphere, 49
Rembrandt, 155, 164
Remmelin, Johannes: *Catoptrum
    microcosmicum*, 205, 208;
    innovations of, 193; Japanese
    adaptation of works of, 205;
    mentioned, 192, 199; moralized
    anatomy of, 201; philosophy of,
    196; *Pinax microcosmographicus*, 183,
    205, 208, 210–11; studies of, 194
reprobos, 47, 54
Resende, André de, 40, 41
Révah, Israël Salvador, 34
Revelation, 5–6
Ricci, Matteo, 12, 14, 17, 18
Richelieu, xi
Ridinger, Johann Elias, 170
Rimmon, 81
Ritsuzan, Shibano, 192

ritual suicide, 62
Rocha, Pedro da, 44
Rodrigues, Estevão, 33
Rodrigues, Paulo, 44
Rodrigues, Simão, 32, 41
Rodrigues de Guevara, Alfonso, 33
Rodrigues (interpreter for Japanese
    envoys), 100
Roëll, Willem, 194
Romain, Jules, 111–12
Le roman de Renart, 10–11
Rondelet, Guillaume, 162
Rosary, invention of, 92
Rousseau, Jean-Jacques, 182
Royal Palace, Madrid, 112
Rubens, Peter Paul, 161
Ruggeri (missionary to China), 14
Rümelin, Johannes. *See* Remmelin,
    Johannes
Ruysch, Frederik, 194, 199
Ryoi, Motoki, 183, 205, 210–11
Ryotaku, Maeno, 184–85, 187, 190, 200
Ryusei, Kishida, xvii

sacraments: Ferreira on, 52, 54; wine
    made from wild grapes, 81–82
Sacrobosco, Joannes de. *See* Holywood,
    John
Sadeler, Raphaël, 103, 106
Saikaku, Ihara, 150
Saint Bartholomew's Day Massacre,
    195
saints, compendium of lives of, 116
Sairan igen (Hakuseki), 179
Sakyamuni Buddha, 92
Sallust, 5
Salzman, Johann, 194
Samson, 95
Sanches, Francisco, 33
Sande, Duarte de, 2, 96
Sannazaro, Jacopo, 5, 104
Santo Domingo, Tomaso de, xi
Saracens, 109–11, 112

Saül (theater), 85
Savery, Roelant, 161
Savonarola, 201
scandal, 79–81
Schambergen, Caspar, 175, 183
School of the Southern Barbarians, 36
Schütte, Josef Franz, 46
Scipion, 111–12
scourging, 124
Scriptures. See Bible
Secret Christians of Japan: about,
    120–25; as authentic Japanese, 135;
    and Beginnings of Heaven and Earth,
    125–30; and Buddhism, 132;
    Christianized Buddhism of, 139–40;
    maintaining own identity, 138–39
secular sphere, distinction from
    religious sphere, 49
Seiyo kibun (Hakuseki), 179
self-control, 63
sendosivistes, 177–82
Seneca, 5
Servetus, Michaël, 195
Shaka, 132
Sheba, Queen of, 98
Shigenaga, Nishimura, 156
Shih-ning, Lang, 158
Shingobei. See Chinzan, Narabayashi
Shintoism: art in temples, 87; and
    impurity, 89; influence on
    Beginnings of Heaven and Earth,
    134–35; in-yo, 24; purification rites
    of, 134–35; rejection of, 178; and
    Secret Christians, 132
Shiseki, So, 158
Shoeki, Ando, 180
Showa-jidä no Sempuku-kirishitan, 125
Shozan, Satake, 163–65, 173
Shrike Calling from a Dead Branch
    (Miyamoto Musashi), xvi
Shuji, Takashina, xvi
Shusaka, Endo, 58
Sidotti, Giovanni Battista, 179

Silius Italicus, 111
Simão, Master, 32
sin by habitus, 79, 80
skeleton illustrations, 201–2, 205, 208
Society of Jesus: artistic representation
    of Crucifixion in Japan, 88–89;
    Bible use in Japan, 115; biblical
    studies, 7; book publishing, 9–11;
    caution in evangelical work, 36; in
    China, 158–59; cultural penetration
    policies, 10; educational system
    restructuring, 4; and Erasmianism,
    39–44; Ferreira's exclusion from,
    57–58; hagiographic literature of,
    116; on Holy Roman Empire,
    96–97; and Islam, 109–10;
    literature instruction of, 84–85;
    and medical practice, 34, 37; "New
    Christians" issue and, 31–33;
    prohibitions of, 3; respect for
    Japanese sensibility, 128; scourging
    practices of, 124; teaching methods
    of, 7–8; textbooks by, 9–10;
    understanding others, 63;
    Valignano as representative to
    Japan, 100; vocation of members, 3
Solomon, 98
Sorai, Ogyu, 178, 179–80
soul: in catechisms, 12–13; in debates,
    22; defining, 17; Japanese feast of
    souls, 78; in Myôtei Mondô, 24, 26;
    theory of, 52–53
So-un, Suzuki, 183
Spinola, Carlo, 125
spiritual goods, 80
spiritual substance, 24
Stradano, Giovanni. See Stradanus,
    Johannes
Stradanus, Johannes, 108, 111
Straet, Jan van der. See Stradanus,
    Johannes
Sturm, Jean, 4
Suárez, Francisco, 6–7, 68, 75, 76